Our DIGITAL WORLD

Second Edition

Introduction to Computing

Jon Gordon • Karen Lankisch • Nancy Muir
Denise Seguin • Anita Verno

PARADIGM
EDUCATION SOLUTIONS

St. Paul

Managing Editor:	Christine Hurney
Senior Editor:	Brenda Owens
Production Editor:	Bob Dreas
Copy Editor:	Carol E. McLean
Cover Designer:	Leslie Anderson
Text Designer and Production Layout:	Jaana Bykonich
Indexer:	Schroeder Indexing Services
Illustrations:	Patrick Gnan, Tim Downs, and Cohographics
Video Production Team:	David Gillette, Mark Heitke, Amanda Day, and Joe Shelton, One Camera Productions, LLC
Flash Movie Script Writer:	Bill Madden, Bergen Community College
Technical Editor:	Alec Fehl

Care has been taken to verify the accuracy of information presented in this book. However, the authors, editors, and publisher cannot accept responsibility for Web, e-mail, newsgroup, or chat room subject matter or content, or for consequences from application of the information in this book, and make no warranty, expressed or implied, with respect to its content.

Trademarks: Some of the product names and company names included in this book have been used for identification purposes only and may be trademarks or registered trade names of their respective manufacturers and sellers. The authors, editors, and publisher disclaim any affiliation, association, or connection with, or sponsorship or endorsement by, such owners.

Photo Credits: Page 4, top, Courtesy of Eastman Kodak Company; right, Courtesy of Motorola Inc.; bottom, Courtesy of Casio America Inc.; left, Courtesy of Apple Inc. Page 6, top, Courtesy of Apple Inc., bottom, Courtesy of Samsung. Page 13, Courtesy of Epson America, Inc. Page 14, top, Courtesy of Intel Corporation; bottom, Courtesy of Dell, Inc. Page 16, left, Courtesy of SanDisk Corporation; right, Courtesy of Seagate Technology LLC. Page 30, bottom, © Simon Jarratt/Corbis. Page 42, Courtesy of Opera Software ASA. Page 46, Reproduced with permission of Yahoo! Inc. ©2011 Yahoo! Inc. YAHOO! and the YAHOO! logo are registered trademarks of Yahoo! Inc. Page 55, Daniel L. Murphy. Page 57, Used with permission from Skype. com. Page 70, top left, Motorola, Inc.; top middle, Courtesy of Nikon, Inc.; top right, Courtesy of Samsung; bottom right, Courtesy of Hewlett-Packard Company; bottom left, Courtesy of Dell Inc. Page 71, Courtesy of ASUSTeK Computer Inc. Page 72, Courtesy of Hewlett-Packard Company. Page 75, Courtesy of Verbatim Americas LLC. Page 76, Courtesy of Logitech. Page 77, top, Courtesy of Hewlett-Packard Company; bottom left, Courtesy of Motorola. Page 78, top, Courtesy of Microsoft Corporation; bottom, Courtesy of National Science Foundation. Page 80, left, Courtesy of Motorola Inc.; bottom, Courtesy of Sony Electronics Inc. Page 81, Courtesy of Epson America, Inc.; Page 82, top, Courtesy of SMART Technologies; bottom, Courtesy of NASA. Page 103, Hagley Museum and Library. Page 104, Used with permission of Microsoft Corporation. Page 105, Used with permission of Microsoft Corporation. Page 106, Used with permission of Microsoft Corporation. Page 108, Used with permission of Microsoft Corporation. Page 109, Courtesy of Linux Online, Inc. Page 111, top, Used with permission of Microsoft Corporation; bottom, Courtesy of Hewlett-Packard Company. Page 114, top, Used with permission of Microsoft Corporation. Page 117, bottom, Used with permission of Microsoft Corporation. Page 118, Used with permission of Microsoft Corporation. Page 121, left, Courtesy of Research in Motion Limited; right, Courtesy of Apple Inc. Page 141, left, Courtesy of Corel Corporation; second from left, Adobe product box shot reprinted with permission from Adobe Systems Incorporated; second from right, Courtesy of Corel Corporation; right, Courtesy of Microsoft Corporation. Page 143, Courtesy of Intuit Inc. Page 155, Courtesy of Lenovo; Page 185, Courtesy of Motorola Inc. Page 186, Courtesty of Nokia. Page 187, bottom right, Courtesy of Motorola Inc. Page 246, Courtesy of SiteTrust Network; Courtesy of TRUSTe Inc.; Courtesy of Validatedsite.com; Courtesy of Council of Better Business Bureaus, Inc. Page 249, left, Courtesy of Kensington Computer Products Group, a division of ACCO Brands; right, U.are.U® 4500 Fingerprint Reader by DigitalPersona, Inc.

We have made every effort to trace the ownership of all copyrighted material and to secure permission from copyright holders. In the event of any question arising as to the use of any material, we will be pleased to make the necessary corrections in future printings. Thanks are due to the aforementioned authors, publishers, and agents for permission to use the materials indicated.

ISBN 978-0-76384-756-2

Contents

Preface

Getting the Most Out of This Book

You've just paid good money for another textbook. It feels like every other textbook. You expect it to be something you have to get through, and something you'll be glad to leave behind when you finish the course.

The truth is, we actually hope you are somewhat surprised by this book.

As in the first edition of *Our Digital World*, we've done a lot of work to make the writing in this book easy to read, to find ways to get you excited about how technology is evolving, and to make computing relevant to your work and personal lives. We've included information about recent technologies such as cloud storage and mobile applications. We've also cut back on the amount you have to read by providing part of the content in multimedia formats that we think you'll find engaging. The result is more than a book—it's a combination of text and technology that together, provides a new learning experience.

The multimedia content of *Our Digital World, Second Edition* is available with the textbook in three package options:

- At the book's Online Companion site: digitalworld2e.emcp.com
- As part of SNAP, a web-based training and assessment system accessed at snap.emcp.com
- On the Core Content DVD

See the About the Components section of preface for a description of each option.

Moving Your Learning Online

One of the fundamental ways that this book provides a different learning experience is by connecting this course with the way you experience computing in the twenty-first century. We have integrated the use of online technology into this textbook through a web-centric educational experience. The activities in this book involve visiting the book's Online Companion website to view videos and Flash movies, play with interactive hands-on tools, connect with fellow students and your instructor by learning how to use collaborative features such as blogs and wikis, and discover where technology is headed by reading stories from today's headlines. To see how this works, take a look at the Chapter Tour beginning on page ix.

Our hope is that you'll not only find our online features informative and interesting, but that you'll also become a more competent participant in our digital world by gaining practice with online technologies. After you finish the course, that practice will continue to help you enjoy computers on a personal and professional level.

Pay special attention to the Core Content activities in this book, which provide required learning in an alternative and visual way. Other activities are up to your instructor to assign to enhance your learning in the way that suits your class environment and interests. This approach makes this textbook uniquely customizable.

Really *Special* Special Features

One way in which we tried to make this book different was by providing special content that answers common questions about planning for the future and using technology wisely. These features include:

- **Computers In Your Career**   We realize that just about every job today involves computers in some way, so rather than focus only on computing careers in IT, we tell you how computers are being used in a wide variety of work settings.
- **Playing It Safe**   Technology offers wonderful opportunities, but it also comes with some risk. In this feature we advise you about staying safe from threats such as ID theft, phishing scams, and virus attacks.
- **Spotlight on the Future**   These fascinating articles and companion podcasts, all new for the second edition, are based on interviews by co-author Jon Gordon, a veteran technology reporter, with one of the country's leading technology journalists, Dwight Silverman. They give you a glimpse of the exciting directions technology is taking and what that could mean for you in your future. All Spotlight on the Future interviews from the first edition will continue to be available as additional podcasts.
- **Ethics and Technology Blog**   This ongoing classroom blog raises interesting ethical questions regarding technology and lets you share your ideas and opinions and engage in ongoing conversations with your classmates.

These features, along with the presentation of key computing concepts, are designed to help you become tech-savvy at home and at work, today and into the future.

Who Are You?

Finally, we know that you aren't one homogenous student so we've tried to address a variety of interests and backgrounds. You are 18 or 28 or 60 years old. You are comfortable with technology or you may be technophobic. You could be juggling a job and family with your education to take the next step in your career, or you could be just starting out on your initial career path. Maybe you recently retired and are looking for a new work experience.

This course could be a basic requirement for your degree that you hope to get through and get a grade. Or it could be a stepping stone to a career that is focused on computing in one of its many forms. Maybe it's simply going to help you keep up with the digital curve so you can explore ways that computers can connect you with friends and family.

Whatever your goals, we believe this book will help you, and we wish you success in exploring the amazing possibilities of our digital world.

Taking a Chapter Tour

Learning objectives establish clear goals and help you focus your study of the chapter.

Why Should I Care? feature provides a context to help you picture the practical reasons for learning the chapter content.

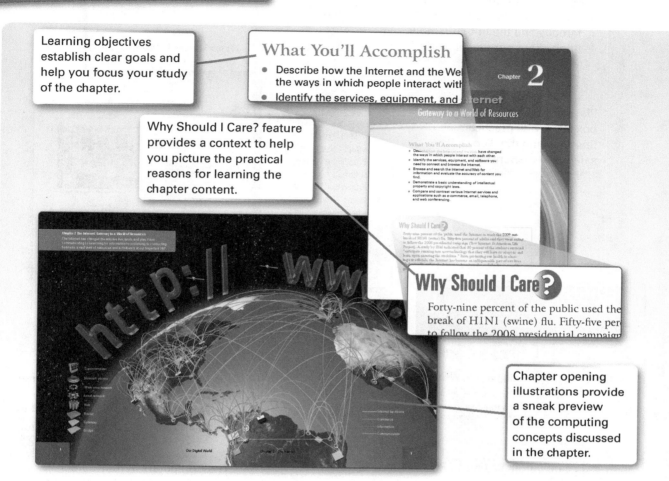

Chapter opening illustrations provide a sneak preview of the computing concepts discussed in the chapter.

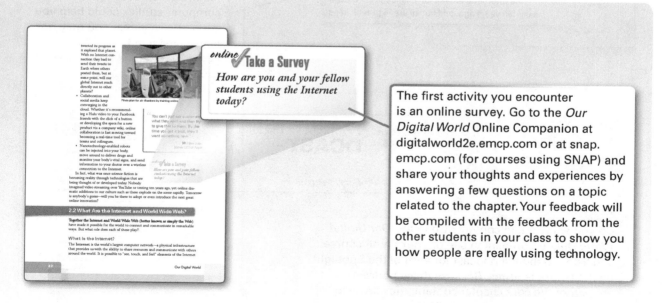

The first activity you encounter is an online survey. Go to the *Our Digital World* Online Companion at digitalworld2e.emcp.com or at snap.emcp.com (for courses using SNAP) and share your thoughts and experiences by answering a few questions on a topic related to the chapter. Your feedback will be compiled with the feedback from the other students in your class to show you how people are really using technology.

Thought-provoking quotes scattered throughout the text provide insights into what the famous and the not-so-famous think about our digital world.

> " The Internet is just a world passing around notes in a classroom. "
>
> ▶▶ Jon Stewart, Comedian

Playing It Safe margin boxes provide practical tips for using the Web safely and responsibly.

Playing It Safe

Email is a wonderful communications tool, but it is also used to deliver a variety of threats such as viruses and financial scams. Use caution when downloading file attachments and read unsolicited emails carefully to understand the sender's intent.

Ethics and Technology Blog *online*

Regulating Web Behavior

Some people think the Web should be regulated by a c... the freedom to say and do what you want on the Web s...

Go to the *Our Digital World* Online Companion site or your SNAP course to blog about some of the thought-provoking ethical questions related to living and working with technology.

Computers in Your Career

The Internet and Web have made available a wi... exist ten years ago, and not all are high-tech in nat...

The Computers in Your Career feature gives ideas for how your computer studies could help you succeed in a career you may not have considered.

online Spotlight on the Future
P▶DCAST

The Web Everywhere

Do you enjoy audio content? Go to the *Our Digital World* Online Companion site or your SNAP course and listen to the full podcast for each of the Spotlight on the Future features. Because these podcasts are part of the core chapter content, they are also available on the Core Content DVD.

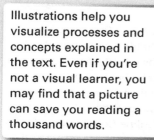

Illustrations help you visualize processes and concepts explained in the text. Even if you're not a visual learner, you may find that a picture can save you reading a thousand words.

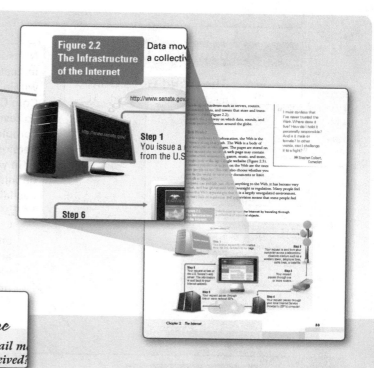

Figure 2.2
The Infrastructure of the Internet

Step 1
You issue a ...
from the U.S...

Step 6

Take the Next Step *online*

Activity 2.7.1
Flash Movie
How are email m... sent and received?

Take the Next Step activities expand what you read in your textbook. These videos, Flash movies, and online research experiences deepen your understanding of computing concepts. Go to the *Our Digital World* Online Companion site or your SNAP course to access these activities. Activities identified as Core Content appear first in the list, and end with a brief online quiz. The Core Content activities and quizzes are also available on the Core Content DVD, for students with limited Internet access.

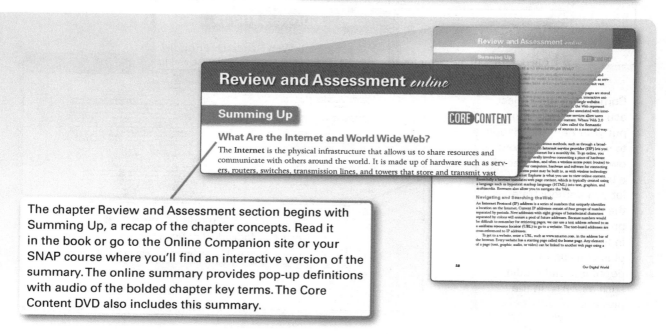

Review and Assessment *online*

Summing Up

CORE CONTENT

What Are the Internet and World Wide Web?

The **Internet** is the physical infrastructure that allows us to share resources and communicate with others around the world. It is made up of hardware such as servers, routers, switches, transmission lines, and towers that store and transmit vast

The chapter Review and Assessment section begins with Summing Up, a recap of the chapter concepts. Read it in the book or go to the Online Companion site or your SNAP course where you'll find an interactive version of the summary. The online summary provides pop-up definitions with audio of the bolded chapter key terms. The Core Content DVD also includes this summary.

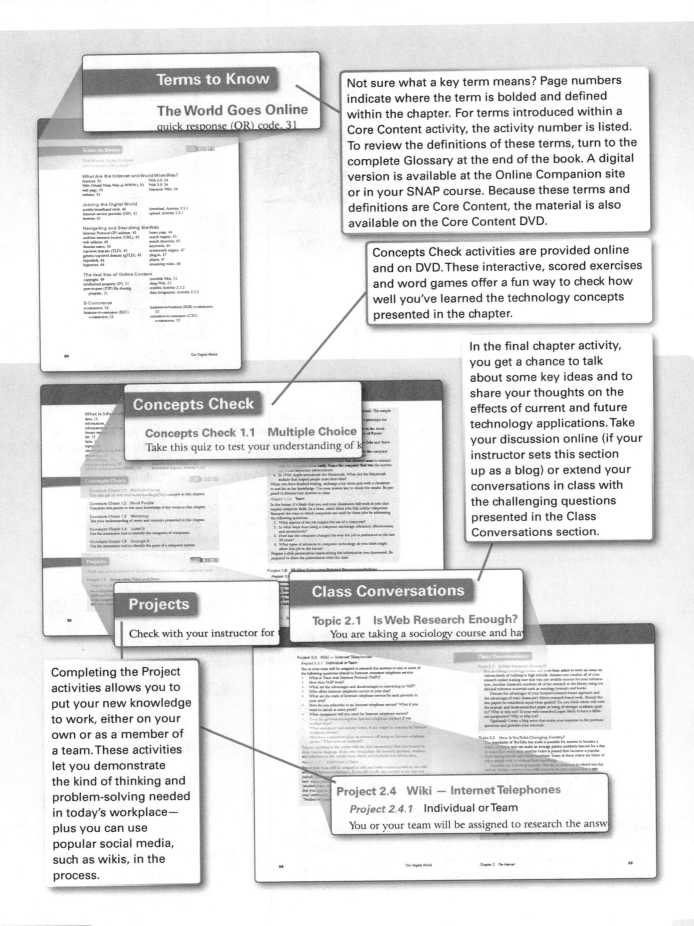

Terms to Know

The World Goes Online
quick response (QR) code, 31

Not sure what a key term means? Page numbers indicate where the term is bolded and defined within the chapter. For terms introduced within a Core Content activity, the activity number is listed. To review the definitions of these terms, turn to the complete Glossary at the end of the book. A digital version is available at the Online Companion site or in your SNAP course. Because these terms and definitions are Core Content, the material is also available on the Core Content DVD.

Concepts Check activities are provided online and on DVD. These interactive, scored exercises and word games offer a fun way to check how well you've learned the technology concepts presented in the chapter.

In the final chapter activity, you get a chance to talk about some key ideas and to share your thoughts on the effects of current and future technology applications. Take your discussion online (if your instructor sets this section up as a blog) or extend your conversations in class with the challenging questions presented in the Class Conversations section.

Concepts Check

Concepts Check 1.1   Multiple Choice
Take this quiz to test your understanding of k

Class Conversations

Topic 2.1   Is Web Research Enough?
You are taking a sociology course and ha

Projects

Check with your instructor for

Completing the Project activities allows you to put your new knowledge to work, either on your own or as a member of a team. These activities let you demonstrate the kind of thinking and problem-solving needed in today's workplace— plus can use popular social media, such as wikis, in the process.

Project 2.4   Wiki — Internet Telephones
Project 2.4.1   Individual or Team
You or your team will be assigned to research the answ

About the Components

As you can see from the Chapter Tour, *Our Digital World, Second Edition* is more than just a textbook. The digital content that is vital to your learning experience is offered in three different forms, as described below.

Online Companion

The Online Companion, available at digitalworld2e.emcp.com, requires an enrollment key, which you will receive from your instructor, and a passcode, which you can purchase with the textbook. Through the Online Companion, you'll be able to access all of the Take the Next Step activity sections as you move through each chapter. Activities with the *Core Content* label include short quizzes. Scores for quizzes are reported automatically to a grade book.

You'll also be able to take the chapter survey, listen to the Spotlight on the Future podcasts, participate in the Ethics and Technology blogs, complete the end-of-chapter Review and Assessment activities, and apply your knowledge playing interactive games.

SNAP Web-Based Training and Assessment

For courses using Paradigm Publishing's SNAP product, the entire contents of the Online Companion are available within the SNAP program. Through the SNAP site at snap.emcp.com, instructors can set up an *Our Digital World* course. Or, they can create courses that combine *Our Digital World* with a book from one of the Microsoft® Office application series: Marquee, Benchmark, or Signature. Like the Online Companion, the SNAP site requires you to log in with an enrollment key, which you will receive from your instructor, and a passcode, which you can purchase with the textbook.

Core Content DVD

If you have limited Internet access, the text with Core Content DVD is a good option. This DVD contains all of the Core Content activities within the Take the Next Step sections. You can print or email your completed quizzes to your instructor for evaluation. Spotlight on the Future podcasts, chapter summaries, and the Glossary fill out the set of required content that, along with the textbook, provide a comprehensive study of introductory computing concepts.

eBook

Don't want to carry around a textbook? Students who want to travel light can access the entire book's contents through the web-based eBook. The eBook features dynamic navigation tools including a linked table of contents and the ability to jump to specific pages, bookmark, highlight, and take notes.

Instructor Resources

Instructor resources are available in print form, on DVD, and at the password-protected instructor area of the Internet Resource Center at www.paradigmcollege.net/digitalworld2e. These materials include:
- Model answers and rubrics for evaluating chapter work
- Teaching hints and lecture tips
- Syllabus suggestions and course planning resources
- **EXAMVIEW®** software and test banks
- PowerPoint® presentations
- Blackboard and distance learning course files

About the Author Team

Jon Gordon

Jon Gordon is an editor at Minnesota Public Radio, where he is responsible for social media and mobile content strategy and execution. Gordon also served 14 years as creator, producer, and host of American Public Media's *Future Tense*, a daily technology report that aired on more than 125 stations across the United States and Canada, and by podcast. Gordon joined Minnesota Public Radio in 1990 and has served as a producer and reporter covering general news, suburban issues, and politics. Gordon's work has been recognized by the Associated Press, the Corporation for Public Broadcasting, and the Northwest Broadcast News Association. He's a recipient of the prestigious Gerald Loeb Award for business journalism from UCLA's Anderson School of Business.

Karen Lankisch

Instructor, Consultant
University of Cincinnati—Clermont College
Cincinnati, Ohio

Karen Lankisch is a Professor at the University of Cincinnati—Clermont College located in Cincinnati, Ohio. She teaches a variety of courses in the Business Information Technology Program. She is also an Adjunct Assistant Professor in the College of Education's graduate program at the University of Cincinnati. She has a PhD in Education with a concentration in technology and adult learning. In addition, Professor Lankisch is certified through AHIMA as a Registered Health Information Administrator (RHIA). Dr. Lankisch presents locally, regionally, and nationally on a variety of technology subjects. She also has served as a national consultant for Paradigm Publishing, giving workshops and presentations to instructors on the SNAP web-based training and assessment tool and the textbooks the SNAP software supports.

Nancy Muir

Writer, Author, Instructor
Seattle, Washington

Nancy Muir is the owner of The Publishing Studio, a technology publishing company. Muir was a co-creator and instructor of a course called Internet Safety for Educators, offered through the distance learning programs at both Washington State

University and The University of Alaska, Anchorage. Previously she was an instructor of Technical Writing at Indiana University/Purdue University in Indianapolis.

In addition to co-authoring *Our Digital World*, Muir has written a number of technology and business books, including *Distance Learning for Dummies* and *Young Person's Guide to Character Education* (winner of the Benjamin Franklin Award for Excellence from the Independent Bookseller's Association). She also runs two websites focused on technology, and is the author of a regular column on Computers and the Internet at www.Retirenet.com.

Denise Seguin

Author, Instructor
Fanshawe College
London, Ontario

Denise Seguin has served on the faculty of Fanshawe College in London, Ontario, since 1986, where she has taught Introduction to Computers courses and a variety of software applications to learners in postsecondary Information Technology diploma programs and in Continuing Education courses. Along with co-authoring *Our Digital World*, Seguin has co-authored texts in Paradigm Publishing's Benchmark Microsoft® Office 2007 and 2010 series, and she has co-authored *Marquee Microsoft® Office 2010* and *Using Computers in the Medical Office*. Other textbooks she has written for Paradigm Publishing include previous editions of the Marquee Series, *Macromedia Flash MX: Design and Application*, and books on Microsoft® Outlook (2000, 2002, 2003, 2007, and 2010).

Anita Verno

Associate Professor
Information Technology Department
Division of Business, Social Sciences, and Public Service
Bergen Community College
Paramus, New Jersey

Anita Verno is an Associate Professor of Information Technology at Bergen Community College and was IT Coordinator/Department Chair from 2000 until 2010. A founding member of the Computer Science Teachers Association (CSTA) (http://csta.acm.org/), Verno was the elected "College Faculty Representative" to its Board of Directors and served as Curriculum Chair from inception until June 2009. She is currently serving on the CSTA Advisory Council. In 2009 she assisted in establishing CSTA's Northern New Jersey chapter to serve computing teachers in her home state. Verno was recently appointed an Associate Member of the ACM Committee for Computing Education in Community Colleges (CCECC) where she is part of a curriculum project team tasked with identifying the nature and breadth of IT-related programs of study in community colleges. Verno was a member of the Board of Directors of the Community College Computer Consortium from 2005-2010 and served as President in 2008–2009. She also sits on the Board of Advisors, BS Engineering Technology, Computer Technology Option for the New Jersey Institute of Technology. Her 35 years of professional experience cover software design and development, teaching in IT/CS, and development of curricula/degrees for high schools and colleges. Along with co-authoring *Our Digital World*, Verno has co-authored *Guidelines for Microsoft Office 2010* for Paradigm Publishing.

Acknowledgements

We would like to thank the following reviewers who have offered valuable comments and suggestions on the content of this textbook.

Becky Anderson
Zane State College
Zanesville, Ohio

Martin S. Anderson, MBA
BGSU Firelands
Huron, Ohio

Roberta Baber
Fresno City College
Fresno, California

Dave Bequette
Butte College
Oroville, California

Shirley Brooks
Holmes Community College
Ridgeland, Mississippi

George Cheng
Hostos Community College
Bronx, New York

Scott Cline
Southwestern Community College
Sylva, North Carolina

James Cutietta
Cuyahoga Community College
Metro Campus
Cleveland, Ohio

Alec Fehl
Asheville-Buncombe Technical
Community College
Asheville, North Carolina

Lisa Giansante, BAS, CMA
Humber College
Toronto, Ontario

Debra Giblin
Mitchell Technical Institute
Mitchell, South Dakota

Glenda Greene
Rowan-Cabarrus Community College
Salisbury, North Carolina

Prosper Hevi, Professor
Kankakee Community College
Kankakee, Illinois

Marilyn Hibbert
Salt Lake Community College
Sandy, Utah

Mardi Holliday
Community College of Philadelphia
Philadelphia, Pennsylvania

Stacy Hollins
Florissant Valley Community College
St. Louis, Missouri

Sherry Howard-Spreitzer
Northwestern Michigan College
Traverse City, Michigan

Annette Kerwin
College of DuPage
Glen Ellyn, Illinois

George Kontos, Ed.D
Bowling Green Community College of
Western Kentucky University
Bowling Green, Kentucky

Kathy Lynch
University of Wisconsin – Oshkosh
Oshkosh, Wisconsin

Lorraine Mastracchio
College of Westchester
White Plains, New York

Dr. Lisa McMillin
East Central Community College
Decatur, Mississippi

Jolene Meyers
Terra Community College
Fremont, Ohio

LeAnn Moreno
Minnesota State College
Southeast Technical
Winona, Minnesota

Larry Morgan
Holmes Community College
Ridgeland, Mississippi

Tammie Munsen, Instructor
Mitchell Technical Institute
Mitchell, South Dakota

Bonnie Murphy
County College of Morris
Randolph, New Hampshire

Gary Muskin
College of Westchester
White Plains, New York

Phil Nielson
Salt Lake Community College
Salt Lake City, Utah

Greg Pauley
Moberly Area Community College
Moberly, Missouri

Stacy Peters-Walters
Kilian Community College
Sioux Falls, South Dakota

Sue VanLanen
Gwinnett Technical College
Lawrenceville, Georgia

Scott Warman
ECPI Technical College
Roanoke, Virginia

Mary Ann Zlotow
College of DuPage
Glen Ellyn, Illinois

Digital Technologies
Exploring a Wealth of Possibilities

What You'll Accomplish

When you finish this chapter, you'll be able to:

- Define what a computer is and identify the various types of computing devices.
- Describe the parts of a computer system and their role in turning data into information.
- Recognize the convergence of computing functionality in devices from phones to appliances.
- Identify the different uses of computers and possible careers in computing.
- Define information technology and explain the information processing cycle.

Why Should I Care?

You encounter computers in their various forms, from desktop computers, to cell phones, to smart appliances, almost every day. In whatever work you do now or are preparing for in the future, understanding the role of computing and the capabilities of computers can help you get ahead. Even an introductory level of technical knowledge gives you an edge in the job market.

Chapter 1 Digital Technologies: Exploring a Wealth of Possibilities

The world of computers includes several types of computing devices that people use for many different purposes. All digital devices process data and produce information that enriches our personal and work lives.

Our Digital World

1.1 Just What Is a Computer?

On the simplest level, a **computer** is an electronic, programmable device that can assemble, process, and store data. An **analog computer** uses mechanical operations to perform calculations, as with an older car speedometer, slide rule, or adding machine. A **digital computer**, which is the category that your laptop or desktop computer falls into, uses symbols that represent data in the form of code. A digital computer has a much higher level of functionality than an analog computing device, including the ability to process words, numbers, images, and sounds.

The combination of digital computing capability with communications has brought us tools such as email and instant messaging, and resulted in new types of computing devices, including mobile phones, gaming devices, and GPS navigation systems.

online **Take a Survey**

How do computers fit into your life?

Today, many devices beyond the traditional desktop or laptop computer have computing capabilities, including your cell phone and gaming devices.

1.2 Computers in All Shapes and Sizes

Although there are many devices that could be considered to have computing capability (which we'll talk about shortly), most of us think of a computer as the desktop or laptop computer we use for work or entertainment. However, nearly two-thirds of Americans (63%) say they use at least two different computing devices (including tablets and smartphones), while 15% use as many as four devices!

Take a stroll down the computer aisle of a well-stocked office superstore and you'll find that there are several kinds of computer models available.

First, as you wander through the store or click through an online store, you'll notice two broad groups of computers: Windows- or Linux-based personal computers (PCs) manufactured by a wide variety of companies such as Hewlett-Packard,

Dell, and Gateway; and Mac computers, available at Apple stores or other authorized retailers. A third, newer category of computers, Chromebooks, run Google's Chrome operating system for web-based computing and are made by manufacturers such as Samsung and Acer.

Table 1.1 lists some common computers categorized by size, which usually correlates with computing power.

Another way to categorize computers relates to their design and size. For example, the computers common in homes and offices range from portable devices to larger units that sit on a desk or table. But the computing world also includes very powerful larger computers used in science and medicine.

Table 1.1 Examples of Computers by Size

Category	Examples
Larger	Supercomputer, mainframe, server
Mid-sized	Personal, workstation, desktop, laptop, netbook
Mobile	Tablet, PDA, smartphone, personal music player, digital audio player, calculator, E-book reader, pocket computer, electronic organizer, handheld game console, wearable computer

Supercomputer

The computing power (that is, the amount of data that can be processed and the speed with which it can be processed) in your laptop today would astound personal computer users of ten years ago. But the fact remains that there are some tasks your personal computer doesn't have the power to handle.

That's where supercomputers and their cousins, mainframe computers (now typically used as servers), come in. A **supercomputer** is a computer with the ability to perform trillions of calculations per second and is usually custom-made for a particular use. For example, when a scientist wants to run a computer model of what happens when a star explodes, or a medical researcher has to process the millions of data points from an MRI scan, he or she turns to supercomputers, because processing the amount of data required could take years on a personal computer. Supercomputer processing power is measured in flops, such as petaflops of processing power. A **petaflop** represents a thousand trillion floating point operations, a measurement often used in scientific calculations.

Supercomputers often function as very large servers in a network. Another model for supercomputers involves **computer clusters**. The moviemaking or computer gaming industries, for example, use clusters of computers joined together with custom-designed connections (known as a **render farm**), to make full-length animated movies that require very high-quality images. These same images would take up to a hundred years to build on a personal computer.

Desktop

A **desktop computer** is a computer whose central processing unit (CPU), might be housed in a tower configuration or in some cases within the monitor, as with the Apple iMac. Though models vary, typically a desktop computer setup includes a CPU, monitor, keyboard, and mouse. Most desktop models would not be considered portable, though you may be able to move some mini-towers or other compact designs around the house with relative ease.

Laptop

Also known as a notebook computer, a **laptop** is essentially portable, though today many are intended as desktop replacements and may come with a large monitor and weigh in at around 15 pounds. Other models weigh only four or five pounds and are designed to be taken on the road. A laptop contains its monitor, keyboard and mouse, along with the CPU and a battery, all in one complete package.

The distinctive design of Macs comes from only one source: Apple.

Tablet

Tablet PCs, which appeared around 2002, are designed to be held like a legal pad, and weigh about three pounds. They are great for taking to meetings or conferences to make notes either by writing on the screen or using an onscreen keyboard. Some models also include a traditional keyboard; you can swivel the unit to go from the pad configuration to a more traditional laptop look. (These are called clamshells.)

In early 2010, a new form of tablet appeared on the scene that essentially replaced Tablet PCs. The Apple iPad hit the market with high demand and created a new niche in computing devices. The tablet is a portable computing device that can be used as an e-reader, web browser, and media content player using a touchscreen interface. Tablets can access a wide world of apps ranging from games to word processors or spreadsheet software. Several tablets are now available, including the Samsung Galaxy, HP TouchPad, T-Mobile G-Slate, ASUS Eee Pad Transformer, and BlackBerry PlayBook and Motorola XOOM. The tablet market is expected to continue to grow in the future.

> " I think if you do something and it turns out pretty good, then you should go do something else wonderful, not dwell on it for too long. Just figure out what's next. "
>
> ▶▶ Steve Jobs, Former CEO of Apple

Tablets enable you to use onscreen controls to navigate by touch.

Netbook

The **netbook** was originally launched as a device for those who mainly wanted to browse the Internet or send and receive email. They are small, usually with screen sizes ranging from eight

Future of the PC

The era of the personal computer—defined here as a separate system unit and CPU, with a large monitor, keyboard, and mouse—is ending, according to many technology pundits.

If that is true, what will our computers look like in the future?

You can expect more tablets, smartphones, and other small devices not yet imagined to handle most of your computing needs, but technology writer Dwight Silverman is not ready to write off the old model that's been with us since the 1970s.

"I think you will always need some kind of very powerful device with a big screen to do heavy lifting," Silverman says.

Listen to the Chapter 1 Spotlight on the Future podcast and then be prepared to answer the following questions.

Talk about It

1. How does Silverman define a personal computer?

2. What does Silverman mean when he talks about a "VPC"?

3. Why does Silverman say the need for a powerful device with a big screen will persist?

4. What company is pushing the idea of a post-PC future?

5. What four components make up Silverman's concept of a personal computer?

inches to ten inches or so, and weigh only two to three pounds. To save on size and weight, netbooks have no optical drive (CD or DVD drive). They do have USB ports that can be used to install applications and to back up files to flash drives (storage devices that slot into a USB port). Next-generation netbooks run operating systems such as Windows 7 and Google Chrome.

The Convergence of Computing Devices

Technological convergence is a term that describes the tendency of technical devices to take on each other's functions. Today computers take many forms beyond the traditional desktop or laptop computer. Some are specialized in their functionality; others tackle some big computer tasks despite their compact design. Many combine communications, media, and information processing features in one package. The ability to access many services online rather than loading applications into a device is helping to make this combination of more features in one small package a reality.

Examples of so-called **convergence devices** include your cell phone, a GPS navigation system, a digital camera, smart appliances that you can program to perform tasks at a certain time, MP3 players, and smartphones. People use these devices for many tasks. It is estimated that by 2014 the number of smartphone users across the globe will be 1 billion. So what are users doing with their convergence devices?

Table 1.2 shows how users are using their smartphones for non-voice data applications. (Note that survey respondents could respond yes to multiple activities.)

Table 1.2 How Smartphones Are Used

Application	Application Percent
Take a picture	76%
Play games	34%
Access the Internet	38%
Play music	33%
Record a video	34%
Send or receive email	34%
Send or receive instant messages	30%
Purchase a product	11%
Make a charitable donation	11%
Status update	10%

Source: Pew Internet Mobile Access 2010, July 7, 2010 - http://pewinternet.org/Reports/2010/Mobile-Access-2010.aspx

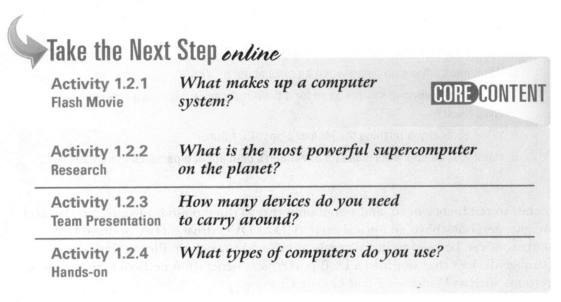

Take the Next Step *online*

Activity 1.2.1 Flash Movie	*What makes up a computer system?*
Activity 1.2.2 Research	*What is the most powerful supercomputer on the planet?*
Activity 1.2.3 Team Presentation	*How many devices do you need to carry around?*
Activity 1.2.4 Hands-on	*What types of computers do you use?*

CORE CONTENT

1.3 Who Is Using Computers and How?

Computers are used in most businesses to create memos and letters, analyze expense and sales figures, research and organize data, and communicate with customers. At home, you may have played a computer game, sent email, or watched a movie on your computer. But you may not be aware of how computers are used by people who work in different industries and have other interests.

Computers Are Everywhere

It's probably easier to give you a list of settings where computers aren't being used than to tell you where they are used. For example, computers are used in government, medicine, publishing, finance, education, arts, law enforcement, social settings, the entertainment industry, gaming, and more.

Our Digital World

Here are a few interesting uses to ponder:

- A fashion show produced by Pitti Imagine used computers to generate images of undersea creatures that the audience could view from both sides of the runway. Models could interact with these images as they showed off the latest fashions.
- Interactive ecosystems in the Netherlands allow children in science museums such as NEMO to interact with the system to make trees out of their bodies and find ways to divert water to them to ensure the health of the forest.
- Philips has produced an interactive window for hotels where a guest can modify the lighting and its pattern. For example, a guest might choose to "draw" the image of a tree outside the window by simply selecting a tree pattern and moving her hand across the window to place the image.
- The ability to archive electronic images such as CAT scans from medical imaging devices and retrieve them from any location, as well as the use of web conferencing to connect specialists at large urban hospitals with healthcare providers in remote locations, is helping doctors diagnose and treat patients more efficiently.
- Korean retailer Tesco used QR codes to enable customers to order groceries for home delivery from subway stations. Users simply scan a product code with their smartphone from a wall display to add the item to their shopping cart. After they check out, the items will be delivered to the customer's home on the same day. Chapter 2 explains what QR codes are and how to use them.
- Thousands of available apps for customizing iPhones, Droid phones, and other smartphones expand the device's capabilities while allowing the user to personalize what the phone can do. Options include travel apps, educational apps, game apps—you name it. Apple even branded this idea with the tagline "There's an app for that."
- Location technologies use GPS or Wi-Fi to track people, fleet vehicles such as delivery vehicles, and products and components in transit from one location to another. Location technologies help ensure that employees and customers have assets where they are needed, find items quickly, avoid excess inventory situations, increase security, and more.

> " The convergence of TV, computer, Net, wireless, telephony across interactive fast real-time broadband networks with GPS information will become a . . . lifestyle. This lifestyle cuts across geography, markets, and cultures. "
>
> ▶▶ Dr. James Canton, Futurist

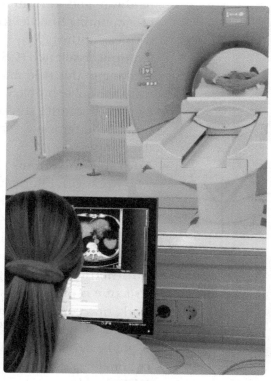

Computer enhanced imaging has allowed medical practitioners to get a clearer picture of patients' health.

Ethics and Technology Blog *online*

Computing All Around You

Ubiquitous computing (also called embedded technology) places computing power in your environment. That means the walls of your house might have the ability to sense your body's temperature and turn up the heat, or sense that you have fallen asleep on the couch and turn down the lighting. If you were a parent, do you think it would be right to monitor your family with such technology?

Finding a Career in Computing

Though you are likely to use computers in your work no matter what your profession, there are several computer-specific fields that exist today. In such a fast-paced field, new career options come up on a regular basis. Even in bad economic times, employers look to information technology workers to save money with more efficient systems and procedures.

Today, there are several computer careers you can prepare for, including:

- **Computer engineering (CE).** This field involves the study of computer hardware and software systems and programming how devices interface with each other.
- **Computer science (CS).** People working in this field may design software, solve problems such as computer security threats, or come up with better ways of handling data storage.
- **Information systems (IS).** Those who work with information systems design technology solutions to help companies solve business problems. An IS professional considers who needs what data to get work done and how it can be delivered most efficiently.
- **Information technology (IT).** IT workers make sure the technology infrastructure is in place to support users. They may set up or maintain a network, or recommend the right hardware and software for their companies.
- **Software engineering (SE).** This field involves writing software programs, which might be developed for a software manufacturer to sell to the public, or involve a custom program written for a large organization to use in-house.
- **Web development.** The World Wide Web provides another group of technology career paths. Programming websites, developing the text and visual content, explaining how clients can use tools such as Search Engine Optimization (SEO) to maximize site traffic, and using social media to pro-

> " With an increase in automation everywhere, the popularity of online social media, the increase in mobile devices, and countries where computing jobs are traditionally off-shored—particularly India—saturating their labor supply, the job prospects for young computing professionals, especially new graduates, are excellent. "
>
> ▶▶| Gopal Gupta, Head of Computer Science, University of Texas

mote goods and services are just a few examples of careers in this area.

- **Geographic information system (GIS) expert.** This field helps us to capture, manage, analyze, and display geographic data. Increasingly used in both the government and private spheres for decision making and problem solving, GIS is a challenging specialty.

A wide variety of careers exists in computer fields, with more being created every day.

According to the *2011 Occupational Outlook Handbook* computer professionals are in demand and it's expected that many new jobs will be created in this field between now and 2018. To prepare for a degree in a computer field, you should consider analytical subjects such as math and science. Usually employers look for a minimum of an associate's degree with a computer science or information technology focus. Because computer technology is constantly changing, employers will be more impressed with your resumé if you stay current with changes by obtaining professional certifications. Some employers will pay for your professional development; others won't.

Take the Next Step *online*

Activity 1.3.1 Video	*What computer jobs has the Web produced?*	**CORE** CONTENT
Activity 1.3.2 Research	*Who provides professional certifications for an IT worker?*	
Activity 1.3.3 Interview	*How have computers redefined some industries?*	
Activity 1.3.4 Research	*How will computers play out in your career?*	
Activity 1.3.5 Hands-on	*What computer-related training will you pursue?*	

The Information Technology (IT) department in an organization is in charge of its most valuable asset: information. IT is a department you are likely to come into contact with, whether as an IT employee or as a user of a company computer system, so it's important for you to understand just what information technology is.

According to the former Information Technology Association of America (ITAA), now merged with other organizations to form TechAmerica, information technology is "the study, design, development, implementation, support, or management of computer-based information systems, particularly software applications and computer hardware."

There are a few basic concepts that will help you understand IT. One is the difference between data and information; the other is what's involved in information processing.

Computers in Your Career

Computer-assisted translation (CAT) is being used by those who translate books or other content. A translator uses software that helps in the translation process. Customized dictionaries in the software contain data that help keep translations accurate and make the work of translators easier. Translation memory programs allow a translator to store phrases that they can retrieve at any time. If you speak another language, consider looking into translating, with the help of CAT, as a possible career.

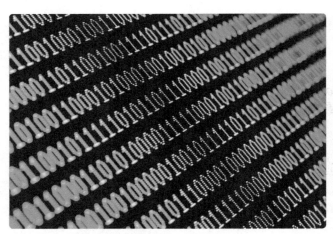

Data such as these numbers may be the basis of information in the form of a graph or table that organizes the data.

Differentiating Between Data and Information

Say that your job is to predict which new toys will prove most popular next holiday season. You might gather data about popular toys, their prices, and their sales to date. When you take that raw data and organize it into a chart or table that compares sales and prices, it becomes information that you can use to make a business decision.

Computers can take data and turn it into useful information by processing and organizing it. **Data** is what you put into a computer. **Information** is what you can get out of it.

The Information Processing Cycle

What happens between obtaining raw data and getting information based on that data from your computer? That is what the **information processing cycle** is all about. This cycle, shown in Figure 1.1, has four parts: input of data, processing of data, output of information, and storage of data and information.

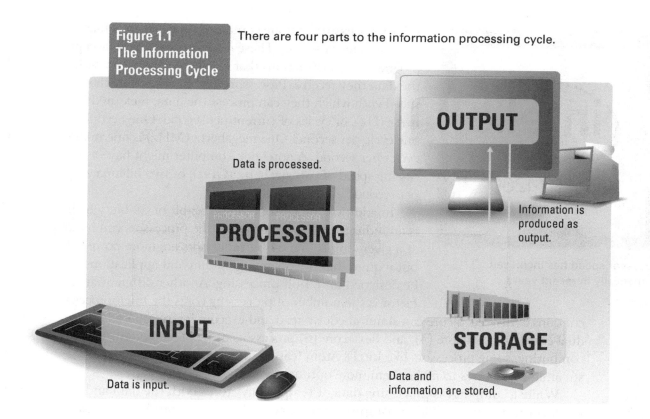

**Figure 1.1
The Information
Processing Cycle**

There are four parts to the information processing cycle.

OUTPUT

Data is processed.

PROCESSING

Information is
produced as
output.

INPUT

STORAGE

Data is input.

Data and
information are stored.

Input In a typical day, you use a decimal system as you go about your tasks. For example, if you have your car repaired and the bill is $321, you've spent three hundreds, two tens, and one dollar. All this is based on a decimal system of ten possible digits, 0 through 9. Computers, on the other hand, use a **binary system** with two possible values, 0 and 1, called binary digits. The term **bit** is a shortening of binary digits. Bits are found together in 8-bit collections. Each collection is called a **byte**. Each byte can store one thing like a digit, a special character, or a letter of the alphabet. You'll hear the terms bits and bytes used in the descriptions of processors (for example, 64-bit Pentium) and data storage capacity (8 gigabytes memory).

When you **input** data in a computer, it is converted to bits and bytes. Though typing data on a keyboard may leap to mind when you think of getting data into your computer, there are actually several methods of inputting data. For example, you might provide your computer with input using a mouse, keyboard, touchscreen, scanner, gaming joystick, bar code scanner, microphone, camera, or the number pad on your smartphone. (You'll learn more about input and output devices in Chapter 3.)

Processing The **central processing unit (CPU)** in your computer is what interprets instructions and performs the **processing** of data. CPUs are made up of integrated electronic circuits called

Devices such as scanners turn existing printed
materials into digital data.

Processor speed has increased dramatically in recent years.

microprocessors that are contained on chips, which are small squares of silicon. These microprocessors can accept programming instructions that tell them what to do with the data they receive. Processors are often rated by the speed with which they can process the data, measured in hertz (Hz), or cycles of current per second. One hertz is one cycle per second. One megahertz (MHz) is one million cycles per second. A notebook computer might have a processing speed of two gigahertz (GHz), or two billion cycles per second.

In addition, processors can be 32-bit or 64-bit, which is an indicator of how much data the processors can handle at a given point. The 64-bit processors are more powerful, but require that the operating system and applications also be designed for 64-bit processing. Another differentiating factor is the number of processing cores the microprocessor contains, where each core can simultaneously read and execute instructions. There are dual-core (2), quad-core (4), and hexa-core (6) processors available today. For mobile computing, some processors like Intel's Atom feature ultra-low-voltage and other streamlined features to make them more optimal for netbooks and tablets.

While a computer is processing data, it temporarily stores both the data and instructions from the CPU in **computer memory** in the form of **random access memory (RAM)**. There is a constant exchange of information between the CPU and RAM during processing. When you turn your computer off, the data temporarily stored in RAM disappears; therefore RAM is also referred to as volatile memory. Think of RAM as similar to a shopping cart—while you're shopping, you can temporarily place items in the cart. If you walk out of the store without buying the items, somebody will empty the cart and the items "disappear."

There is also an area of computer memory between RAM and the processor called cache memory. **Cache memory** is a holding area for the most frequently used data. As illustrated in Figure 1.2, your processor checks the cache memory first, because it is located on or near the microprocessor chip and therefore quicker to access. This procedure saves time trolling through the entire RAM holding area for what the processor needs.

Monitors come in a variety of sizes and types. This 27-inch widescreen monitor provides a large-screen view of computer programs and data, and is especially beneficial for users who work with detailed drawings.

Output Once you've put a lot of data into your computer, you'll typically want to see that data in some form. **Output** is the information that results from computer processing. Output might include the information you view on your monitor, a printed hard copy of a document, or an x-ray produced by a medical imaging computer. Your mobile phone screen can also provide output.

A monitor can display your computer's output at various resolutions. **Resolution** refers to the number of **pixels** (short for picture elements, which relates to the

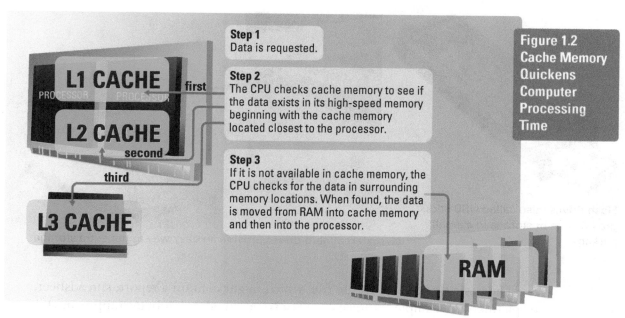

Figure 1.2
Cache Memory
Quickens
Computer
Processing
Time

Step 1
Data is requested.

Step 2
The CPU checks cache memory to see if the data exists in its high-speed memory beginning with the cache memory located closest to the processor.

Step 3
If it is not available in cache memory, the CPU checks for the data in surrounding memory locations. When found, the data is moved from RAM into cache memory and then into the processor.

L1 CACHE   first
L2 CACHE   second
third
L3 CACHE
RAM

number of dots of color) used to generate an image on your screen. The higher the number of pixels, the more clearly defined the image.

Speakers are another form of output device. You might receive output of audio files through your computer or cell phone speakers, for example.

Printers are another method of output that create a permanent hard copy record of your computing results. Though there have been predictions of a paperless office for years, people seem to cling to their paper copies of documents to keep records or make notes on. Many printer types are available, such as laser and deskjet, which you will learn more about in Chapter 3.

Storage **Storage** is a key part of the information processing cycle. If you have ever spent hours typing on a keyboard only to discover that your work was somehow lost, you know how important storage is. Your computer temporarily stores data while it runs processes, but that temporarily stored data is lost when you turn your computer off. You use a permanent storage device, such as a flash drive, to save a copy of your data or information that's available long after you have shut your computer off. Early permanent storage media included paper punch cards, followed by floppy plastic disks and then floppy disks in hard cases. The most common long-term storage medium is your computer's internal hard drive, which is a metallic disk that uses magnetic storage technology to store data. You can also store data on removable media (for example a flash drive or DVD) so you can retrieve it from any computer. An increasingly popular storage medium is cloud storage. **Cloud storage** involves storing information on the Web. Users access the stored information from any computer using a username and password. A popular cloud storage service is SkyDrive. SkyDrive is free and users get up to 25 GB of storage. Any type of file may be uploaded and may be private, shared, or public. Other popular cloud storage services are Dropbox, iCloud, Box.net, and ADrive.

Playing It Safe

It's a good idea to get in the habit of saving your files as you work and backing up your files on a regular basis. The cost in time and money of losing your work could be tremendous. In addition, in your working life you may be required to keep backup copies of files for a period of time to meet government regulations or prove your ownership of the work. Always keep a backup separate from your computer hard drive (for example on a DVD, flash drive, or in the Cloud) in case your hard drive fails.

Flash drives (also called USB sticks) provide lots of storage in a small package.

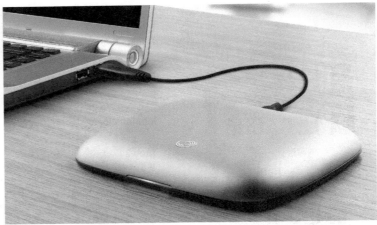

External hard drives provide an easy way to get extra storage capacity.

The basic storage unit is the **file**, which might contain a report, spreadsheet, or picture, for example. Storage capacity is measured in kilobytes (approximately 1,000 bytes), megabytes (approximately 1 million bytes), gigabytes (approximately 1 billion bytes) and terabytes (approximately 1 trillion bytes).

Storage devices include your computer's hard disk, CD or DVD discs (also called optical discs), USB or flash drives (thumb-sized cartridges that slot into a USB port on your computer), and external hard drives (small boxes that connect to your computer via a cable connected to a USB port). Future forms of computer memory and storage may be made of conductive gels, making them suitable for environments that would destroy current types of memory and storage, such as wet environments.

Take the Next Step *online*

Activity 1.4.1 Flash Movie	*What are the various types of RAM?*	**CORE**CONTENT
Activity 1.4.2 Video	*What is the machine cycle?*	**CORE**CONTENT
Activity 1.4.3 Research	*How big can data get?*	
Activity 1.4.4 Team Presentation	*Is it data or information?*	
Activity 1.4.5 Video	*Why should you consider backing up files online?*	
Activity 1.4.6 Hands-on	*What does the term* computer *mean to you?*	

Just What Is a Computer?

On the simplest level, a **computer** is a programmable device that can assemble, process, and store data.

An **analog computer** uses mechanical operations to perform calculations, as with an older car speedometer or slide rule. A **digital computer** uses symbols that represent data in the form of code.

The combination of digital computing capability with communications has brought us tools such as email and instant messaging and new types of computing devices, including mobile phones, gaming devices, and GPS navigation systems.

Computers in All Shapes and Sizes

Computers fall into three broad groups based on operating system and manufacturer: Windows- or Linux-based personal computers (PCs) manufactured by a wide variety of companies such as Hewlett-Packard, Dell, and Gateway; Mac computers available only through Apple; and Chromebooks using Google's Chrome OS.

Computing power is the amount of data that can be processed and the speed with which it can be processed. A **supercomputer** is a computer with the ability to perform trillions of calculations per second and is usually custom-made for a particular use.

A **desktop computer** includes a central processing unit (CPU), which might be housed in a tower configuration or in some cases within the monitor, as with the Apple iMac.

Also known as notebook computers, **laptops** are usually portable, though today many are intended as desktop replacements and may come with a large monitor and weigh as much as 15 pounds.

Tablets are manufactured by several companies and enable you to navigate by touching easy-to-use onscreen tools. Tablets run several newer operating systems, such as Apple's iOS and Android.

The **netbook** was originally designed for users who mainly wanted to browse the Internet or send and receive email. They are small, usually with screen sizes ranging from eight inches to ten inches or so, and weigh only two to three pounds.

Technological convergence is a term that describes the tendency of technical devices to take on each other's functions, resulting in communications, media, and information computing features in one package. So-called **convergence devices** include your cell phone, a GPS navigation system, a digital camera, MP3 players, and smartphones.

Who Is Using Computers and How?

Computers are used in government, medicine, publishing, finance, education, arts, law enforcement, social settings, the entertainment industry, gaming, and more.

Though you are likely to use computers in your work no matter what your profession, there are several computer-specific fields that exist today. **Computer engineering (CE)** involves the study of computer hardware and software systems and programming devices to interface with each other. **Computer science (CS)** workers may design software, solve problems such as computer security threats, or come up with better ways of handling data storage. **Information systems (IS)** workers identify the kinds of data company employees need and design the technology systems to solve business problems. **Information technology (IT)** workers make sure the technology infrastructure is in place to support users. They may set up or maintain a network, or recommend the right hardware and software for their companies. **Software engineering (SE)** involves writing software programs that a software manufacturer sells to the public, or custom programs that a large organization uses in-house. There are also a number of **web development**-focused career tracks, as well as the need for **geographic information system (GIS)** experts.

What Is Information Technology?

According to the former Information Technology Association of America (ITAA), now part of TechAmerica, information technology is "the study, design, development, implementation, support or management of computer-based information systems, particularly software applications and computer hardware."

Computers take **data** and turn it into useful **information** by processing and organizing it. For example, if you take raw data about sales and prices and put it into a chart, it becomes information that you can use to make a business decision.

The **information processing cycle** has four parts: input of data, processing of data, output of information, and storage of data and information. Computers use a **binary system** of data based on two possible values, 0 and 1, called binary digits or **bits**.

You provide your computer with **input**-using devices such as a mouse, keyboard, scanner, gaming joystick, bar code scanner, or the number pad on your smartphone.

The **central processing unit (CPU)** in your computer interprets instructions and performs the **processing** of data. CPUs are made up of integrated circuits called **microprocessors** contained on chips. Processors are often rated by the speed with which they can process data, measured in hertz (Hz), megahertz (MHz), or gigahertz (GHz). The 64-bit processors generally can handle more data at once than 32-bit processors, and require matching 64-bit software. The number of cores indicates how many simultaneous program instructions the processor can execute, with dual-core (2), quad-core (4), and hexa-core (6) processors available today. For mobile computing, some processors such as Intel's Atom feature ultra-low-voltage and other streamlined features to make them more optimal for netbooks and tablets.

While a computer is processing data, it temporarily stores both the data and instructions from the CPU in **computer memory** in the form of **random access**

memory (RAM), also called volatile memory. When you turn your computer off, the data temporarily stored in RAM disappears. There is also an area of computer memory between RAM and the processor called cache memory. **Cache memory** is a holding area for the most frequently used data.

Output is the information that results from computer processing. Output can include the information you view on your monitor or a printed hard copy of a document.

Storage is a key part of the information processing cycle. Your computer temporarily stores data while it runs processes, but that temporarily stored data is lost when you turn your computer off. You use a permanent storage device to save a copy of your data or information that's available long after you have shut your computer off. The basic storage unit is the **file**. Storage devices include your computer's hard disk, CD or DVD discs (also called optical discs), USB or flash drives, and external hard drives. **Cloud storage** involves storing information on the Web. Future memory and storage technologies might use conductive gels that can stand up in wet environments.

Terms to Know

CORE CONTENT

Just What Is a Computer?

computer, 4

analog computer, 4

digital computer, 4

Computers in All Shapes and Sizes

supercomputer, 5

petaflop, 5

computer cluster, 5

render farm, 5

desktop computer, 5

laptop, 6

tablet, 6

netbook, 6

technological convergence, 7

convergence device, 7

Who Is Using Computers and How?

ubiquitous computing, 10

computer engineering (CE), 10

computer science (CS), 10

information systems (IS), 10

information technology (IT), 10

software engineering (SE), 10

web development, 10

geographic information system (GIS) expert, 11

webmaster, Activity 1.3.1

Internet law, Activity 1.3.1

web designer, Activity 1.3.1

What Is Information Technology?

Concepts Check

CORE CONTENT

Concepts Check 1.1 Multiple Choice
Take this quiz to test your understanding of key concepts in this chapter.

Concepts Check 1.2 Word Puzzle
Complete this puzzle to test your knowledge of key terms in this chapter.

Concepts Check 1.3 Matching
Test your understanding of terms and concepts presented in this chapter.

Concepts Check 1.4 Label It
Use the interactive tool to identify the categories of computers.

Concepts Check 1.5 Arrange It
Use the interactive tool to identify the parts of a computer system.

Projects

CORE CONTENT

Check with your instructor for the preferred method to submit completed work.

Project 1.1 Computers Then and Now

Project 1.1.1 Individual

As a computer user, you may be curious as to the history of the personal computer and its changing purposes and functions. To gain a better understanding of the computer's evolution, research the Internet to help you formulate questions for a trivia quiz for your classmates. You will want to create 15 to 20 test questions and a separate answer key (including reference sources). The sample questions below will give you a head start.

1. Who developed the first model that would serve as the prototype for computers?
2. What are the names of the two men who played a part in the development of the PC that was first advertised on the cover of *Popular Electronics*? What company did they later form?
3. What is the name of the computer company that Steve Jobs and Steve Wozniak formed in 1976?
4. In 1981, a computer was released that would dominate the computer market. What was the name of this personal computer?
5. Name the operating system advancement that allowed users to interact with the computer more easily. Name the company that was the innovator of this important advancement.
6. In 1984, Apple introduced the Macintosh. What did the Macintosh include that helped people store their files?

When you have finished writing, exchange your trivia quiz with a classmate to test his or her knowledge. Use your answer key to check the results. Be prepared to discuss your answers in class.

Project 1.1.2 Team

In the future, it's likely that you and your classmates will work in jobs that require computer skills. As a team, select three jobs that utilize computers. Research the ways in which computers are used for these jobs by addressing the following questions:

1. What aspects of the job require the use of a computer?
2. In what ways does using a computer encourage efficiency, effectiveness, and productivity?
3. How has the computer changed the way the job is performed in the last 20 years?
4. What types of advances in computer technology do you think might affect this job in the future?

Prepare a slide presentation summarizing the information you discovered. Be prepared to share the presentation with the class.

Project 1.2 Making Computer-Related Recommendations

Project 1.2.1 Individual

As a manager for a pharmaceutical sales company, you oversee a staff of sales representatives who frequently travel to call on doctors, hospitals, and research teams. Your staff uses laptops with broadband access cards, but you are considering a switch from laptops to either tablets or netbooks. Research the pros and cons of three different types of devices and document your resources. Then prepare a table that addresses the following questions:

1. What is the cost of each selected device?
2. What features are included with each device?
3. What components may be added?

Use the information from your table to determine which device would be a better option for your sales representatives. Summarize your decision in writing. If you decide to make the switch from laptops to another device, specify which device you would recommend purchasing and why.

Project 1.2.2 Team

The owners of a toy manufacturing company believe that new computer input and output devices will result in improved worker efficiency. Your IT team has been asked to study the issue and make a recommendation. To accomplish this project, you and your teammates should complete the following tasks:

1. Prepare a list of all possible input/output devices in general use.
2. Describe what type of training each input/output device requires.
3. Identify which company departments (such as marketing, sales, finance, manufacturing, customer service) might use a specific input/output device.
4. List the cost of each device, assuming that mice and keyboards do not need to be purchased. Include your reference sources.
5. Recommend three input/output devices that should be purchased.

Prepare a table that displays your research findings, and attach a summary of your written recommendation.

Project 1.3   Understanding Work-Related Injuries

Project 1.3.1 Individual

Substantial evidence indicates that individuals who frequently use computers at work are at risk for computer-related injuries. As you start your new data entry job, you want to ensure that you do not become another statistic. Research the topic of work-related injuries for computer users. Prepare a blog posting that lists common injuries, the causes of these injuries, and suggestions for creating a safe working environment.

Project 1.3.2 Team

As members of the human resources department, your team has been assigned to investigate an increase in employee work-related injuries. Specifically, employees who work at computer workstations have reported chronic musculoskeletal problems. To help these employees, your team will prepare a slide presentation on how to create an ergonomic workstation. Your presentation should address chair requirements, including height adjustments and lumbar support; monitor and keyboard locations and settings; ergonomic accessories; and training. Be prepared to share your presentation with the class.

Project 1.4   Storage and Processing

Project 1.4.1   Individual

There are a variety of storage devices such as disk storage, cloud storage, CDs and DVDs, tapes, off-site backups, and flash memory. As a consultant to a large city hospital, you must select the most dependable storage devices to meet the hospital's needs. What type of storage devices would you recommend for private patient records? What type of storage devices would you use for very large files such as x-ray images? What type of storage devices would you use that you can save data to and retrieve data from (read/write)? How does retrieval speed affect your choice of media? Write a summary of your research, and include a recommendation of storage devices that will meet the hospital's needs. Be sure to document your resources.

Project 1.4.2   Team

Your team has been assigned to apply the information processing cycle to the car design industry. The information processing cycle includes four steps: input, processing, output, and storage. Research the various applications, and share your findings in a classroom slide presentation.

Project 1.5   Wiki Project — Backing Up Data

Project 1.5.1   Individual

Interview one person who works at your college or a local business to find out how and why they back up data. If possible, pursue interesting industries that might have unique data needs such as nuclear power facilities, hospitals, or the stock exchange. Post your interview in podcast or transcript form on the class wiki. Be sure to include references for verification of content.

Project 1.5.2   Team

As a class, design a structure for a wiki database of industry backup procedures. The database might include the industry, backup methods, and comments about why these methods are important in that industry. Break into small teams. Everybody on your team should post the information they gathered about backup methods on the class wiki. If two people post information about the same industry, they should combine the entries. In addition to posting an entry, add a comment or more information to other students' postings. When you post or edit content, make sure you include a notation with the page that includes your name or team name and the date you posted or edited the content.

Project 1.6   Choosing a Computer

Project 1.6.1   Individual

You are offered a position as a graphic designer. Your new employer tells you that you can select the computer you need, as well as submit a list of specifications for your computer system. Research your computer options. Identify a base system you feel would work, and prepare a table or spreadsheet listing the specifications and costs. Include any upgrades or additional components (along with their costs) that would enhance your system. In a memo addressed to your employer, state your computer system preferences and include your table or spreadsheet showing cost analysis. In addition, provide a list of informational resources.

Project 1.6.2   Team

More and more students are using tablet devices in the classroom. Your institution has been asked to recommend a tablet for incoming students. The director of the IT department at your institution has recommended that the IT Club take on this project. The club has decided to work in teams to research the advantages and disadvantages of each tablet device such as an iPad, Galaxy, or any other brand of tablets. Each team will prepare a presentation to the director of IT at your institution comparing the various brands of tablet devices. Your presentation should include an overview of each device, and a picture of the tablet, as well as specific information such as weight, cost, available apps and software, ease of use, battery life, screen size, storage, wireless connectivity, special features, and options for input/output peripheral devices. Your presentation should include both advantages and disadvantages of each brand of tablets. After your team has compiled the research, prepare your presentation and make a recommendation. Make sure you include a justification for your team's recommendation.

Class Conversations

Topic 1.1   Computers and Efficiency

Computers have changed the way we work. Most employees would say that computers have helped them become more effective and efficient in the workplace. Some think that computers just create more work and cause problems when they crash or slow down. Discuss a career or place of employment where you think computers have actually decreased effectiveness and efficiency. Why do you think this is the case? Be prepared to support your position.

Topic 1.2 The Computer of the Future

Technology changes rapidly. Since the first personal computer appeared on the cover of *Popular Electronics* in 1975, the computer has changed in performance, cost, size, and capabilities. The personal computer has morphed from a desktop to a handheld device. The Chapter 1 Spotlight on the Future podcast on page 7 discusses possibilities regarding the future of computers. Consider what you think the computer of the future will be like. Discuss what the computer might look like, its functionality, capacity, and performance.

Topic 1.3 Globalization of the Computer Industry

Many companies have outsourced specific types of computer work to other countries. There is a cost benefit to using overseas employees, but an economic toll on domestic companies. Discuss the advantages and disadvantages of outsourcing computer work to other countries. How could this decision have an impact on the U.S. and Canadian economies and the job market in the future?

Chapter 2

The Internet
Gateway to a World of Resources

What You'll Accomplish

- Describe how the Internet and the Web have changed the ways in which people interact with each other.
- Identify the services, equipment, and software you need to connect and browse the Internet.
- Browse and search the Internet and Web for information and evaluate the accuracy of content you find.
- Demonstrate a basic understanding of intellectual property and copyright laws.
- Compare and contrast various Internet services and applications such as e-commerce, email, telephone, and web conferencing.

Why Should I Care?

Forty-nine percent of the public used the Internet to track the 2009 outbreak of H1N1 (swine) flu. Fifty-five percent of adults said they went online to follow the 2008 presidential campaign (Pew Internet & American Life Project). A study by IBM indicated that 80 percent of the students surveyed "anticipate running into new technology that they will have to adapt to and learn upon entering the workforce." From protecting our health to electing our officials, the Internet has become an indispensable part of our lives. Understanding what the Internet is, how it works, and the dynamics of its growth will help you succeed personally and professionally in our digital age.

Supercomputer

Network access

Wide area network

Local network

Hub

Router

Gateway

Bridge

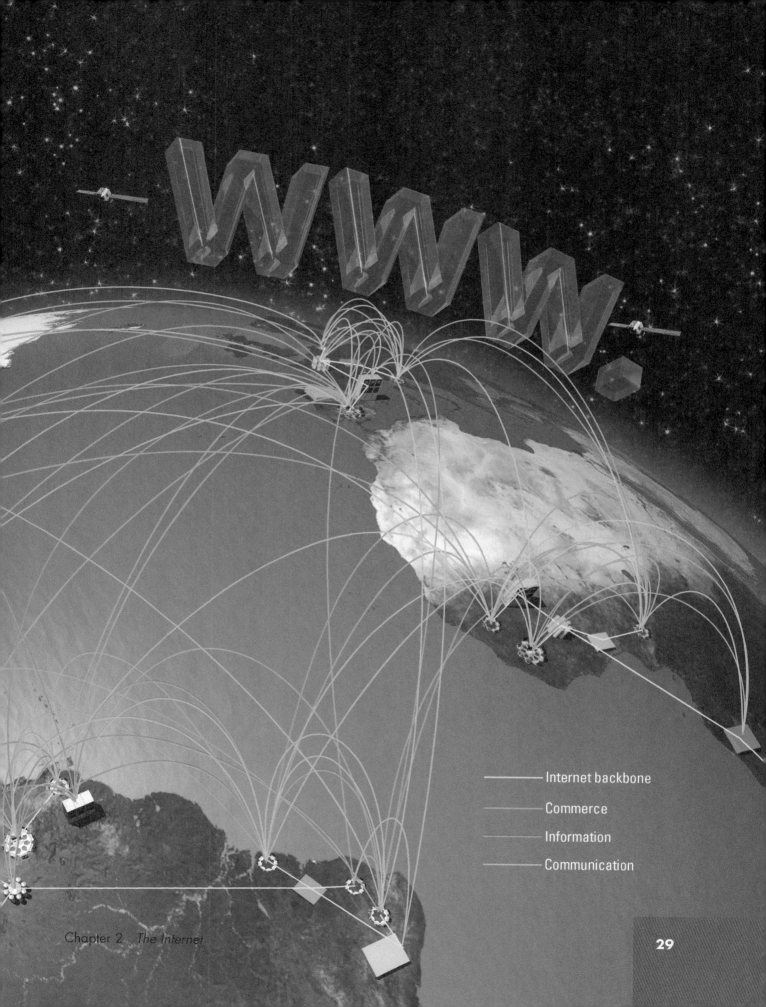

Internet backbone

Commerce

Information

Communication

Many people, for much of their day, use the Internet for a wide variety of activities. People learn, work, play, and connect with others using several types of devices, such as computers, cell phones, PDAs, and even gaming devices and information kiosks. We can even connect our own electronic devices with one another to keep our data up to date. That enables us to do things like view our calendar and contacts on our PC or on our smartphone and post to Facebook from any Internet-connected device.

In a survey conducted by IBM's Academic Initiative, which polled 1,613 college-enrolled undergraduates nationwide in 2009, 99 percent own a cell phone, 97 percent have a profile on a social networking site, and 93 percent own a laptop. A survey of students from Kansas State University revealed that students view an average of 2,300 web pages a year and read over 1,200 Facebook postings. All these activities on various devices take advantage of the Internet to do things that would have seemed miraculous only a dozen years ago.

Your cell phone is a tiny computer with enormous potential.

Cutting-Edge Internet

Activities such as shopping, communicating, and researching online are probably familiar to you, but there are some uses of the Internet that could be new to you. For example:

- Today, scientists share the use of extremely expensive, specialized microscopes over the Internet.
- Doctors learn surgery through online cyberscalpel simulations.
- Airline pilots practice landing a plane on water with web-based flight simulators.
- NASA, through a program called NASA Quest, offers web-based, interactive explorations of space to students.
- iPhones can act as electronic airline tickets—the airline sends you an email or text message that

Many colleges are phasing out computer labs and requiring that freshmen have a laptop computer to do coursework and communicate with instructors.

contains a bar code. Open the message and then scan your phone at the airport rather than handing over a paper boarding pass.

- A **quick response (QR) code** provides a shortcut you can use to go to a website using your smartphone. Rather than entering the web address, you use your phone (with a reader application installed) to scan this 2D bar code and let the code connect your phone to the site. Figure 2.1 shows how this process works. QR codes work well in marketing for bringing potential clients or customers to a target website. A school library can use a QR code to direct a student to a website to search for a particular book.
- Cloud computing lets you access your files and programs from anywhere in the world via the Internet. Because the files and programs reside on the web, they are always available. For example, say your class is cancelled which means that you now have time to finish your research paper before your next class. Even if you don't have your laptop with you, you could use a lab computer to open the document that contains the research paper from the cloud and work on it using cloud-delivered software, such as GoogleDocs.
- Microblogging sites such as Twitter are pushing the boundaries of citizen journalism as participants often send out updates on current news stories before news agencies do.

What remarkable uses of the Internet are you aware of?

**Figure 2.1
A QR Code
in Action**

Scanner software enables your smartphone to read the code and go to the destination website.

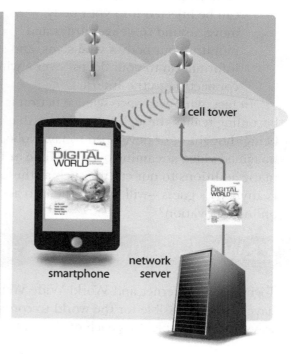

The Future of the Internet

Some current uses of the Internet are amazing, and in the future, this technology will only become more ingrained in your daily life. Consider the possibilities:

- In 2009 astronauts sent the first tweets (Twitter messages) from the space shuttle Atlantis and the International Space Station. The Mars Phoenix lander tweeted its progress as it explored that planet. With no Internet connection they had to send their tweets to Earth where others posted them, but at some point, will our global Internet reach directly out to other planets?

Pilots plan for air disasters by training online.

- Collaboration and social media keep converging in the cloud. Whether it's recommending a Hulu video to your Facebook friends with the click of a button or developing the specs for a new product via a company wiki, online collaboration is fast moving toward becoming a real-time tool for teams and colleagues.
- Nanotechnology-enabled robots can be injected into your body, move around to deliver drugs and monitor your body's vital signs, and send information to your doctor over a wireless connection to the Internet.

In fact, what was once science fiction is becoming reality through technologies that are being thought of or developed today. Nobody imagined video streaming over YouTube or texting ten years ago, yet online dramatic additions to our culture such as these explode on the scene rapidly. Tomorrow is anybody's guess—will you be there to adopt or even introduce the next great online innovation?

" You can't just ask customers what they want and then try to give that to them. By the time you get it built, they'll want something new. "

▶▶I Steve Jobs, former CEO of Apple

online ✓ **Take a Survey**
How are you and your fellow students using the Internet today?

2.2 What Are the Internet and World Wide Web?

Together the Internet and World Wide Web (better known as simply the Web) have made it possible for the world to connect and communicate in remarkable ways. But what role does each of these play?

What Is the Internet?

The **Internet** is the world's largest computer network—a physical infrastructure that provides us with the ability to share resources and communicate with others around the world. It is possible to "see, touch, and feel" elements of the Internet because it's made up of hardware such as servers, routers, switches, transmission lines, and towers that store and transmit vast amounts of data (Figure 2.2).

The Internet is the pathway on which data, sounds, and images flow from person to person around the globe.

What Is the Web?

If the Internet is a pathway for information, the Web is the content that travels along that path. The **Web** is a body of content that is available as web pages. The pages are stored on Internet servers around the world. A **web page** may contain text, images, interactive animations, games, music, and more. Several web pages may make up a single **website** (Figure 2.3).

The documents you choose to put on the Web are the ones you want other people to see. You can also choose whether you want everyone in the world to view your documents or limit access to a few close friends.

Because anyone can publish just about anything to the Web, it has become very popular very fast, and has grown with little oversight or regulation. Many people feel that what makes the Web appealing is that it is a largely unregulated environment. However, that very lack of regulation and supervision means that some people feel

> " I must confess that I've never trusted the Web. Where does it live? How do I hold it personally responsible? And is it male or female? In other words, can I challenge it to a fight? "
>
> ▶▶I Stephen Colbert, Comedian

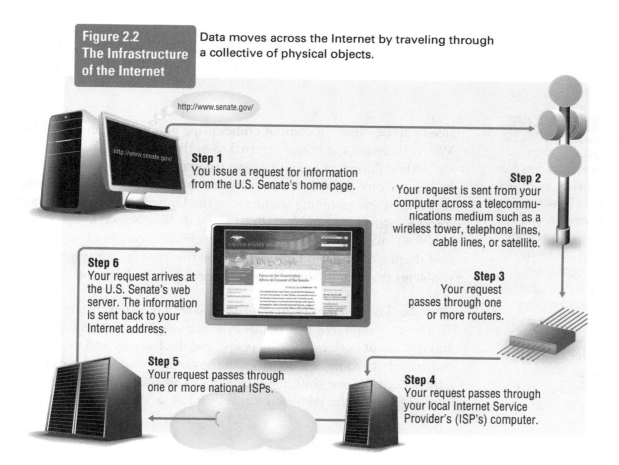

**Figure 2.2
The Infrastructure of the Internet**

Data moves across the Internet by traveling through a collective of physical objects.

http://www.senate.gov/

http://www.senate.gov/

Step 1
You issue a request for information from the U.S. Senate's home page.

Step 2
Your request is sent from your computer across a telecommunications medium such as a wireless tower, telephone lines, cable lines, or satellite.

Step 3
Your request passes through one or more routers.

Step 4
Your request passes through your local Internet Service Provider's (ISP's) computer.

Step 5
Your request passes through one or more national ISPs.

Step 6
Your request arrives at the U.S. Senate's web server. The information is sent back to your Internet address.

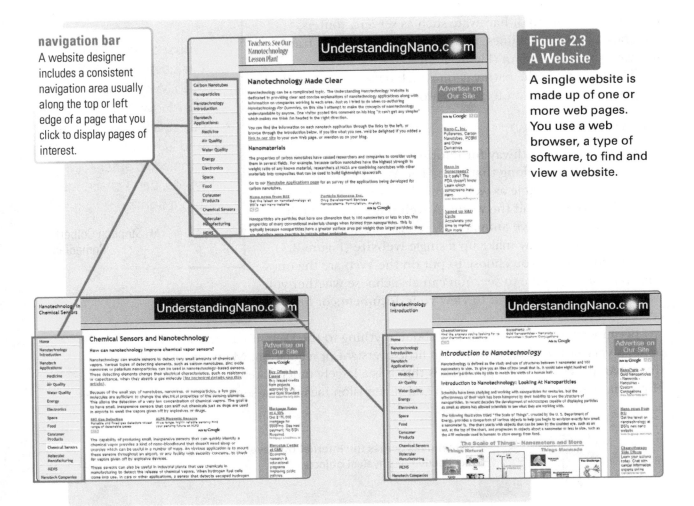

**Figure 2.3
A Website**

A single website is made up of one or more web pages. You use a web browser, a type of software, to find and view a website.

free to abuse others or commit crimes using online tools and sites. The Web is therefore sometimes referred to as the wild, wild West.

Although certain countries have regulations and laws in place, it is hard to enforce them across borders and cultures. For example, many forms of online gambling are illegal in the United States, but it's easy for U.S. citizens to gamble online using off-shore hosted online casinos. Still, many people feel that the benefits of freedom of expression and sharing of ideas and information on the Web far outweigh the problems that result from the lack of regulation and control.

Web 2.0 The different phases of the Web are not like software releases. Rather, they represent new trends in online usage and technologies, brought about both by the way people use the Internet and the technologies that enable new activities in the online world. We have already experienced the first shift in online usage. This shift is considered the second phase of the Web, and it is referred to as Web 2.0. **Web 2.0**

Ethics and Technology Blog *online*

Regulating Web Behavior

Some people think the Web should be regulated by a central body. Other people think the freedom to say and do what you want on the Web should be protected. What do you think? Should the Web be under anybody's control?

Take the Next Step *online*

Activity 2.2.1 Research	*If anyone can post content to the Web, who manages the Web and in what ways?*	**CORE CONTENT**
Activity 2.2.2 Research	*Who founded the Web?*	

Computers in Your Career

The Internet and Web have made available a wide variety of careers that didn't exist ten years ago, and not all are high-tech in nature. Consider jobs such as web content writer, Internet law expert, and online trainer. If you are more technically inclined, a variety of developer jobs allow you to work with tasks from programming an e-commerce shopping cart to creating environments in virtual reality worlds.

marks a change from people simply reading information online to people interacting by both reading and writing online content.

The concept of Web 2.0 came out of the "dot-com collapse" of 2001, when many online businesses failed. Internet users appeared to be unwilling to pay fees to use online services such as email and news and sought a more collaborative experience. New applications and websites began popping up with surprising regularity, marking a turning point for the Web, according to an article by Tim O'Reilly, founder of O'Reilly Publishing.

Over time, Web 2.0 has become associated with interactive web services such as Wikipedia and Facebook that provide users with a way to collaborate by sharing and exchanging ideas, and adding or editing content. The premise of this generation of web usage is that one is not passively viewing but actually interacting with content.

Web 2.0 spawned an entire conference dedicated to defining it.

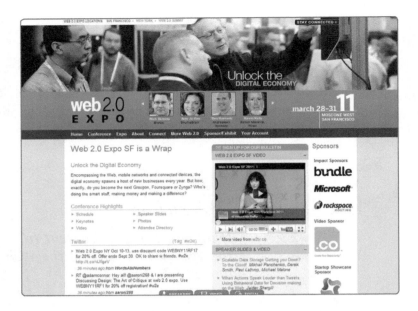

Web 3.0 **Web 3.0** is seen as the next phase in online usage. Web 3.0 will host collaborative content that is connected in meaningful ways. For example, where today you can post a photo from your vacation online and also keep an online calendar with your trip itinerary, in the world of Web 3.0 your photos appear within the calendar on the date and at the time you took them. Web 3.0 is also called the **Semantic Web**, appropriately named because semantics is the study of meaning in language.

In Web 3.0, machines can talk to machines. For example, TiVo searches the Internet and gathers information about programs that you might like to watch from various websites. In Web 3.0, machines go beyond just gathering information; they can also draw conclusions about the data they share. The Semantic Web will make it possible for websites to "understand" the relationships between elements of web content. An intelligent agent, or search program, can even update and modify your documents on the fly based on information you read on the Internet. For this to come about, we have to find common formats so that data can be integrated, rather than just exchanged.

Web 3.0 will have an impact on how we search. In 2009 Google introduced Google Squared, a tool that can break down research into columns and rows to

Computers in Your Career

Huge volumes of patient data create a record keeping challenge in the medical field. Medical informatics professionals work to tame the mountains of data by designing medical information systems that make it easier to enter, update, and retrieve medical data. Today's expert systems not only make data retrieval easier, but also present and summarize information in a way that assists medical professionals in diagnosing and treating illnesses.

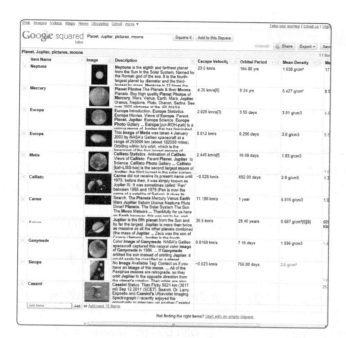

Google Squared is just one of several new approaches to searching that allows you to collect and compare different results.

help users organize information they find on the Web. Microsoft's Bing search service finds information and provides recommendations to help you make choices and decisions for shopping, travel, and more. Stephen Wolfram's Wolfram Alpha appeared in 2009 as a new kind of search engine that lets you ask questions in natural human language rather than entering keywords. Instead of simply searching for matches, this engine computes answers to your questions.

Ethics and Technology Blog *online*

Good Business vs. an Invasion of Privacy

The advertising and marketing world are eager to find new opportunities for collecting information about how people use the Internet. Do you think the ability of online stores to track your actions and to sell that information to others is "business as usual" or an invasion of your privacy?

Take the Next Step *online*

Activity 2.2.3 Video	*How is Web 2.0 changing our world?*	**CORE** CONTENT
Activity 2.2.4 Video	*What might the Web of the future look like?*	

The Web Everywhere

The Internet: It's not just for computers anymore.

The Internet began as a Pentagon research project that connected a few computers through a bunch of tangled wires. It grew through the research and educational establishments until it finally made the leap to personal computers. Then the Internet and the World Wide Web became available over wireless connections.

More recently, consumers started accessing the Web on devices such as smartphones and tablet computers.

Did you know the Internet might be in your fridge, too? And down the road, in the gallon of milk in your fridge?

"The Web will be ubiquitous," says technology writer Dwight Silverman. "It will be everywhere you are."

Listen to the Chapter 2 Spotlight on the Future Podcast with Dwight Silverman, and be prepared to answer the following questions.

Talk about It

1. What are some places, other than computers, where you can find the Web today?
2. Where might you encounter the Web in the future?
3. What is meant by the term *internet of things*?
4. What are the privacy implications of the internet of things?
5. How might people end up paying for access to online content and services when the Web is everywhere?

2.3 Joining the Digital World

You may have been going online for many years and it may seem as natural as turning on a television set, or you may have only skimmed the surface of the Internet, which came into the public mainstream a mere dozen or so years ago.

Whichever the case, you are probably aware that today, the Internet is truly a global phenomenon. In 2011, Nielsen Online and the International Telecommunication Union estimated that 2.1 billion people (30.2 percent of the world's population) are now online, up from 360 million people in 2009. This represents 480.4 percent growth over approximately 10 years. (http://www.internetworldstats.com/stats.htm)

According to recent data from www.InternetWorldStats.com summarized in the graph in Figure 2.4:

- Asia has the highest number of Internet users, at 922,329,554.
- North America, including the United States and Canada, comes in third at 272,066,000.

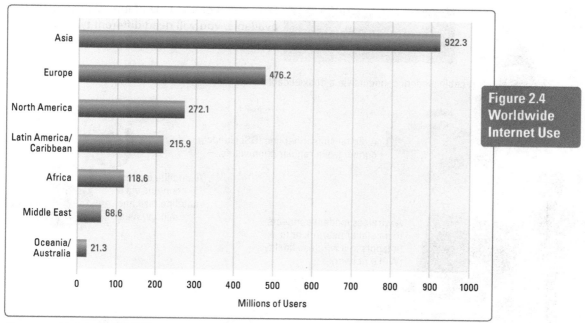

Figure 2.4 Worldwide Internet Use

Source: www.InternetWorldStats.com, March 31, 2011.

However, these statistics can be misleading. In fact, relative to the size of our population, North America has the greatest penetration of Internet usage: 78.3 percent of us are online, compared to 23.8 percent of the population of Asia.

To appreciate how the online world works, it's useful to understand how we all connect to this vast community with a combination of hardware and software and technology.

Hardware to Make the Connection

Most of today's computers come ready to connect to the Internet, and many also offer wireless technology. After you establish an account with an Internet service provider (ISP), you will need hardware such as a DSL, cable, or satellite modem to connect (see Figure 2.5). If you want to connect wirelessly, you will need additional hardware such as a router.

You might connect in a number of ways:

- You can get access via a cable modem that connects your computer via a coaxial cable (the same type of cable that carries a cable TV signal) or a high speed digital subscriber line (DSL) modem that connects your computer via regular phone lines. You can share either type of connection over a wireless router.
- With WiMAX, you connect your wireless computer to a WiMAX tower. The WiMAX tower connects directly to the Internet or transmits to one or more additional towers that then connect to the Internet. This technology provides high-speed long distance connectivity when cable and DSL are not available.
- Use a wireless modem (most newer computers offer this option) to go online by way of a cellular network.
- Tap into a wireless fidelity (Wi-Fi) network, which uses radio signals for a wireless connection from hotspots located in places such as hotels, airports, and Internet cafes. These may be free or may require that you pay a fee to connect.

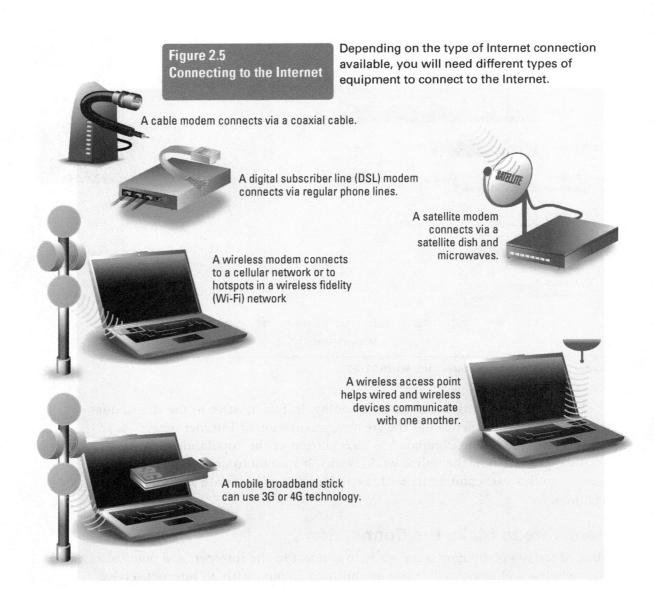

**Figure 2.5
Connecting to the Internet**

Depending on the type of Internet connection available, you will need different types of equipment to connect to the Internet.

A cable modem connects via a coaxial cable.

A digital subscriber line (DSL) modem connects via regular phone lines.

A satellite modem connects via a satellite dish and microwaves.

A wireless modem connects to a cellular network or to hotspots in a wireless fidelity (Wi-Fi) network

A wireless access point helps wired and wireless devices communicate with one another.

A mobile broadband stick can use 3G or 4G technology.

- **Mobile broadband sticks** are essentially portable modems about the size of a USB stick (the size of a piece of gum). They use 3G or 4G technology to connect via a provider such as T-Mobile or Vodafone for a monthly fee. 3G is the third generation of cellular technology; it is also used on cell phones and provides expanded

Many ISPs, such as Earthlink, provide a variety of connection methods that vary in price. The higher your connection speed, the more you will pay.

bandwidth. 4G is fourth generation technology that provides increased speed and bandwidth.

You may still occasionally come across an old-fashioned modem that is used for a low-speed connection method called dial-up. With dial-up Internet connection you plug a phone line into your computer and dial a local access number provided by your Internet service provider (ISP) to go online. The connection is usually slow and you can't use your phone for calls while you're connected.

Paying for the Privilege: Internet Service Providers

An **Internet service provider (ISP)** lets you use their technology (servers and software) to connect to the Internet for a fee. Your ISP might be your phone or cable company. There are also national ISPs such as EarthLink and local and regional ISP companies that use technologies such as DSL and fiber optic access provided by local utility companies.

Depending on your connection method, your ISP may provide you with a modem and/or router and instructions for using it to make your connection. ISP accounts typically include a variety of services, such as an email account, news and other information services, and security services such as a firewall, virus scans, and spam management for your monthly subscription fee. Email and information services may be identified and displayed on your ISP start page, which is often personalized with your name and a weather report for your area. You can personalize your start page further by choosing which news services, for example, send news to the page.

How Browsers View What's Online

You use browser software such as Internet Explorer (IE), Firefox (Figure 2.6), Safari, Google Chrome, and Opera to view online content. Essentially, a **browser** renders web pages, which are typically created using a language such as HTML (HyperText Markup Language) into text, graphics, and multimedia.

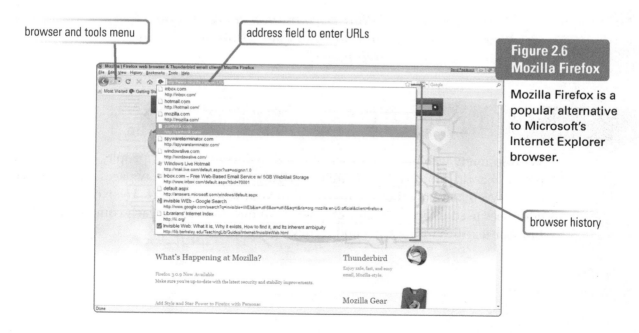

browser and tools menu

address field to enter URLs

browser history

Figure 2.6 Mozilla Firefox

Mozilla Firefox is a popular alternative to Microsoft's Internet Explorer browser.

Browsers allow you to move around the World Wide Web, moving from page to page and retaining favorite sites and a record of your browsing history. Browsers have become an ally in protecting your privacy online with built-in filters and security features.

Mobile devices use web browsers designed to display web pages on smaller screens. For example, Opera Mobile allows a smartphone running the Windows, Symbian, or Android operating systems to browse the Web on the go. (Chapter 4 provides more information about mobile phone operating systems.) Web 2.0 sites such as ChaCha allow you to text questions from your cell phones and get nearly immediate answers.

Mobile phones and smartphones allow you to browse the Web with mini-browsers, such as Safari or Opera Mobile.

Take the Next Step *online*

Activity 2.3.1
Flash Movie
Why choose one Internet connection method over another?

CORE CONTENT

Activity 2.3.2
Video
What is your Internet connection and how does your browser display web pages?

2.4 Navigating and Searching the Web

With so many web pages out there created by lots of different people, it ought to be pretty chaotic. However, there are underlying systems as to how pages are organized on the Web and how they are delivered to your computer. This involves unique addresses used to access each web page, a unique address for each computer, and browser features for locating and retrieving online content.

IPs and URLs: What's in an Address?

An **Internet Protocol (IP) address** is a series of numbers that uniquely identifies a location on the Internet. An IP address consists of four groups of numbers separated by periods; for example: 225.73.110.102. A nonprofit organization called ICANN keeps track of IP numbers around the world.

Due to the explosion of Internet users and websites, the number of available unique four-group addresses (under IPv4) has been nearly consumed. A new standard known as IPv6 uses addresses with eight groups of hexadecimal characters separated by colons and should provide enough available addresses for the foreseeable future.

Because numbers would be difficult to remember for retrieving pages, we use a text-based address referred to as a **uniform resource locator (URL)** to go to a website (Figure 2.7). A URL, also called a **web address**, has several parts separated by a colon (:), slashes (/), and dots (.). The first part of a URL is called a protocol and identifies a certain way for interpreting computer information in the transmission process. *Http*, which stands for hypertext transfer protocol, and *ftp*, for file transfer protocol, are examples of protocols. Some sites use a secondary identifier for the type of site being contacted, such as *www* for a World Wide Web site, but this is often optional.

The next part of the URL is the **domain name**, which identifies the group of servers (the domain) to which the site belongs and the particular company or organization name (such as emcp in the Figure 2.7 example).

A suffix, such as *.com* or *.edu*, further identifies the domain. For example, the *.com* in the URL example shown in Figure 2.7 is a **top-level domain (TLD)**. There are a number of TLDs such as *.com*, *.net*, *.org*, *.edu*, and *.gov*. These TLDs with three or more characters are also called **generic top-level domains (gTLDs)**, in contrast to two-character country code TLDs such as .jp and .de. Table 2.1 provides a rundown of common gTLDs being used today. To accommodate future growth, ICANN recently announced a plan to increase the number of available gTLDs. It will be gathering suggestions for the new gTLDs in early 2012.

> " The goal has always been the same. The progression is from data to useful information to knowledge that answers questions people have or helps them do things. Knowledge is the quest. "
>
> ▶▶ Amit Singhal, Head of Google Search

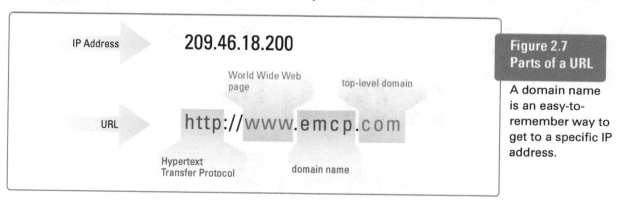

Figure 2.7 Parts of a URL

A domain name is an easy-to-remember way to get to a specific IP address.

Table 2.1 Common Generic Top-Level Domain Suffixes Used in URLs

Suffix	Type of Organization	Example
.biz	business site	Billboard: http://www.billboard.biz
.com	company or commercial institution	Intel: http://www.intel.com
.edu	educational institution	Harvard University: http://www.harvard.edu
.gov	government site	Internal Revenue Service: http://www.irs.gov
.int	international organizations endorsed by treaty	World Health Organization: http://www.who.int
.mil	military site	U.S. Department of Defense: http://www.defenselink.mil
.net	administrative site for ISPs	Earthlink: http://www.earthlink.net
.org	nonprofit or private organization	Red Cross: http://www.redcross.org

Browsing Web Pages

You may already be quite comfortable with browsing the Internet, but you may not have pondered how browsers move around the Web and retrieve data.

Any element of a web page (text, graphic, audio, or video) can be linked to another page using a hyperlink. A **hyperlink** describes a destination within a web document and can be inserted in text or a graphical object such as a company logo. Text that is linked is called **hypertext**.

A website is a series of related web pages that are linked together as in Figure 2.8. You get to a website by entering the URL, such as www.amazon.com, in your browser. Every website has a starting page, called the **home page**, which is displayed when you enter the site URL. You can also enter a URL to jump to a specific page on a site, such as the Instant-Video page at Amazon's site, http://www.amazon.com/Instant-Video/b/ref=sa_menu_aiv_vid0?ie=UTF8&node=2858778011.

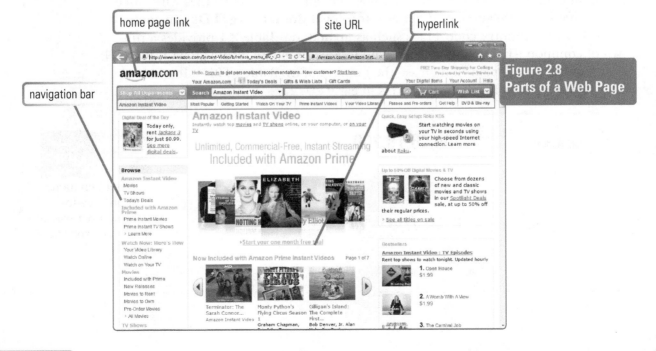

Figure 2.8
Parts of a Web Page

Searching for Content Online

A **search engine**, such as Google.com, Ask.com, and Yahoo.com, catalogs and indexes web pages for you. A type of search engine, called a **search directory**, can also catalog pages into topics such as *finance, health, news, shopping,* and so on.

Search engines may seem to be free services, but in reality they are typically financed by selling advertising. Some also make money by selling information about your online activities and interests to advertisers.

The newest wave of search engines, including Microsoft Bing and Google Squared, not only search for content but make choices among content to deliver more targeted results. Such search engines allow you, for example, to ask for a list of female tennis stars from 1900 on and they then assemble a table of them for you.

Table 2.2 shows some common search tools with their URLs and an indication of whether they offer the ability to catalog pages in directories.

Table 2.2 Common Search Tools

Search Tool	URL	Type
Ask	www.ask.com	engine
Bing	www.bing.com	engine
Dogpile	www.dogpile.com	engine
Google	www.google.com	engine/directory
MSN	www.msn.com	engine/directory
Yahoo!	www.yahoo.com	engine/directory

Ethics and Technology Blog *online*

Sharing Information from Search Directories

Do search engine companies such as Google have the right to make your personal information (a picture of your home, your phone number, or whatever) available to others? Should you have the right to opt out of being included in these directories?

links to narrow searches to images, maps, news, or video

search results

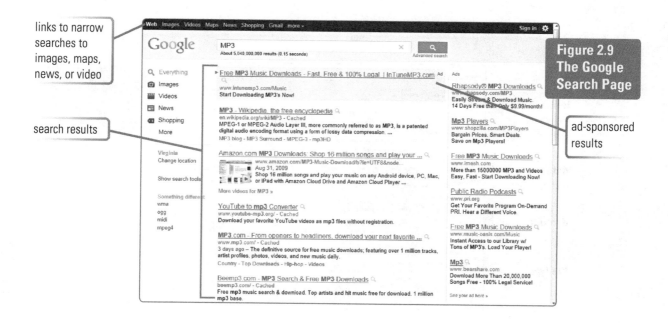

Figure 2.9 The Google Search Page

ad-sponsored results

Searches That Succeed So how do search engines work? You can search for information by going to the search engine's website and typing your search text, which is comprised of one or more **keywords** or keyword phrases.

For example, to find information about the international space station you could type *space station* in the search engine's search text box and press Enter. You can narrow your search by specifying that you want to view links to certain types of results such as images, maps, or videos, as on Google's site shown in Figure 2.9.

You can get more targeted search results by honing your searching technique. Effective searching is a skill that you gain through practice. For example, typing *space station* in a search engine's web page could easily return more than 80 million results. If what you really need is the cost to build the station, consider a more targeted keyword phrase like "space station cost." Search engines provide advanced search options that you can use to include or exclude certain results. For example, you can exclude pages with certain domain suffixes (such as .com and .net) to limit your search results to educational and government sites. Table 2.3 offers some ways you can narrow your search by entering your keywords in various ways. Figure 2.10 shows Yahoo!'s advanced search parameters which included specifying when a site was last updated, the domain name, or file format.

Table 2.3 Advanced Search Parameters

Item	What It Does	Example
Quotes ("")	Instruction to use exact word or words in the exact order given	"Pearl Harbor"
Minus symbol (-)	Excludes words preceded by the minus symbol from the search	jaguar -car
Wildcard (*)	Treat the asterisk as a placeholder for any possible word	*bird for bluebird, redbird, etc.
Or	Allow either one word or the other	Economy 2006 or 2007

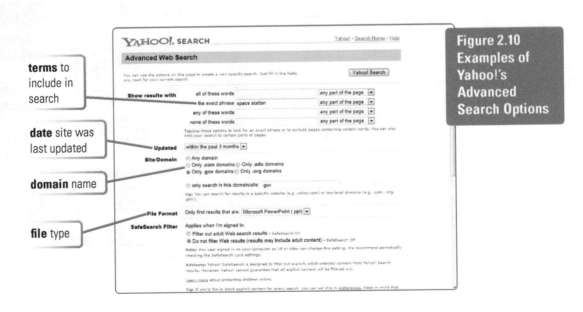

terms to include in search

date site was last updated

domain name

file type

Figure 2.10 Examples of Yahoo!'s Advanced Search Options

Our Digital World

A **metasearch engine**, such as dogpile.com, searches keywords across several websites at the same time. This helps optimize the search by providing the top results from the best search engines. For example, imagine you need to write a report on cocoa production. Instead of checking several search engines individually, you can use a metasearch engine, which will initiate searches on several engines at the same time.

Specialized Search Sites Many services online are essentially specialized search services. Some simply provide you with information while others use your search results to sell you merchandise or services. Here are some examples:

- Mapquest lets you look for locational information including maps and driving directions.
- Expedia is a travel site that searches a multitude of resources for rates on airfares, hotels, and rental cars to help you plan a trip. Similarly, KAYAK searches hundreds of travel websites so you can compare results and find the best deal.
- BizRate is a site you can use to compare and shop by gathering results for prices at dozens of retailers.
- Sites such as Google Video index videos that have been posted online from around the world.

Some of these sites charge a fee. For example, if you book a trip on Expedia, you pay for the trip plus a small fee to Expedia for providing your itinerary. Other sites such as Mapquest are free.

Playing It Safe

Most people don't realize how much information about them exists online. Maybe you posted a resume or made some blog entries on a publicly viewable page. Perhaps schools, employers, friends, or the government placed your information online. Do a web search of your name. If you find information about you that you'd rather not have online, ask the host site to remove it.

BizRate is a metasearch engine that allows you to compare information on several retailers to find the best price available on a product.

The Role of Plug-ins and Players Some multimedia components on a web page may require that you install a **plug-in** or **player** on your computer to view or hear content. Many players are installed with your browser; however, you've probably come across a web page that uses a plug-in or player that you need to download and install. These programs are free and simply require that you go to the publisher's site to download and install them.

For example, to play **streaming video**, which is video that is delivered to your computer as a constant stream of content, you may need a media player. To play certain kinds of animations, you need to install the Adobe Flash animation plug-in. To read a file saved in PDF format, you must install the Adobe Acrobat Reader. Table 2.4 contains a list of some of the most common plug-ins and players.

Table 2.4 Common Plug-Ins and Players

Name	Home Page	Purpose
Adobe Reader	www.adobe.com	Read and print PDF files
Adobe Flash Player	www.adobe.com	Play animations
QuickTime	www.apple.com	Play MP3 music, animations, and video files
RealPlayer	www.real.com	Play streaming audio and video files
Shockwave	www.adobe.com	Play interactive games and various multimedia files online
Windows Media Player	www.microsoft.com	Play streaming audio, video, animations, and multimedia presentations on the Web

Apple's QuickTime player allows you to play a variety of multimedia files.

Take the Next Step *online*

Activity 2.4.1 Flash Movie	*How do servers interpret URLs?*	CORE CONTENT
Activity 2.4.2 Research	*Can somebody steal a URL?*	
Activity 2.4.3 Tutorial	*How can I become a better searcher?*	

2.5 The Vast Sea of Online Content

Though it's difficult to calculate exactly how many websites and web pages exist today, information from the Netcraft Secure Server Survey in 2009 indicated an increase of over six million websites just between March and April of that year. With that kind of constant activity, it's logical to conclude that not all of the content that is online is of the same quality or accuracy. In addition, some of that content is free for the taking, while other content is protected by **copyright**, or legal ownership of that content. It's important that you learn how to evaluate the quality of content, learn to respect laws that govern your use of that content, and understand when free exchange of content is allowed and encouraged.

Some information posted online occurs in social transactions such as blogs on social networking sites. Chapter 7 takes a look at the social Web and the kinds of content and activity you'll find there.

Playing It Safe

If a window appears on a website telling you to install a plug-in, it's better to go to the plug-in maker's site and download it from there than to click a link in a pop-up window. Using these links sometimes downloads spyware (a type of malicious software) to your computer.

Evaluating Web Content

There is a wealth of accurate and useful information online. However, not all information found online is true, just as newspaper stories can contain inaccuracies or, in some cases, be fabricated. As in the offline world, you have to consider the source of online content. If you trust technology information from *Wired* magazine in print, you can have a similar level of trust in its online site. If you don't know a source at all, you may have to do some digging to discover if it is reputable by looking at the source's credentials (what individuals or organizations are involved in the venture), methods (for example, is the information based on surveys and experiment, or personal opinion?), and reputation (what do other online users say in reviews of the site or the company's products?).

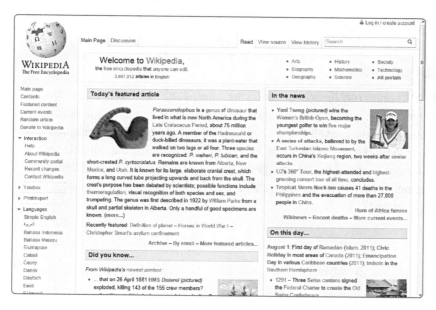

Some academics prefer more authoritative sources than the collaborative Wikipedia. Still, many people find the shared knowledge it provides innovative and valuable.

Because anyone can publish to the Web, to gauge the accuracy of what you read, you have to verify the three Ws (or WWW) of online content (Figure 2.11):

- WHO is the author or publisher? Is the source credible?
- WHAT is the message? Is the information verifiable? Is there a possibility of bias? Always try to crosscheck the information with other sources. Look for sponsors of a site to determine if they have a bias.
- WHEN was this published? Is this information current? If no date is published, is it possible to figure out how current the information is from the text? Online information can stay put for a very long time. Always look for the most current information on any topic.

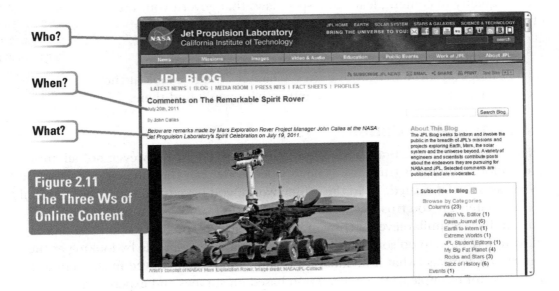

**Figure 2.11
The Three Ws of
Online Content**

Computers in Your Career

A wide variety of careers rely heavily on using the Internet for research. Librarians, government policy analysts, economists, insurance risk analysts, and others make use of online encyclopedias, survey results, and online professional journals on a regular basis. Human resource workers search online for the latest compensation models for different jobs in different areas of the country. Purchasing agents search for vendors and the best prices online. What career are you considering and how could online research help you succeed?

Intellectual Property

Some information or works online are placed there to be shared and passed on. Other content falls into the category of intellectual property, much of which is copyrighted. According to the World Intellectual Property Organization (WIPO), **intellectual property** (IP) refers to "the creations of the mind; inventions, literary and artistic works; and symbols, names, images, and designs used in commerce." It is illegal to copy or distribute intellectual property without appropriate permission.

> " You can't say that you work in research and not worry about IP because as soon as you do any research you are doing intellectual property – it goes with the research and you have a responsibility to look after it. "
>
> ▶▶| Dr. Philip Graham, Director of the Association for University and Industry Links

The Internet has brought the issue of illegal treatment of intellectual property front and center. Because it's so simple to copy and paste content online, many people who would never dream of stealing a CD from a music store or a book from a bookstore download music illegally or plagiarize by using text or images from a website and representing that content as their own work.

Peer-to-peer (P2P) file sharing programs such as BearShare are used by millions of people to share music, video, and other types of files by downloading them from each others' hard drives, rather than from the Internet. This type of sharing is ripe for copyright abuse because materials that might be downloaded from a legitimate source by paying a fee are instead exchanged freely with no payment going to the copyright owner.

However, some people feel that copyright law in the digital age has gone too far. There's a strong sense among many Internet activists that laws such as the Digital Millennium Copyright Act distorts the balance between fair use (the right to reuse content that is available to all) and intellectual property rights and are a threat to creativity and technological innovation.

The Invisible Web (aka Deep Web)

The content you typically find online is only the tip of the Web content iceberg. There are huge "hidden" collections of information that are collectively known as the **invisible Web** or **deep Web**. A typical search engine won't return links to these databases or documents when you enter a search keyword. To get to some databases on the invisible Web, libraries and companies have to pay for access to them.

In the future you will probably be able to more easily find this content as search engines get more sophisticated. You can try now by entering the word "database" after your keyword(s) in services such as Google and you may locate some of this content. You can also try to locate this content in directories such as the Librarians' Internet Index, free and paid-for databases such as LexisNexis for legal research, and some specialized search engines such as Scirus, a science search engine. If you're willing to pay for help accessing the invisible Web, companies such as BrightPlanet specialize in harvesting information.

Take the Next Step *online*

Activity 2.5.1 Research	*What is copyright?*	**CORE CONTENT**
Activity 2.5.2 Video	*How and why is the deep Web hidden from us?*	**CORE CONTENT**
Activity 2.5.3 Research	*Which source do you trust?*	
Activity 2.5.4 Research	*Is it legal for me to use these images, songs, and videos?*	
Activity 2.5.5 Team Research	*What happens when intellectual property protection crosses borders?*	

2.6 E-Commerce

Electronic commerce, or **e-commerce**, involves using the Internet to transact business. When you're buying downloadable music or software, shopping for shoes, or paying to access your credit report, for example, you're involved in e-commerce.

There are three main kinds of e-commerce that describe how money flows in an online business. Money can flow from business-to-consumer (B2C), business-to-business (B2B), or consumer-to-consumer (C2C). Sometimes more than one of these models occurs on a single site (for example, when a consumer on eBay buys a product from another consumer (C2C), but eBay makes money from advertisers (B2B).

B2C E-Commerce

Business-to-consumer (B2C) e-commerce is probably the kind you're most familiar with. It involves companies that sell products and services to individual consumers, such as Amazon.com and Zappos.com. This is the model that most resembles those stores in the mall that you go to when purchasing books or finding shoes.

The steps in the online shopping process are shown in Figure 2.12.

B2B E-Commerce

Business-to-business (B2B) e-commerce involves businesses selling to businesses. In some cases, a business provides supplies or services to another business, such as a plumbing supply site that caters to building contractors.

In another B2B model, businesses provide a service to consumers but do not charge those consumers directly. Instead, their business model involves making money from selling ad space to advertisers, or selling information about their customers to advertisers. Given that e-commerce models are defined by how money

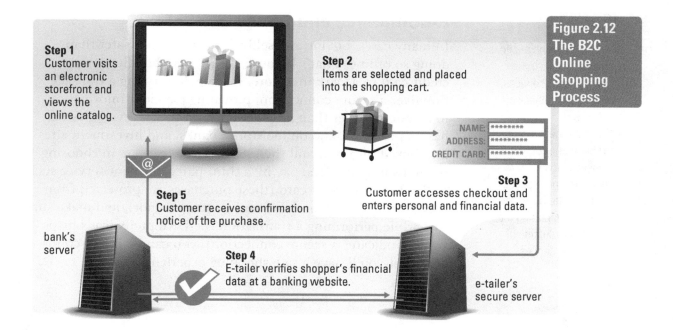

Step 1
Customer visits an electronic storefront and views the online catalog.

Step 2
Items are selected and placed into the shopping cart.

NAME: ********
ADDRESS: ********
CREDIT CARD: ********

Step 3
Customer accesses checkout and enters personal and financial data.

Step 5
Customer receives confirmation notice of the purchase.

bank's server

Step 4
E-tailer verifies shopper's financial data at a banking website.

e-tailer's secure server

Figure 2.12 The B2C Online Shopping Process

flows, Facebook is an example of this second kind of B2B site because it gets no money from its members, only from advertisers (other businesses).

C2C E-Commerce

Consumer-to-consumer (C2C) e-commerce activity occurs on sites such as Craig's List or eBay where consumers buy and sell items from each other over the Internet. Though the host site provides the infrastructure, the money flows from one consumer to another. What e-commerce model do you think supports the companies that host C2C sites? If you guessed B2B (they get their money from advertisers) you'd be right!

eBay is a popular auction site with B2B, B2C, and C2C characteristics because transactions can occur between two consumers, two businesses, or a business and a consumer.

E-Commerce and Consumer Safety

In many cases, buying and selling items online is safer than doing so offline. That's because, rather than handing your credit card to a clerk in a store, you are performing a transaction over a secure connection, providing payment information to a system rather than an individual. Of course, every system has its problems, and online stores, banks, and investment sites are hacked into now and then. Still, if you use care in choosing trusted shopping sites, pay by a third-party payment service such as PayPal or by credit card (these purchases are protected from theft, while a check or debit card purchase is not), and make sure that while performing a transaction the URL prefix reads https (which indicates a secure connection), you can be pretty confident that you'll have a safe shopping experience.

Computers in Your Career

Many people have become online entrepreneurs by starting their own eBay store or creating a website about a special interest such as baking bread or children's books. Others become affiliates or associates; they get a small fee for sending online browsers to a partner site. Whether you use e-commerce to supplement your regular job or as your main source of income, it can offer interesting challenges and rewards.

Take the Next Step *online*

Activity 2.6.1 Video	*What are the differences among the three kinds of e-commerce?*	

| Activity 2.6.2 Presentation | *How do online auctions work?* | |

2.7 Connecting in Cyberspace

The Internet offers a variety of ways to communicate that people are using to get work done or stay in touch with family and friends. Working people send an average of 36 emails a day and receive 74 emails a day according to about.com. Voice over Internet Protocol (VoIP) allows subscribers to make phone calls via the Internet; VoIP provider Skype had a record 27 million users signed on simultaneously on January 10, 2011. Skype is also adding call minutes at twice the rate of all other phone companies combined worldwide. Individuals and companies are also taking advantage of combinations of technologies to work collaboratively using web conferencing and collaborative learning and working spaces. Social networking tools provide a variety of ways to network and collaborate, both professionally and personally. Chapter 7 will cover social networking in more detail.

Email

Electronic mail (**email**) was one of the first services available on the Internet, even before consumers started coming online and the Web appeared on the scene. In fact, the first email was sent between two computers in 1971. Following the advent of the commercially available Internet, email soon became the standard method of communication for businesses and individuals. Today, email allows people to communicate with one another almost instantaneously from anywhere on the planet that offers an Internet connection.

The computer used to send the first email in 1971 was huge by today's standards.

Many ISPs provide a web-based method that you can use to access your email (a service typically included free with your account, or you can use an email client application such as Outlook on your computer). You use **web-based email** to create and send messages, add attachments, receive and reply to messages, store contact information, and manage messages in folders. Hotmail and Gmail are examples of popular web-based email services. Many email programs include calendaring options.

An **email client** such as Microsoft's Outlook or Apple's Mail can perform the same functions as a web-based email service and can also manage messages that come to any number of email accounts you might have created on the Internet. For example, if you have a Gmail account for work, an AOL account for personal messages, and a Hotmail account you use to make online purchases, you can access and manage them all using an email client.

Services such as MobileMe from Apple go a step further. They help you to access multiple email accounts and sync your email and contacts among multiple devices such as a PC, iPhone, and iPod (Figure 2.13).

You may have already observed that email services use a specific address format for sending messages, but you may not know what each piece of that address means. An **email address** includes a user name, the domain name for the email service, and the domain suffix, as in YourName@gmail.com. The user name and domain name are

Playing It Safe

Email is a wonderful communications tool, but it is also used to deliver a variety of threats such as viruses and financial scams. Use caution when downloading file attachments and read unsolicited emails carefully to understand the sender's intent.

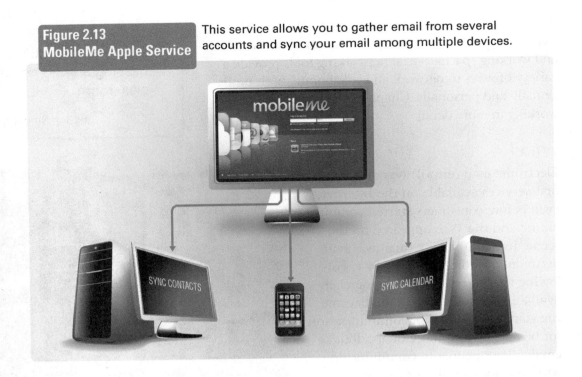

**Figure 2.13
MobileMe Apple Service**

This service allows you to gather email from several accounts and sync your email among multiple devices.

SYNC CONTACTS

SYNC CALENDAR

separated by the @ symbol. Email addresses are all unique, and a user name can be made up of a combination of letters and numbers and some special characters such as the underscore and period.

Text Messaging

Messaging between mobile phones and other portable devices is another growing form of communication. When you send a **text message**, you are exchanging a written message of 160 characters or less with another person using **Short Message Service (SMS)**. Sending a text message is called **texting**. According to the U.S. Census (Statistical Abstract of the United States: 2010), text messaging increased from 48 billion messages in the month of December 2007 to 110 billion in the month of December 2008.

More recently, according to a June 9, 2011, article in the *Wall Street Journal*, U.S. cellphone users sent/received more than a trillion texts in the last half of 2010. While that's a lot of texting, it represents only an 8.6% increase over the first half of 2010, the smallest increase in 10 years. These statistics suggest that we are moving from SMS text messages (sent over the phone) to Internet-based text messages, sent using messaging apps such as BBM (Blackberry's Instant Messaging) and Apple's iMessage. According to the *Wall Street Journal*, texting is no longer "cool" while messaging is in.

Internet Voice Services

Voice over Internet Protocol (VoIP) is a transmission technology that allows you to make voice calls over the Internet using a service such as Skype. When you speak into a microphone, software and hardware convert the analog signals of

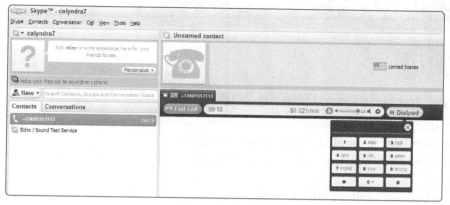

Skype was one of the early leaders in VoIP. The company offers various tiers of Internet calling services; some are free, and some are fee based.

your voice into digital signals that are then transferred over the Internet. VoIP is also used for collaborative services such as **web conferencing**, a technology that allows companies to conduct live meetings and presentations over the Internet with employee groups or clients across the country.

Services such as ViaTalk provide free calls to other ViaTalk users and may charge a monthly fee if you want to call landline numbers that run through a phone network. Even traditional phone providers such as AT&T are now offering VoIP service.

Email and VoIP are only two of the ways people are connecting using their computers and other devices. Today people are using text, video, audio, and images to share with others in creative and exciting ways. You'll hear about many of these as you explore other chapters in this book.

Take the Next Step *online*

Activity 2.7.1 Flash Movie	*How are email messages sent and received?*	**CORE** CONTENT
Activity 2.7.2 Video	*How does VoIP work?*	**CORE** CONTENT
Activity 2.7.3 Team Presentation	*Should your email be private in your workplace?*	
Activity 2.7.4 Research	*Which VoIP provider would you choose?*	

What Are the Internet and World Wide Web?

The **Internet** is the physical infrastructure that allows us to share resources and communicate with others around the world. It is made up of hardware such as servers, routers, switches, transmission lines, and towers that store and transmit vast amounts of data.

The **Web** is a body of content that is available as web pages. The pages are stored on servers around the world. A **web page** may contain text, images, interactive animations, games, music, and more. Several web pages make up a single **website**.

The Web continues to evolve, and the different phases of the Web represent shifts in online usage and technologies. **Web 2.0** has become associated with interactive web services such as Wikipedia and Facebook. These services allow users to collaborate—share, exchange ideas, and add or edit content. Where Web 2.0 focused on *exchange* of data by individuals, **Web 3.0** (also called the **Semantic Web**) will involve *integration* of data from a variety of sources in a meaningful way.

Joining the Digital World

You can connect to the Internet through various methods, such as through a broadband cable or DSL phone connection. An **Internet service provider (ISP)** lets you use their hardware to connect to the Internet for a monthly fee. To go online, you need an Internet account, which generally involves connecting a piece of hardware such as a cable, DSL, or satellite modem, and often a wireless access point (router) to share the connection. With newer computers, hardware and software for connecting to your Internet modem or access point may be built in, as with wireless technology.

A **browser** such as Internet Explorer is what you use to view online content. Essentially a browser translates web page content, which is typically created using a language such as hypertext markup language (HTML) into text, graphics, and multimedia. Browsers also allow you to navigate the Web.

Navigating and Searching the Web

An **Internet Protocol (IP) address** is a series of numbers that uniquely identifies a location on the Internet. Current IP addresses consist of four groups of numbers separated by periods. New addresses with eight groups of hexadecimal characters separated by colons will ensure a pool of future addresses. Because numbers would be difficult to remember for retrieving pages, we can use a text address referred to as a **uniform resource locator (URL)** to go to a website. The text-based addresses are cross-referenced to IP addresses.

To get to a website, enter a URL, such as www.amazon.com, in the address bar of the browser. Every website has a starting page called the **home page**. Any element of a page (text, graphic, audio, or video) can be linked to another web page using a hyperlink. A **hyperlink** describes a destination within a web document and can be added to text or to an image such as a company logo. Text that is linked is called **hypertext**. Navigating among pages using a browser is called browsing the Web.

A **search engine** allows you to search for information by going to the search engine's website and typing one or more **keywords** or keyword phrases.

Some components on a web page may require that you install a **plug-in** or **player** on your computer to view or hear content. These programs are free and simply require that you go to the publisher's site to download and install them.

The Vast Sea of Online Content

As in the offline world, you have to consider the source of content online. Look at the credibility of who has written and published the information, the quality of the information, and how current it is to evaluate its quality and accuracy.

Some online content is free to exchange, share, and remix. **Intellectual property**, which includes inventions and literary and artistic works, cannot be copied or distributed without permission. Much of this material has the additional legal protection of a **copyright**. The Internet can make it easy to copy and use other people's property, so intellectual property abuse is rife.

Databases and other collections of information on the Web that are hidden or are not catalogued by most search engines are collectively known as the **invisible Web** or **deep Web**. To get to some databases on the invisible Web, libraries and companies have to buy access to them.

E-Commerce

Electronic commerce, or **e-commerce**, involves using the Internet to transact business such as shopping and banking. E-commerce sites are classified based on the flow of money. There are three main kinds of e-commerce: **business-to-consumer (B2C)**, **business-to-business (B2B)**, and **consumer-to-consumer (C2C)**.

Connecting in Cyberspace

You use an **email** program to create and send messages, add attachments, receive and reply to messages, store contact information, and manage messages in folders.

Voice over Internet Protocol (VoIP) is a transmission technology that allows you to make voice calls over the Internet using a service such as Skype.

Text messaging enables you to send brief messages of up to 160 characters between mobile phones using SMS.

Web conferencing is a service that combines several technologies such as VoIP and webcams to conduct live meetings or presentations over the Internet.

The World Goes Online
quick response (QR) code, 31

What Are the Internet and World Wide Web?
Internet, 32
Web (World Wide Web or WWW), 33
web page, 33
website, 33

Web 2.0, 34
Web 3.0, 36
Semantic Web, 36

Joining the Digital World
mobile broadband stick, 40
Internet service provider (ISP), 41
browser, 41

download, Activity 2.3.1
upload, Activity 2.3.1

Navigating and Searching the Web
Internet Protocol (IP) address, 43
uniform resource locator (URL), 43
web address, 43
domain name, 43
top-level domain (TLD), 43
generic top-level domain (gTLD), 43
hyperlink, 44
hypertext, 44

home page, 44
search engine, 45
search directory, 45
keywords, 46
metasearch engine, 47
plug-in, 47
player, 47
streaming video, 48

The Vast Sea of Online Content
copyright, 49
intellectual property (IP), 51
peer-to-peer (P2P) file sharing
    program, 51

invisible Web, 51
deep Web, 51
crawler, Activity 2.5.2
data integration, Activity 2.5.2

E-Commerce
e-commerce, 52
business-to-consumer (B2C)
    e-commerce, 52

business-to-business (B2B) e-commerce,
    52
consumer-to-consumer (C2C)
    e-commerce, 53

Connecting in Cyberspace

Concepts Check

CORE CONTENT

Concepts Check 2.1   Multiple Choice
Take this quiz to test your understanding of key concepts in this chapter.

Concepts Check 2.2   Word Puzzle
Complete this puzzle to test your knowledge of key terms in this chapter.

Concepts Check 2.3   Matching
Test your understanding of terms and concepts presented in this chapter.

Concepts Check 2.4   Label It
Identify the component of the URL for each numbered item.

Concepts Check 2.5   Make the Connection
Match the label to the correct device.

Projects

Check with your instructor for the preferred method to submit completed project work.

Project 2.1   Visiting a Tourist Attraction Near Your School

Project 2.1.1   Individual

Pick a tourist attraction near your school, such as a national or state park, historical site, zoological or botanical garden, museum, theme park, or aquarium. Use Google maps to search for the attraction's location. Then manipulate the street view and generate a map. Finally, get driving directions from your school to the location.

Project 2.1.2   Team

As a team, share the individual travel destinations that were completed in Project 2.1.1, and choose one as the focus of this project. Your team's assignment is to plan a school field trip, including an overnight stay, to your selected destination. To begin this task, use the Internet to research the destination and help your team create a trip itinerary, including overnight accommodations and points of interest. Then prepare a budget spreadsheet for each student that outlines entrance fees for all attractions listed in the itinerary, the cost of overnight accommodations, approximate costs for meals, and estimated costs for miscellaneous items such as snacks and souvenirs. (Your team may assume that your school will cover the transportation costs.) Finally, create a short slide presentation that includes information about your field trip destination.

Project 2.2   Net Neutrality—Should Everyone on the Internet Be Considered Equal?

Project 2.2.1   Individual

You have been assigned to research the principle of net neutrality. To start your investigation of this controversial topic, go to www.emcp.net/Berners-Lee and watch a video discussion of net neutrality by Tim Berners-Lee. Following the video, conduct an Internet search to learn more about this principle. When you have finished these steps, prepare a summary that defines net neutrality, covers its main concepts, and explains the controversy surrounding this topic. Include any necessary text citations and a list of Internet sources.

Project 2.2.2   Team

Discuss with your team the results of your individual research from Project 2.2.1. Next, address the following questions with team members: Are the concerns of Tim Berners-Lee justified? Should corporations be able to treat Internet users differently depending on the services to which the users have subscribed? Why or why not? Based on your discussion, arrive at a joint conclusion that either supports or opposes net neutrality. Prepare a summary explaining your team's position and the information that led your group to reach this conclusion. Have one person submit the document to your instructor with all team members' names included.

Project 2.2.3   Team

Using your summary from Project 2.2.2, prepare an oral presentation and a brief slideshow to present your team's position and rationale on net neutrality. First, write a script for an oral presentation and assign each team member a speaking part. Then create a series of slides to accompany your presentation. The slides should highlight the main points of your position and provide effective visuals. Give your oral presentation to your classmates and provide an opportunity for student discussion.

Project 2.3   U.S. Healthcare Reform

Project 2.3.1   Individual

On March 21, 2010, the U.S. House of Representatives narrowly passed a healthcare reform bill after much controversy and fierce debate. This legislation represents the biggest change to the U.S. healthcare system since the creation of Medicare. Use your favorite search engine to find two articles on the healthcare reform legislation and its implementation: One article should clearly support the legislation, and the other article should present opposing views. Apply advanced search techniques so that the articles you choose to read have been published since January 1, 2010. When you have finished locating and reading the articles, write a one-paragraph summary of each article and include the URL below each summary.

Project 2.3.2   Individual

Evaluating the credibility and accuracy of articles on the Internet is an important part of the research process. Using the three Ws (or WWW) technique you learned in this chapter, evaluate the credibility and accuracy of the two articles that you read for Project 2.3.1. To your existing document, add a table after each article that includes your three Ws analysis of the article's content.

Project 2.3.3   Team

Each team member should search the Internet to find a web page that has inflammatory or provocative content regarding the recent U.S. healthcare reform. Team members should share their web pages with their group, and choose one of the pages to analyze for this project. As a team, write a one-page document that summarizes the content of the page and offers the reasons for your team's decision that the content is unreliable or not credible. Include a second page that lists the URLs and brief summaries of the other articles that were found by team members.

Project 2.3.4   Team

Prepare a short slide presentation for the class that displays the web page and then presents your reasons for finding the content unreliable or not credible.

Project 2.4   Wiki — Internet Telephones

Project 2.4.1   Individual or Team

You or your team will be assigned to research the answers to one or more of the following questions related to Internet consumer telephone service:

- What is Voice over Internet Protocol (VoIP)?
- How does VoIP work?
- What are the advantages and disadvantages to converting to VoIP?
- Who offers Internet telephone service in your area?
- What are the costs of Internet telephone service for each provider in your area?
- How do you subscribe to an Internet telephone service? What if you want to cancel at some point?
- What equipment will you need for Internet telephone service?
- Does the government regulate Internet telephone service? If yes, in what ways?
- What emergency and security issues, if any, might be concerns in Internet telephone service?
- How does a subscriber place an overseas call using an Internet telephone service? What costs are incurred?

Prepare a posting to the course wiki site that summarizes what you learned in clear, concise language. Make sure you include the research question, citations, and references to the articles from which you obtained your information.

Project 2.4.2   Individual or Team

You or your team will be assigned to edit and verify content posted on the wiki site about Internet telephones. If you add or edit any content, make sure you include a notation within the page that includes your name or the team members' names and the date you edited the content—for example, "Edited by [student name or team members' names] on [date]." Keep a list of references that you used to verify your content changes. When you are finished with your verification, include a notation at the end of the entry—for example, "Verified by [student name or team members' names] on [date]."

Class Conversations

Topic 2.1   Is Web Research Enough?

You are taking a sociology course and have been asked to write an essay on various kinds of bullying in high schools. Assume you conduct all of your research online making sure that you use credible sources for your information. Another classmate conducts all of her research at the library using traditional reference materials such as sociology journals and books.

Discuss the advantages of your Internet-research-based approach and the advantages of your classmate's library-research-based work. Should the two papers be considered equal when graded? Do you think others will view the journal- and book-researched paper as being of stronger academic quality? Why or why not? Is your web-researched paper likely to have a different perspective? Why or why not?

Optional: Create a blog entry that states your response to the previous questions and provides your rationale.

Topic 2.2   How Is YouTube Changing Society?

The popularity of YouTube has made it possible for anyone to become a media publisher and can make an average person suddenly famous for a day. It seems that every week another video is posted that becomes a popular topic among friends and family members. Some of these videos are taken of other people with or without their knowledge.

Consider the following scenario. You are on your way to school one day and are having a conversation with someone in your carpool that is getting rather animated. You are momentarily distracted when someone in the back seat makes a funny joke in an attempt to lighten the atmosphere. You turn around to speak to the person and the next thing you know you have jumped the curb and hit a stop sign. Meanwhile, a friend driving by who witnessed the accident thought it was funny and filmed the accident with her cell phone. She posted the video on YouTube with the title "Lousy Driver Alert!"

a.   What is the likelihood you would know this video existed on YouTube?

b.   Should the motorist who filmed the accident be required to get your release before posting the video? Why or why not?

c.   Does this scenario violate any guidelines provided by YouTube?

d.   If you became aware of the video, what would you do?

e.   Should someone be allowed to capture video of you without your knowledge? If you answer no, how could society police this action?

Topic 2.3   What's after Web 3.0?

If the evolution of the Web makes it possible for intelligent agents to locate information for you on the Internet based on your preferences and even update and modify your documents when you read a related article, what will that mean for the role of the Internet in learning? If student work is updated automatically, what will be the role of individual contribution and how much inaccuracy could be introduced? What role will humans play in the development of information on the Web in future?

Computer Hardware and Peripherals
Your Digital Toolbox

What You'll Accomplish

When you finish this chapter, you'll be able to:

- Identify and explain the functions of the major components of the computer system and the parts of the motherboard.
- Understand how a computer system uses memory.
- Identify various input and output devices.
- Explain what features to look for when purchasing a computer.

Why Should I Care?

We live in a time when digital devices rule. If you love gadgets, you don't need to ask why you should care, you just enjoy playing with all the new technology. But even if you're not one to jump on the latest gadget, you should still realize that these devices, from the computer at your office to an Xbox in your living room, are an important part of your life. Understanding the parts of the hardware that make up these devices, how you get information in and out of them, and how to make wise technology buying choices can help you cope and prosper in our digital age.

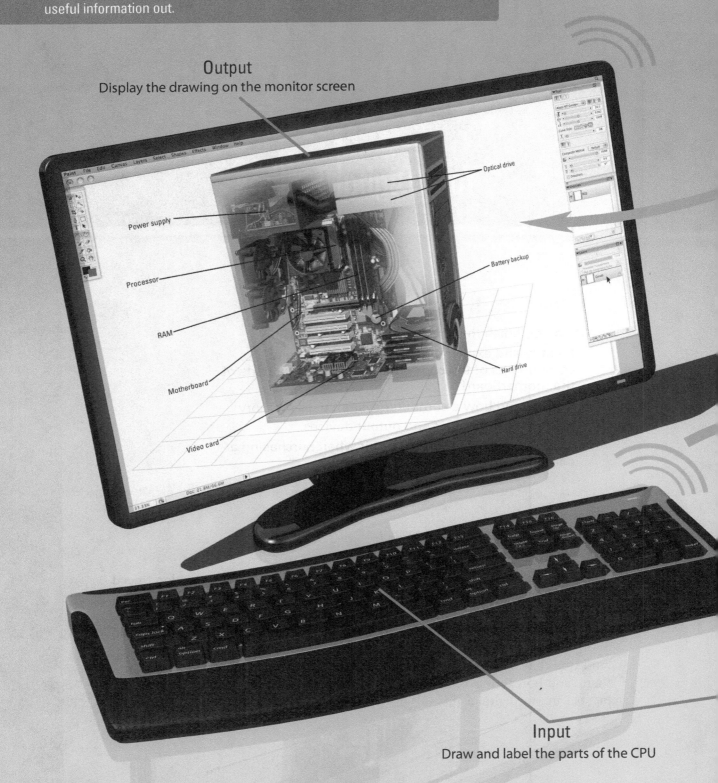

Chapter 3 Computer Hardware and Peripherals: Your Digital Toolbox

The tangible part of computing starts with hardware. Components for input, processing, output, and storage allow you to put data in and get useful information out.

Output
Display the drawing on the monitor screen

Optical drive

Power supply

Battery backup

Processor

RAM

Hard drive

Motherboard

Video card

Input
Draw and label the parts of the CPU

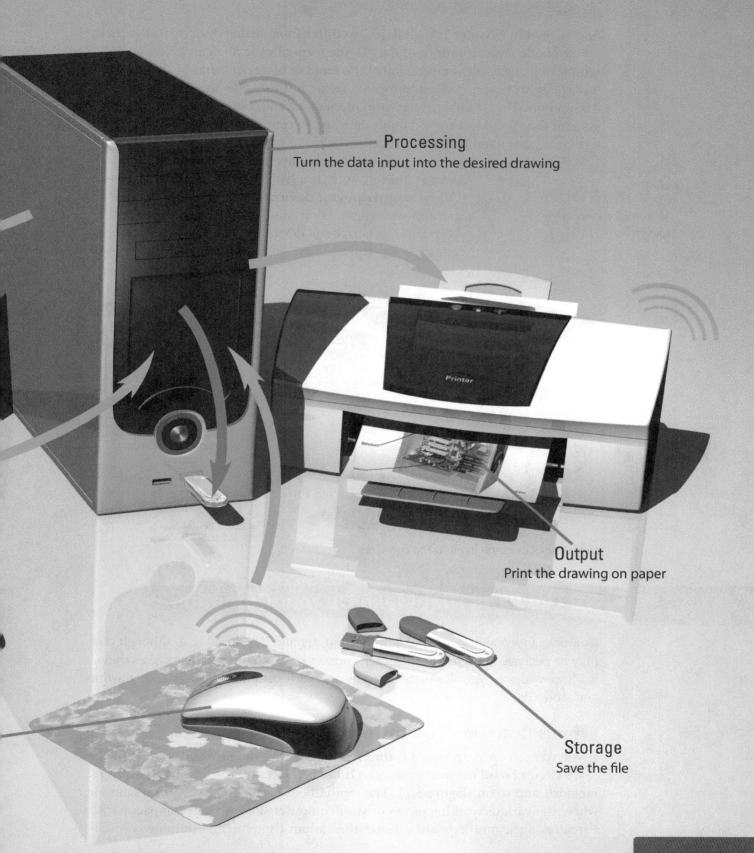

Processing
Turn the data input into the desired drawing

Output
Print the drawing on paper

Storage
Save the file

3.1 A World of Digital Devices

As you read in Chapter 1, digital devices differ from analog devices in that they use symbolic representations of data in the form of code and can process words, numbers, images, and sounds. Today the number of devices that fit that definition has expanded beyond your desktop computer, but these devices have certain things in common. They all have some form of memory and, however basic, an operating system; they provide a way to input data and output information; and they have a source of power and the ability to store data.

Some digital devices have input devices and/or output devices built in, such as a laptop computer or cell phone. Others use **peripheral devices** that physically or wirelessly connect with them. For example, your desktop computer keyboard is a peripheral device used to input data, and your printer is a peripheral device used to produce printed output.

Digital devices come in all forms and sizes.

3.2 The Parts That Make Up Your Computer

Compare a typical desktop and laptop computer and you'll find that although they may be packaged differently, they each contain similar hardware that makes them work, provides power, allows them to connect with peripheral devices and networks, and stores data.

What's Contained on the Motherboard?

If you were to open up your PC tower you'd see that the **motherboard** is the primary circuit board on your computer. It holds the central processing unit, BIOS, memory, and so on (Figure 3.1). The motherboard is really just a sort of container where the various working pieces of your computer slot into one compact package. Circuits on the motherboard connect the various components contained on it.

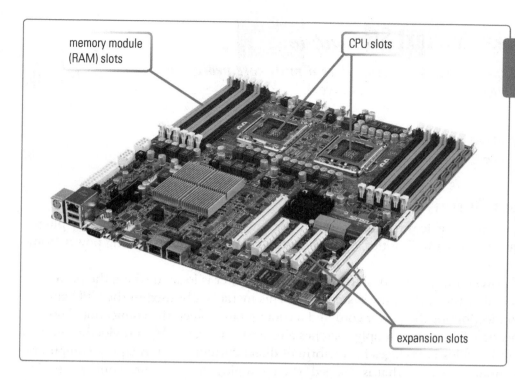

memory module (RAM) slots

CPU slots

expansion slots

**Figure 3.1
The Operations of the Motherboard**

The motherboard is a container for various processors and expansion slots for cards that add functionality such as sound, graphics, or memory.

The central processing unit (CPU), which is a microprocessor (also called by the shorter terms *processor* or *core*), sits on the motherboard. The CPU processes a user's requests, such as opening documents or formatting text. A CPU is a thin wafer or "chip" made up of a semiconducting material such as silicon. It contains an integrated circuit (a very small electronic circuit) and is considered to contain the system's computing power. (Note that the term *central processing unit* is also commonly used to refer to the case that contains the processor and everything else within this case.)

The motherboard also holds different types of memory. **Read-only memory (ROM)** is the permanent, or nonvolatile, memory of a computer hardwired into a chip. In a PC, the read-only memory stores the **BIOS**, which stands for basic input/output system. During the boot-up sequence, the BIOS checks devices such as your memory, monitor, keyboard, and disc drives to insure they are working properly and to start them up. It also directs the hard drive to boot up and load the operating system (OS) to memory.

Random access memory (RAM) chips are slotted into the motherboard and are used to store programs and data while the computer is in use. This memory is temporary, or volatile. Each memory location in RAM can be accessed in any order, which speeds up processing. (This differs from storage devices that store and retrieve data in a specific order.)

While some computers have built-in sound or graphics cards, others include them as **expansion cards**. These cards enable input and output of sound or images. Your laptop computer can also accommodate **PC Cards** that slot into a built-in card reader to provide other kinds of functionality such as additional USB ports or wireless networking capabilities.

Activity 3.2.1 Video	*How does a multicore processor system work?*	**CORE CONTENT**
Activity 3.2.2 Video	*What types of expansion cards are available?*	

Power Supply

All computing devices require power to work, whether that power comes by plugging a cord into a wall outlet, operating off a charged battery, or using power from solar cells.

A **power supply** in a desktop or laptop computer is located where the power cord is inserted at the back of the system unit. This metal box housed in the CPU contains the connection for the power cord and a cooling fan to keep the connection from overheating. The power supply switches alternating current (AC) provided from your wall outlet to lower voltages in the form of direct current (DC). A laptop computer also contains a battery that is charged when you plug the cable into your wall outlet.

Batteries provide portable power.

Your operating system is capable of sending a signal to the power supply to instruct it to sleep or hibernate. This action puts your computer into a lower power mode or no power mode without losing your current, unsaved work. To take some computers out of sleep or hibernation mode, you can move the mouse or press any key. For most systems, however, you have to press the system's power button.

Ports

A computer uses a **port** to connect with a peripheral device such as a monitor or printer or to connect to a network. There are several different types of ports. A **physical port** connects a computer to another device, sending a signal via a cable (as for a USB port), infrared light (as with an infrared port), or a wireless transmitter (as with a wireless USB device).

> " Researchers at IBM have created computer chips that behave more like actual brains when processing information. Systems built with these chips will be called "cognitive computers"... Cognitive computers are expected to learn through experiences, find correlations, create hypotheses and remember. "
>
> ▶▶ Rob Spiegel, TechNewsWorld, 8/2011

Some types of physical ports (commonly called just ports) in use today, shown in Figure 3.2, are serial, USB, FireWire, and infrared.

A **serial port** is a port, built into the computer, used to connect a peripheral device to the serial bus, typically, by means of a plug with 9 pins. Network routers use serial ports for administration, although they are replaced by web-based administration interfaces.

USB hubs increase the number of available USB ports.

A **universal serial bus (USB) port** is a small rectangular slot that has quickly become the most popular way to attach everything from wireless mouse and keyboard dongles (the small device that transmits a wireless signal to a wireless device) to USB flash drives for storing data. USB first came out in version 1.0, which supported a 12 megabits per second (Mbps) data rate (the measurement of the speed at which data can be transmitted). USB 3.0 became available in 2010, providing a transfer rate of up to 5 Gbps.

Usually a computer has two to four USB ports that you can use to attach peripheral devices. Often users need more ports. You can add a hub that increases the number of available USB ports. Plug the USB hub into one of your computer's USB sockets, and then you can plug USB devices into the ports on the hub. Most USB hubs offer four ports, but some offer more.

A **FireWire port** is based on the same serial bus architecture as a USB port. (A bus is essentially a subsystem of your computer that transfers data between the various components inside your computer). It provides a high-speed serial interface for high-end digital cameras, camcorders, set-top boxes (connects to your TV), and audio and video. The newest version of FireWire supports an 800 Mbps data rate.

An **Infrared Data Association (IrDA) port** allows you to transfer data from one device to another using infrared light waves. Today the ability to transmit wirelessly between devices using Bluetooth (a wireless communications standard) is making IrDA ports obsolete. You can add Bluetooth connectivity via a device that connects to the USB port.

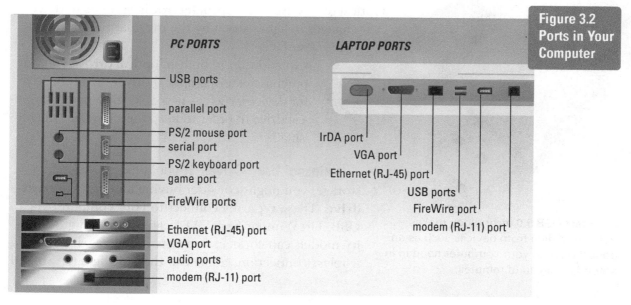

PC PORTS

- USB ports
- parallel port
- PS/2 mouse port
- serial port
- PS/2 keyboard port
- game port
- FireWire ports
- Ethernet (RJ-45) port
- VGA port
- audio ports
- modem (RJ-11) port

LAPTOP PORTS

- IrDA port
- VGA port
- Ethernet (RJ-45) port
- USB ports
- FireWire port
- modem (RJ-11) port

Figure 3.2
Ports in Your Computer

MIDI is a protocol that allows computers and devices, such as musical synthesizers and sound cards, to control each other. Game ports on older computers allowed the connections of the MIDI device to a computer.

Storage

Because saving the work you've done on your computer is so important, computer manufacturers have devised several ways to store all kinds of data, from numbers and images to words and music. All storage media have methods for reading the data from the media (input) and for writing the data to the media (output).

The various storage media used on a computer are accessed using **drives**, which are identified on a Windows-based computer by a unique letter. For example, your computer's hard disk is typically identified as your C drive, while a DVD or USB stick drive might be labeled E, F, or G. Mac computers give each drive a name such as Mac HD for the hard drive and DVD_VIDEO for a DVD drive in which you have inserted a video. If you are connected to a network, you may also be able to access shared network drives.

Hard Disks The first place most of us save a copy of our work is on our computer **hard disk**. When you save a file to your Documents library in Windows 7 and later, for example, it is saved to your hard disk drive. This is the disk drive that is built into your computer. The platters or disks in the drive rotate and one or more so-called "heads" read and write data to them.

Because all hard disks eventually fail, the wise person will use other storage media to make backup copies.

Optical Drives Your computer is likely to have a built-in drive where you can place a **CD** or **DVD** to read content stored there or store data of your own. Another type of storage drive that is built into some computers is a **Blu-ray disc** drive, mostly used for high-definition movies and games. This type of drive is called an **optical drive**. Discs placed in optical drives are covered with tiny variations, or bumps, that can be read as data by a laser beam in the drive. Optical drives use these **optoelectronic sensors** to detect changes in light caused by the irregularities on the disc's surface.

In addition to built-in optical drives, you can purchase external optical drives; this is handy for devices, such as netbooks, that have no optical drive in order to keep their size and weight small.

Ultra-fast USB 3.0 technology makes transfer of data from devices such as an optical drive to your computer happen in seconds, instead of minutes.

External Hard Drives If you'd like additional storage, you might consider buying an **external hard drive**. These typically connect to your computer via a USB, FireWire, or Serial ATA cable. Select high-capacity models can connect to a network via a wired or wireless connection. Some call these devices networked external hard drives while others refer to them as **network attached storage (NAS)**.

External hard drives are useful to back up your entire computer system, or for computers such as netbooks that have a smaller amount of internal storage. Some portable models don't need a separate power source. Networked models can provide centralized storage for multiple teammates or family members, or can serve as a "jukebox" for storing various forms of media such as music or videos.

Flash drives are very portable storage devices that are gaining larger capacities all the time.

Flash Drives Call them **flash drives**, USB sticks, or thumb drives, these conveniently small devices are a great way to store your data and take it with you. As of this writing, they come with capacities as big as 64 gigabytes (bigger than most hard drives just a few years ago), and this amount will have probably changed by the time you read this book.

Flash drives use **flash memory** to record and erase stored data and to transfer data to and from your computer. Flash memory is also used in tablets, mobile phones, and digital cameras because it is much less expensive than other types of memory. Flash memory is also non-volatile, meaning that it retains information even in a powered-off state.

Solid-State Drives (SSDs) A **solid-state drive (SSD)** is essentially a flash-based replacement for an internal hard disk. These drives are lighter and more durable than traditional hard disks, and should pave the way for smaller, portable computers with longer battery life as these become more common and prices come down. Some notebook models already use SSDs. Apple introduced them in new MacBook Air and MacBook Pro models, and a handful of Windows-based systems also ship with SSDs rather than traditional hard disks.

Cloud Storage In addition to using physical storage, many users increasingly rely on cloud storage. Cloud storage is where data is stored and managed on a web-connected server operated by a third party. You can access your files stored in the cloud from any location using any computer with an Internet connection. Cloud storage may be used not only for storage but also for backing up information, as well as sharing files with others. If you've ever lost or damaged your flash drive, you can appreciate how valuable it would be to have backup copies of your information that you could access via the Web from your school, on a trip, or in your office. Depending on your needs, you can choose either a fee-based cloud storage service, or free services such as SkyDrive. Some of the most popular cloud storage services today are Dropbox, Amazon S3, Box.net, Carbonite, and iStorage. In the fall of 2011, Apple released its version of a cloud storage service, iCloud, which allows users to share content across a range of Apple devices.

Activity 3.2.3 Flash Movie	*What devices can be built into your computer to enable communications?*
Activity 3.2.4 Hands-on	*How does a wireless or network device connect to your computer?*
Activity 3.2.5 Research	*What's the difference between static and dynamic RAM?*
Activity 3.2.6 Research	*How do I keep my storage media safe?*

CORE CONTENT

3.3 Input and Output Devices

Your computer is capable of processing and storing data, but if you can't get data into your computer and get information out of it, it's not much use. That's where input and output come in. Examples of **input devices** are your keyboard to enter text or a microphone to record sound. **Output devices** produce information in one of several forms: printed text, sound from a speaker, an image on your monitor, for example.

A Wide Assortment of Input Devices

A computer **keyboard** contains keys that you press to activate electronic switches. Today's computer keyboards also allow you to combine some keystrokes to accommodate additional commands (the familiar Ctrl, Shift, or Alt combinations and function keys, for example). Some keyboards also include shortcut keys that allow you to manage media such as video or audio playback.

Key presses are interpreted by the software program that controls the keyboard, called a device driver. The operating system then provides the key press information to the currently active program, such as a word processor or email client. Keyboards can plug into your computer, be built into a laptop, or use a wireless connection.

Your **mouse**, also referred to as a pointing device, detects motion in relation to the surface you rest it on and provides an onscreen pointer representing that motion. You might think of a mouse as being like the lever that a crane operator moves to control the crane, which moves up or down in the air according to

What goes into your computer in the form of digital files may come out as printed text, a movie, an image, or sound.

The option to use wireless input devices permits greater flexibility in positioning your keyboard and mouse.

the movements of the lever. A mouse prototype was invented in 1964 at Stanford University. The first mouse was sold with a computer when the first Apple Macintosh appeared in 1984.

A mouse can plug into your computer, be built into a laptop, or use a wireless connection. However it is connected to your computer, a mouse can function in several different ways. It can use:

- a mechanical device, such as a ball that rolls on a surface, to track motion.
- a light-emitting diode or **infrared technology (IR)** to sense motion (used by optical mice).
- an optoelectronic sensor that actually takes pictures of the surface.
- ultrasound technology to detect movement, as with 3D mice.

Finally, a **touchpad**, which senses finger movement, or a track pointer, which senses finger pressure, may be built into many computing devices. Other devices such as smartphones and tablets include touchscreens. These input devices use the motion and position of a person's finger to locate a position on the computer screen, either directly (touchscreen) or indirectly (touchpad).

Webcams are often used with online calling or meeting services so both callers can see each other as they chat.

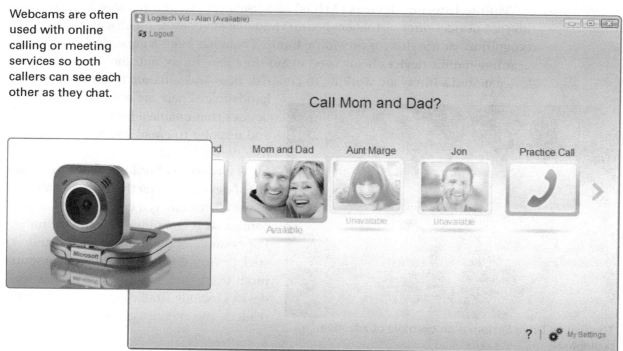

The **scanner** has a very descriptive name, as its function is to optically scan hard copy of text or images to convert them into electronic files. Scanners may sit on your desktop (called flatbed models), be built into an all-in-one printer, or be handheld. In the world of industrial design, 3D scanners can scan all sides of an object and produce three-dimensional models of them.

A **webcam** is a video camera that can be built into your computer monitor or purchased separately and mounted onto your computer. Both webcams and digital cameras can become input devices when they interface with your computer to upload photos or videos in digital file formats.

Gaming devices such as Xbox and Wii provide controllers you can use to input moves in a game. The controllers often combine multiple buttons, a joystick, and even motion sensors. Virtual reality systems that are used to simulate situations for learning, such as for astronauts, offer **wired data gloves** that allow users to communicate with the system.

Xbox and other gaming consoles can be stand-alone devices or connected to the Internet for interactive gaming.

Speech recognition turns the user's voice into an input device. Leading voice recognition programs include Dragon Naturally Speaking and MacSpeech. The user typically completes a setup process to train the voice recognition software to understand his or her voice. The software then understands the user's speech patterns, enabling that person to give commands and create documents, such as spreadsheets and emails.

Mobile Internet devices (MIDs) also use a variety of input devices. Mobile Internet devices offer virtual keyboards, foldable keyboards, touchscreens, voice recognition, or a stylus for providing input. There has been a great deal of debate regarding mobile devices being used in automobiles. Today, automobile and mobile device manufacturers are working to create devices and software that can be used hands-free. There are currently voice devices that enable a user to open, create and respond to email and SMS messages totally hands-free.

Assistive technologies include a variety of devices and methods that enable physically challenged computer users to control their computer and provide input. For example, sip-and-puff or wand and stick devices enable users to give computer input using their mouths. Other assistive devices include Braille embossers, screen readers, and speech synthesizers.

The Tongue Drive System is an example of adaptive technology.

Computers in Your Career

If you work in a retail store, you may be asked to use a bar code reader. These are the devices that are used to scan the little series of lines, or bar code, on most packaged products. Most kinds of bar code readers use light beams to scan the bars and read their widths; the black bars absorb light while the white portions between the bars reflect light. Camera-based readers actually take a picture of the bar code. The scanned code is then sent to a connected computing device to track sales. Learning to use a bar code reader isn't hard, and if your employer uses such a reader, it can save you and fellow workers lots of time otherwise spent in tracking inventory and sales manually.

Tablet PCs provide a special **electronic pen** (also called a stylus) you can use to write on their special screens.

Retail store or manufacturing employees often use bar code readers and RFID readers. **Bar code readers** optically scan a set of lines to identify a product. **RFID readers** scan an embedded tag that emits a radio frequency. Both are used to provide input to a computer system so software can track inventory and sales activity.

A **microphone** is an input device for getting sounds, from narrations to music, into your computer in the form of audio files. Microphones might be built into your computer, be plugged in via a cable, or be part of a headphone set.

" Garbage in, garbage out. "

▶▶ George Fuechsel, IBM Technician, advising that bad input results in bad output.

Playing It Safe

Keystroke logging software is a kind of malware that can be delivered to your computer in several ways, but most commonly is downloaded when you go to an untrustworthy site or click on an attachment in an email. The software records your keystrokes as you type and sends the information to a remote location. In this way someone might obtain your bank account password and account number, for example. Antivirus and antispyware software can help you locate such a program on your system and get rid of it.

Getting Things Out of Your Computer with Output Devices

Any device that displays, prints, or plays content stored in your computer is an output device, including your monitor, speakers, headphones, printer, or a projector.

Monitors and Speakers You may not think of your **monitor** as an output device, but it is. That's because information stored inside your computer is delivered to you in the form of images. In the case of a mobile phone or gaming device, the screens are output devices. Monitor output is temporary; once you turn the monitor off, there is no record of what was displayed.

Monitors sometimes include a **speaker** to add audio output. Another way to get audio from your computing device is by plugging a headset into your phone, CPU, or laptop or by using a wireless **Bluetooth headset**. Notebook computers typically include an internal speaker, while a desktop system may or may not include a sound card and external speakers that you can plug into it.

Monitors come in a variety of sizes, from a few inches on your cell phone to 8-inch netbooks to huge screens over 30 inches across. Display size is the measurement between two diagonally opposite corners. The

Bluetooth headsets let you talk on a mobile phone handsfree.

latest USB 3.0 cables are enabling lightning-fast transfer of data such as high-definition 3-D video to your computer monitor or TV screen.

Computer monitors in use today use one of three technologies:

- **TFT active matrix liquid crystal display (LCD)** is the most prevalent type of monitor today. It uses a thin film transistor (TFT) to display your computer's contents.
- **LED displays** use light-emitting diodes. They both conserve power and provide a truer picture than LCD models.
- **Plasma displays** are flat panel displays mainly used for televisions, but can be multifunction monitor/TV devices. They use a great deal of power but have a very true level of color reproduction compared with LCDs.

Some new display technologies beginning to appear on computer monitors and television sets include:

- **Surface-conduction electron-emitter display (SED)** using nanoscopic electron emitters (extremely tiny wires smaller than human hairs) to send electrons that illuminate a thin screen.
- **Organic light emitting diodes (OLED)**, which project light through an electroluminescent (a blue/red/green-emitting) thin film layer made of organic materials.

Plasma displays are often used in television sets. Some computers can connect to a TV display to output contents.

- 3D or 3D-ready technology uses polarized lens to display images. Usually, the viewer must purchase special glasses and may have to install separate IR equipment for use with the computer in order to view the 3D effect. This 3D technology is being used for both computer monitors and televisions.

Printers and Faxes A **printer** is the main way in which you can get so-called "hard copy" (print on paper) out of your computer. The foundation for today's printers was a dry printing process called electrophotography commonly called a Xerox (hence the company of the same name). When the use of a laser beam was added, we saw the introduction of the laser printer in 1971 and inkjets (printers that spat little jets of ink onto paper) in 1976. Hewlett-Packard threw their entry into the printer ring in 1984 with the first commercially available laser printer.

A **photo printer** that prints high-quality photos directly from a camera storage card and a **thermal printer** which heats coated paper to produce an image, like the kind you've seen printing receipts in retail stores, are also part of the printed output world. You may also encounter high-end commercial printers like the ones you see at your local copy store, and **plotters** used to print large blueprints and other technical drawings.

You can also use fax programs to send content from your computer that comes out as printed copy at the receiving end. If you use a **fax machine** to scan content and then send it, the machine converts the scanned content into an electronic file and then sends it to the recipient's fax machine, which prints it into hard copy on the other end. In this case, the sending fax machine is an input device and the receiving one an output device.

Devices That Project Computer Content You may send your computer contents out into the world in the form of a presentation. In that case, equipment such as LCD projectors, document cameras often used in educational settings, or monitors used to view Web presentations are the output devices.

LCD, or liquid crystal display, **projectors** involve projecting light through panels made of silicone colored red, green, and blue. The light passing through these panels displays an image on a surface such as a screen or wall. By blocking pixels or allowing light to pass through pixels on the panels, these projectors can accommodate a huge range of colors.

A **document camera** is another output device that is often used in educational settings. This output device can be used to display text from a book, slides, a 3D object, or any other printed material.

If you give presentations, you will encounter LCD projectors, popular for displaying PowerPoint slides and other types of content.

An **interactive whiteboard (IWB)** is a display device that receives input from the computer keyboard, a pen, a finger, a tablet, or other device. The IWB may connect directly to a computer to show the computer desktop, or you might need a projector to show the desktop on the IWB. IWBs help make points clearer and improve communication in settings such as the classroom, the corporate world, sports coaching, and broadcasting. Information displayed on an IWB may be saved as a document and shared or printed later. Popular IWB brands include SMART Board, Promethean, mimio, eBeam, and PolyVision.

An interactive whiteboard display device.

Virtual Reality Displays A **virtual reality system** connects you to a computer-simulated world. Most provide visuals to the user and some provide sound as well. The user wears a head-mounted display and headphones if sound is being provided. In the more sophisticated systems, gloves with wiring allow you to control actions with your hands. Virtual reality is a connection between user and computer that allows both input and output. This technology is used to train pilots, astronauts, doctors, and others in dealing with simulated situations.

Though not yet inexpensive nor user-friendly, virtual reality equipment is helping people in various industries to simulate situations they might encounter in their work and prepare for them.

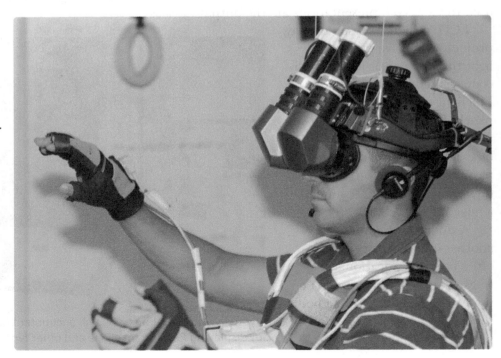

Our Digital World

Ethics and Technology Blog *online*

Free for the Taking

I bought a computer from this guy and was surprised to see that he left a bunch of software and files on it, including his assignments from a course I'm taking next year. I'm definitely gonna use the software, but I'm thinking of changing his assignments slightly and submitting them. Is that too sleazy?

Take the Next Step *online*

Activity 3.3.1 Flash Movie	*How do touchscreens work?*
Activity 3.3.2 Research	*How are assistive technology devices being used in the workplace?*
Activity 3.3.3 Team Presentation	*What new monitor technologies are on the horizon?*

CORE CONTENT

3.4 Purchasing a Computer

Many people get overwhelmed trying to figure out all the features and tech terms when faced with buying a new computer. The challenge is compounded because the specifications for what makes up the latest and greatest computing device keep changing as manufacturers try to outdo each other. However, there are certain questions you can answer to make an intelligent computer purchase.

What Are Your Computing Needs?

Not everybody needs the newest, fastest, most high-powered computer, so don't let sales hype sway you into buying more computer than you need.

Activities that require speed and high performance include:

- Working with high-end graphics such as photo manipulation or web design.
- Working with audio and video.
- Online tasks that involve uploading or downloading very large files (more than 20 MB, for example).
- Rich multimedia experiences such as gaming.

Also consider how much time you will spend on the computer. If you work at home and will use the computer eight hours a day, five days a week, you need a better quality (which often means more expensive) model. But if you only log on to read email a few days a week and manage your checkbook with a financial program once a month, a lower-end model will probably do. Efficient power consumption is one last consideration. Many systems do comply with Energy Star requirements, but double-check the labeling and specifications to make sure.

Also consider how your choices create a larger impact. Think about how the rapid change and constant upgrading of these devices has an impact on the environment. Technology doesn't seem green when you think about all the computer monitors, cases, keyboards, hard drives, and printers that get disposed of each day. The green computing movement focuses on several important factors:

- Reduce hazardous materials
- Make computing devices energy efficient
- Recycle outdated computing devices
- Limit factory wastes

Technology companies have been developing products that are more energy efficient and promoting recycling efforts to make computing more green.

What Processor Speed Do You Need?

As you learned earlier in this chapter, computers contain a processor that is located on a computer chip. Your computer **processor speed** influences how fast your computer runs programs and completes various processing tasks.

Those who want to play games and work with graphics require a more powerful computer system.

Processor speed is measured in **gigahertz (GHz)**. The more gigahertz, the faster the processor speed. Processor speed gets faster all the time. As of the writing of this textbook, 2.5 to 4.0 gigahertz was the higher end for the average computer, though some have reached 5 gigahertz.

Gordon Moore, one of the founders of Intel, is the creator of **Moore's Law**, which states that over time the number of transistors that can be placed on a chip will increase exponentially, with a corresponding increase in processing speed and memory capacity. Since proposing this idea in 1970, Moore has largely been proved correct.

How Much Memory and Storage Is Enough?

Your computer has a certain amount of **memory capacity** that it uses to run programs and store data. When you buy a computer, you'll notice specifications for the amount of RAM and hard drive storage each model offers.

- As you read previously, RAM is the memory your computer uses to access and run programs. RAM chips come in different types, including DRAM, SRAM, and SDRAM. Most modern computer memory is some variation of SDRAM including DDR-SDRAM, DDR2-SDRAM, and DDR3-SDRAM. Performance has steadily improved with each successive generation. The more sophisticated programs you run and the more you want to run several programs at one time, the higher RAM you should look for.

- RAM chips are rated by **access speed**. This rating involves how quickly a request for data from your system is completed. Your computer will also use some RAM to run the operating system and application programs. RAM access speed is measured in **megahertz (MHz)**. For example, 800 MHz is a typical access speed that would be sufficient to run most computers. In early 2012, Intel will release a new processor that will operate up to 1600 MHz. Adding RAM to your computer is simple to do and one of the least expensive ways to improve the speed of your computer.
- The average computer's hard drive capacity for data storage is measured in **gigabytes (GB)**. A typical consumer PC might have anywhere from 250 GB to 750 GB of storage capacity. Large systems used by business and research institutes and very powerful consumer devices may have storage measured in terabytes (TB, measured in thousands of gigabytes). Likewise, data storage size is an issue for smartphones and tablets. Many smartphones feature up to 64 GB of storage. Tablets start at 16 GB and go to 64 GB or more.

online Spotlight on the Future
PODCAST

Can You Future-Proof Your New Digital Device?
Even though personal computers are much less expensive than they used to be, you still have to make a significant financial investment to buy one.

It's good news, then, that PCs seem to be lasting longer before they become outdated.

"The traditional PC is a pretty future-proofed machine now, so long as you don't really cheap out" on the machine you buy, according to technology writer Dwight Silverman.

So, you can shop for a PC with good confidence that it will be able to run your software, play your favorite games or connect to the Internet several years down the road. But as people move their computing to smartphones and tablets like the iPad, the outlook changes.

Listen to the Chapter 3 Spotlight on the Future podcast and then be prepared to answer the following questions.

Talk about It
1. How has the lifespan of a typical PC changed over the years?
2. What are the things you should look for in a PC to ensure that it will last as long as possible?
3. Does innovation suffer when people are holding on to their PCs longer?
4. Why do smartphones and tablet computers have a shorter life span at the moment?
5. When might the life cycle of smartphones and tablet computers increase significantly?

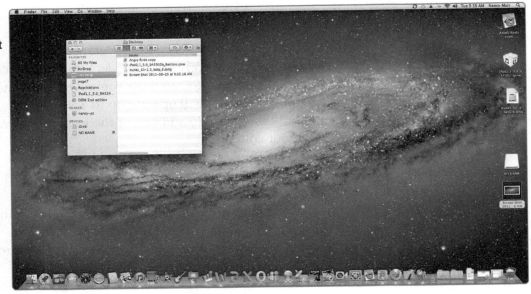

Operating systems are getting better at allowing users to interact with files created on other systems.

Which Operating System Is Right for You?

Chapter 4 of this book goes into operating systems in detail, but when you go out shopping for a computer you should consider which operating system to use for a few reasons.

All new computers come with an operating system installed, so the cost of the operating system (OS) isn't usually a factor. However, if you are buying OS software, there are variations in cost to consider.

Windows is a popular operating system, but if you are buying the software (as opposed to buying a computer with it already installed), it is costly (up to a few hundred dollars for an upgrade package) when compared with the free open source Linux OS (though some packaged versions of Linux may charge a subscription fee). Also, because of its popularity, Windows computers are more often the target of viruses (though Macs are gaining in both popularity and virus problems).

Linux is a Windows-like operating system that comes in different "flavors" such as Red Hat and Ubuntu. You can use the free, open-source version of Linux or you can purchase a packaged edition. For a packaged edition, the company may charge a fee and add something extra, such as support and documentation. The Linux community offers lots of applications and add-ins to choose from.

Mac computers are manufactured by Apple and use the Mac OS X operating system. Macs use software written by Apple, but there are other popular software products you can buy in a Mac version. Many software applications originally written for Windows are also available in Mac versions, such as Microsoft Office. You can also set up your Mac to run the Windows operating system, so you can take advantage of a wide variety of software.

How Do You Want to Connect with the Online World?

Computers come with various features that allow them to connect to the Internet. Dial-up modems were built into older computers but are less popular now. Today's standard is to include a port for connecting a cable to your computer and a built-in **wireless adapter**.

What Are You Willing to Spend?

Computers range in price from a few hundred dollars to several thousand. Often, buying a base model and customizing it with additional memory and an upgraded monitor will get you the system you need. Laptops are still slightly more expensive than desktop models, but tiny laptops such as netbooks have leveled the playing field. It's a good idea to use online sites to check out the best prices and read consumer reviews before buying.

Where you shop can have an impact on price. You can shop for a computer in an online store, in a traditional retail store, or use online auctions or classifieds to find deals on new or refurbished models. Retail stores provide the ability to try before you buy. You can spend time with the computer, getting the feel of the keyboard and viewing the display to see if it meets your needs. Manufacturer sites allow you to customize computers to your requirements.

Check to see whether memberships in organizations such as your university or member-discount retail stores such as Costco give you access to good deals. Also, think about shipping costs if you buy online. Retail stores often charge a restocking fee if you return a computer.

Should You Opt for Higher-End Graphics and Sound?

Those who work with a lot of visual elements (for example, photographers, gamers, or movie buffs), should opt for a better quality graphics card. Movies and games also use sound, so a high-end sound card is a plus.

Computers that have higher-end sound and image capabilities are referred to as gaming or multimedia models. Besides more sophisticated sound and video cards, they usually have higher memory specifications.

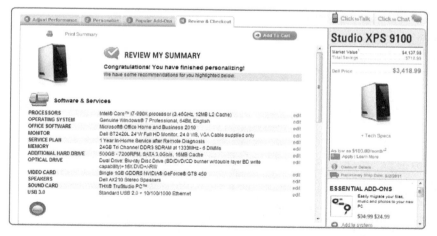

Companies such as Dell and Gateway offer buyers the opportunity to build a custom machine online.

Take the Next Step *online*

Activity 3.4.1 Video	*What affects your computer's speed?*	**CORE CONTENT**
Activity 3.4.2 Flash Movie	*How do you install external devices and update drivers on your system?*	**CORE CONTENT**
Activity 3.4.3 Research	*How do different styles of computers compare for weight, size, and portability?*	
Activity 3.4.4 Team Research	*How much battery life is enough for a computing device?*	
Activity 3.4.5 Research	*Which operating system is right for me?*	
Activity 3.4.6 Research	*What can I customize in a computer?*	

CORE CONTENT

A World of Digital Devices

Some digital devices have certain features built into one unit, such as a laptop computer or cell phone. Others use other **peripheral devices** that physically or wirelessly connect with them.

The Parts That Make Up Your Computer

The **motherboard** is the primary circuit board on your computer, and holds the central processing unit (CPU), BIOS, memory, and so on. The motherboard is a sort of container where the various working pieces of your computer slot into one compact package. Circuits on the motherboard connect the various components contained on it.

The central processing unit (CPU), which is a microprocessor, sits on the motherboard. The CPU processes a user's requests. A **multicore processor** contains more than one CPU, which in this situation is referred to as a core.

The motherboard also holds different types of memory. **Read-only memory (ROM)** is the permanent, or nonvolatile, memory of a computer hardwired into a chip. In a **PC**, the **BIOS** is stored in ROM. BIOS stands for basic input/output system. This is code embedded in a memory chip also residing on the motherboard. During the boot-up sequence, the BIOS checks devices to insure they are working properly and to start them up. It also directs the hard drive to boot up and load the operating system (OS) to memory. Random access memory (RAM) chips store data and programs and allow access in any order, which speeds up processing.

While some computers have built-in sound or graphics cards, others include them as **expansion cards**.

A **power supply** in a desktop or laptop computer is located where the power cord is inserted at the back of the CPU. The power supply switches alternating current (AC) provided from your wall outlet to lower voltages in the form of direct current (DC).

A computer uses a **port** to connect with a peripheral device such as a monitor or printer or to connect to a network. A **serial port** is used to connect a peripheral device to the serial bus via a cable with a plug that typically contains nine pins. A **universal serial bus (USB) port** is a small rectangular slot that provides a popular way to attach peripherals and storage devices. You can add a hub to expand the number of available USB ports. A **FireWire port** is based on the same serial bus architecture as a USB port. It provides a high-speed serial interface for high-end digital cameras, camcorders, set-top boxes, and audio and video. An **Infrared Data Association (IrDA) port** allows you to transfer data from one device to another using infrared light waves.

All storage media have methods for reading the data from the media (input) and for writing the data to the media (output). The various storage media used on a computer are accessed using **drives**.

Storage media include the **hard disk** built into your computer; an **optical drive** to read a **CD**, **DVD**, or **Blu-ray disc**; an **external hard drive** or a **network attached storage (NAS)** shared external hard disk; a **flash drive**; and a **solid-state drive (SSD)**. Third party cloud storage systems store and manage on a web-connected server.

Input and Output Devices

You use **input devices** to get data into your computer and **output devices** to get information out.

Input devices include a computer **keyboard**, a **mouse**, a **scanner**, digital cameras and **webcams**, **gaming devices**, special **electronic pens** used to write on tablet PCs, touchscreens and foldable keyboards for **mobile Internet devices (MIDs)**, **assistive technology devices**, devices often used in retail or manufacturing settings such as **bar code readers** and **RFID readers**, and **microphones** for getting sounds into your computer in the form of audio files.

Output devices include any device that displays, prints, or plays content stored in your computer, including your **monitor**, **speakers**, headphones, **printer**, or an **LCD projector**.

Some devices provide both input and output functionality, such as a **fax machine**.

Purchasing a Computer

When buying a computer, you should consider the following questions:
- What are your computing needs?
- What **processor speed** do you need?
- How much memory and storage is enough?
- What operating system is right for you?
- How do you want to connect to the Internet?
- What are you willing to spend?
- Should you opt for higher-end graphics and sound?

Your computer has a certain amount of **memory capacity** that it uses to run programs and store data. When you buy a computer you'll notice specifications for the amount of RAM and hard drive storage each model offers. RAM **access speed** is measured in **megahertz (MHz)**. The average computer's hard drive capacity for data storage and the storage capacity for smartphones and tablets is measured in **gigabytes (GB)**.

All new computers come with an operating system installed, so consider whether you want Windows, Linux, or a Mac OS X system. Computers also come with various features that allow them to connect to the Internet.

Computers range in price from a few hundred dollars to several thousand. Often, buying a base model and customizing it with additional memory and an upgraded monitor will get you the system you need. Laptops are still slightly more expensive than desktop models. Where you shop can have an impact on price.

Those who work with a lot of visual elements (for example, photographers, gamers, or movie buffs) should opt for a better quality graphics card. Movies and games also use sound, so a high-end sound card is a plus.

Terms to Know

A World of Digital Devices

The Parts That Make Up Your Computer

Input and Output Devices

Purchasing a Computer

Concepts Check

Concepts Check 3.1   Multiple Choice
Take this quiz to test your understanding of key concepts in this chapter.

Concepts Check 3.2   Word Puzzle
Complete this puzzle to test your knowledge of key terms in this chapter.

Concepts Check 3.3   Matching
Test your understanding of terms and concepts presented in this chapter.

Concepts Check 3.4   Label It
Use the interactive tool to identify objects on a motherboard.

Concepts Check 3.5   Label It
Use the interactive tool to identify the parts of a computer.

Projects

Check with your instructor for the preferred method to submit completed work.

Project 3.1   Understanding Your Computer System and Performance

Project 3.1.1   Individual

Knowing the parts of your computer system will be helpful when you need to upgrade your system or buy a new computer. Using the list of computer parts below as a guide, create a table and include descriptions of the features of your current computer. If you don't own a computer, use a public computer or a friend's computer to perform this task. Note any hardware features that you want to upgrade for increased performance. (You can find information about the computer system in the Control Panel of Windows under the category of System and Maintenance, or by looking at your user manual or visiting your manufacturer's website and searching for your computer model.) Be prepared to discuss your findings in class.

CPU processor

CPU speed

RAM

Hard drive capacity

DVD drive

CD drive

Monitor type

Monitor size

Sound card

Video card memory

Speakers

Ports (types and numbers of each)

Size

Weight

Style (desktop/laptop/ other)

Project 3.1.2 Team

Using a Windows-based computer, have your team visit the Microsoft website and search the term "Windows Experience" to learn about Windows base scores for your system's performance. Analyze the performance of the computer. Prepare a table that lists the processor subscore, RAM subscore, graphics subscore, gaming graphics subscore, primary hard disk, and the base score. Then discuss two suggestions that would improve the performance of the computer's system, such as adding RAM or removing viruses. Determine, for example, whether the computer system's base score would support the installation of a new software suite that requires a base score of 3.0. Create a memo to your instructor that includes the table, recommendations to improve performance, and information about the software suite upgrade.

Project 3.2 Purchasing a Computer

Project 3.2.1 Individual

You have decided to purchase a new computer to launch a home business. Because your current computer works fine, you would like to donate it to a charitable organization. Before making the donation, you know that your computer must be wiped clean of data. You realize that simply deleting files or reformatting your hard drive doesn't remove all the data, so you decide to research the proper way to permanently erase computer data. Based on your research, prepare a list of instructions for wiping your computer clean of data.

Project 3.2.2 Team

Your Introduction to Computers class has volunteered to help people in the community who need to buy new computers. Your instructor will divide the class into three groups:

- Group A is purchasing a computer for a senior citizen for personal use.
- Group B is purchasing a computer for a teenaged gamer.
- Group C is purchasing a computer for a business person who travels regularly and needs Internet access and basic business functionality.

Your group's task is to meet the needs of your assigned community member by researching a variety of computer options. To begin the process, consider the user's likely computer needs and cost limitations. Then investigate different computer systems that satisfy those requirements. Use the table format created in Project 3.1.1 to guide you in your research, and keep a list of your reference sources. Prepare a group presentation that shares your research findings and computer recommendation.

Project 3.3 Exploring Data Storage

Project 3.3.1 Individual

With an increased need for computer users to access information from any location, online data storage is becoming a popular service. Research several cloud storage companies, and examine the pros and cons of the service, the costs, and any security issues. Write a report about online data storage and include a recommendation for an online storage company. Be sure to provide your instructor with a list of references for your information.

Project 3.3.2 Team

As a help desk member of an information technology department, you observe some risky data handling practices. In particular, you have noticed that many employees have CDs, DVDs, flash drives, and external hard drives lying around on their desks. You have also observed some employees placing CDs and flash drives in their pockets to carry them home. After speaking with your supervisor about the potential for damaged or lost data, your supervisor asks you to prepare a slide presentation about the proper use of data storage devices. As a team, select three storage devices and provide guidelines that address how to keep the devices and the data stored on them safe. Be prepared to present these guidelines to your class, and to submit a list of resources to your instructor.

Project 3.4 How Much RAM Is Enough?

Project 3.4.1 Individual

Your classmate is having a hard time understanding RAM. To help your classmate, you have been asked by your instructor to research RAM and to create an outline covering its basic concepts. Your outline should include the definition of RAM, the types of RAM, the location of RAM, and the amount of RAM a well-equipped computer should contain. Keep a list of references that you used in your investigation. After you have completed the outline, work with a partner to review each other's outline and to solicit feedback on its usefulness. Record any comments on each other's outlines, and submit your outline and list of references to your instructor.

Project 3.4.2 Team

A local school has received a donation of computers that are in excellent shape but are operating slowly and need a new software suite installed. A school employee, Tony, has volunteered to install the software. Tony realizes that the computers need more RAM to run the new software and address the slow operating speed, but he has never installed RAM. To help Tony with this task, prepare a tutorial presentation (supported with text and screen captures) on the installation of RAM. Be sure to include a list of references for your information.

Project 3.5 Wiki — Exploring New Computer Technologies

Project 3.5.1 Individual

Research the Internet to find an article about a new computer device released in the current calendar year. If possible, focus your search on devices that use a new technology that wasn't available a year earlier. Read the article and write a summary of the device, including a description of the device, its purpose and functions, the total cost of the device (including all components), and its availability. Attach a list of references that you used to write your summary, and post the summary on the course wiki site.

Project 3.5.2 Individual or Team

You or your team will be assigned to edit and verify the content posted on the wiki site from Project 3.5.1. If you add or edit any content, make sure you include a notation within the page that includes your name or team members' names and the date you edited the content—for example, "Edited by [student name or team members' names] on [date]." Keep a list of references that you used to verify your content changes. When you are finished with your verification, include a notation at the end of the entry—for example, "Verified by [student name or team members' names] on [date]."

Project 3.6 Green Computing

Project 3.6.1 Individual

The increasing use of computer technology has had a significant impact on the environment. As a result, many companies have implemented policies that support green computing. Research the term "green computing" and the major initiatives behind this environmental movement. Write a report that discusses the definition and main concepts of green computing. Address the measures being taken by companies to support this movement and their positive impact on the environment. Be sure to offer a recommendation in your report as to how computer users can support the green computing movement. Submit your report and a list of your references to your instructor.

Project 3.6.2 Team

Your information technology team has been assigned to prepare a slide presentation on green computing for the board of directors of your school. This presentation should provide the broad definition and purpose of green computing as well as specifically define and address the major concepts of this environmental initiative: green use, green design, green disposal, and green manufacturing. Be sure to include in your presentation a recommended green computing plan for your school to implement.

Class Conversation

Topic 3.1   What Happens to Old Computers?

The personal computer began to become a household fixture in the early 1990s. In the last twenty years, computers have gained improved productivity, increased in speed, decreased in size, and continue to get better and faster year after year. What happens to all the old computers? What impact will these old computers have on our environment in the next ten years?

Topic 3.2   When Will Technology Slow Down?

Technology changes rapidly. Do you think the development of new technology will slow down at some point? At some point will consumers be satisfied with the current technology, or is it human nature to continually want change? What impact does a desire for new technology have on our economy?

Topic 3.3   Compare Online Shopping with Buying a Computer Retail

Computers are sold in a variety of settings, such as specialty computer stores, large discount retailers, or online at retail stores or auction sites. What are the benefits of purchasing a computer at a specialty computer store? Do you feel secure about purchasing a computer online? Is the support you can get for your computer better if you buy it at a brick-and-mortar store? What support options do you think exist for a computer purchased online?

System Software
The Control Center of Your Computer

What You'll Accomplish

When you finish this chapter, you'll be able to:

- Define the role of system software and identify tasks it performs.

- Explain the functions of an operating system in a computer or mobile device and describe the basic features of today's popular operating systems.

- Identify the tasks of the operating system package and how the utilities in the package monitor system performance.

- Describe various utility programs that are used to optimize and maintain a computer.

- Outline the history of the development of operating systems and identify future trends.

Why Should I Care?

Hardware without system software is like a powerful new car without a driver. The computer may have the latest gadgetry under the hood, but without system software, the gadgetry can't do anything. Every computer, from a small mobile device to a large mainframe computer, needs system software, which includes the operating system and various utility programs, to work. Understanding how an operating system package such as Windows manages the various devices, programs, and files on your computer will help you make choices when purchasing a computer, troubleshoot your system when things go wrong, keep your data secure, and perform regular maintenance to keep your computer performing well.

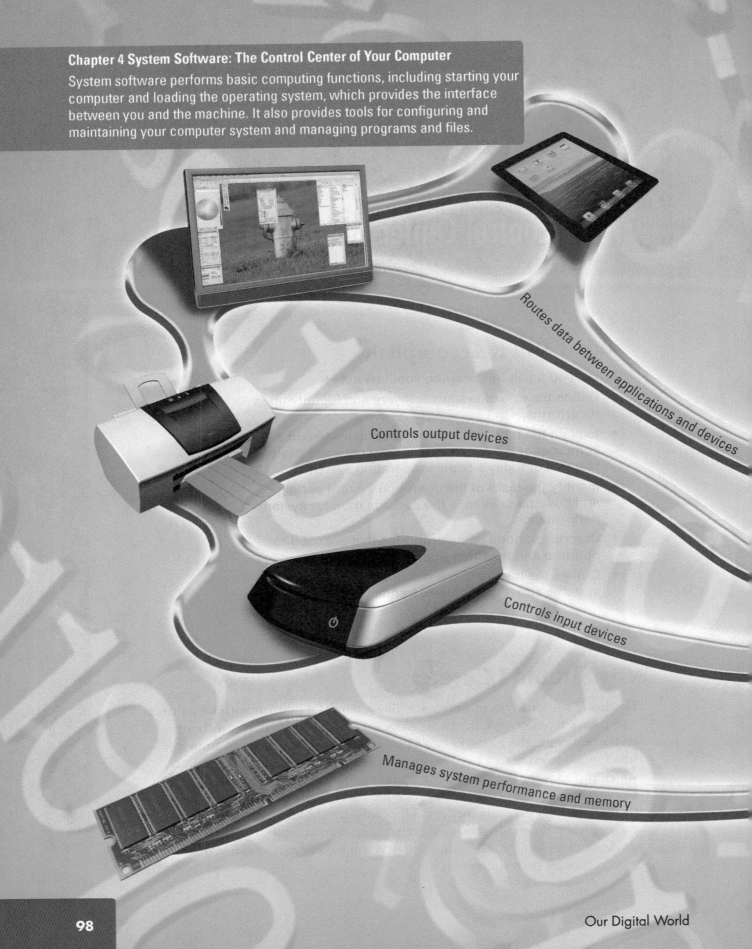

Chapter 4 System Software: The Control Center of Your Computer

System software performs basic computing functions, including starting your computer and loading the operating system, which provides the interface between you and the machine. It also provides tools for configuring and maintaining your computer system and managing programs and files.

Routes data between applications and devices

Controls output devices

Controls input devices

Manages system performance and memory

Provides a user interface

Creates and manages files

Configures hardware

Shuts computer off

Maintains computer

Operating System

Provides search and help

The first instructions your computer uses when you turn on the power are stored in a ROM BIOS chip located on your computer's motherboard (the circuit board that holds the various elements of your computer). These instructions are called firmware. **Firmware** in a computer system contains code that is used to start your computer and load system software.

System Software

System software includes your operating system (OS) and several types of utility software. The OS provides you with an interface to work with your computer hardware and applications, while utilities optimize and maintain your computer. The OS and utilities are typically combined in an operating system package such as Windows, Linux, UNIX, the Mac OS X, Android, and Chrome OS. More portable devices such as tablet devices and smartphones typically use a mobile operating system that provides similar functionality to the OS on your desktop or laptop computer.

The **operating system (OS)** part of system software allows you to organize and control your computer hardware and software. It's in charge of loading files, deciding which applications get to do what and when as you work, and shutting down your computer. The OS is essential for you to interact with your computer because software and hardware simply can't run without an OS in place. Your OS translates your commands and performs appropriate actions.

Utility software, or utilities, although included in an operating system package such as Windows, aren't *essential* to the functioning of the OS but are *useful* to the OS and to the user. **Disk Cleanup** in Windows, for example, helps the OS function by maintaining your computer and getting rid of unused or unusable files.

Figure 4.1 shows the devices that communicate with the OS.

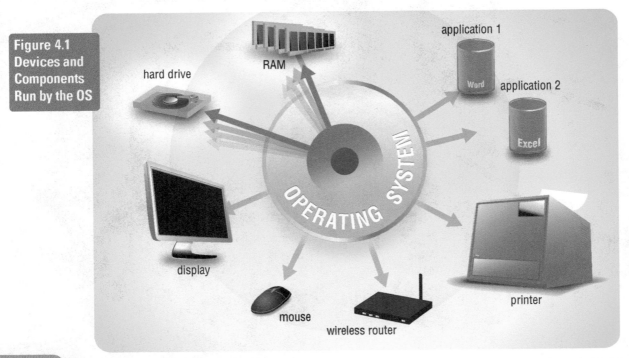

Figure 4.1 Devices and Components Run by the OS

hard drive

RAM

application 1

Word

application 2

Excel

OPERATING SYSTEM

display

mouse

wireless router

printer

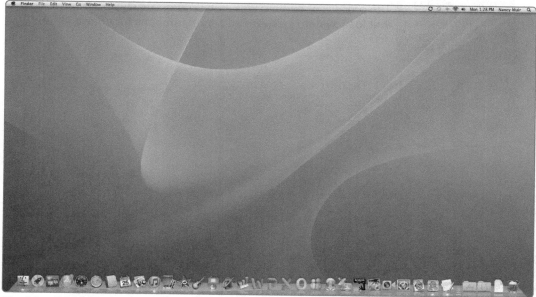

The Mac OS X, though outsold by Windows, has a loyal and growing following. This is the Mac OS X desktop.

Starting Your Computer

The process of starting your computer, called **booting**, is handled by instructions that reside on the BIOS chip slotted onto the motherboard. These instructions load the OS, which then loads the remaining system and software files into RAM (memory). If you start a computer when the power is turned off, you're performing a **cold boot**; if you restart the computer (shut it down and then turn it on again without turning the power off), that's called a **warm boot**. A new specification for booting your computer called **UEFI (Unified Extensible Firmware Interface)** is just beginning to be adopted; UEFI replaces the aging BIOS firmware and could make booting computers a much speedier process.

Figure 4.2 shows the steps in booting a computer. During this procedure the following components are involved:

- The motherboard, which holds the central processing unit (CPU) and other chips.
- The CPU, or microprocessor chip, which is the brains of your computer.
- The BIOS, which stands for basic input/output system. This is code embedded in a memory chip on the motherboard. The BIOS code (firmware) is used by your computer to load the operating system and communicate with hardware devices.
- **System files**, which run when you start up your computer. They provide the instructions that the operating system needs to run.
- **System configuration**, a definition or means of defining your entire computing system, including the identity of your computer, the devices connected to it, and some essential processes that your computer runs.

> " The BIOS is an integral part of any computer since it initializes a machine before the OS takes over, but it has changed little in 25 years and was never designed with the long term in mind. "
>
> ▶▶ Emil Protalinski, Techspot.com

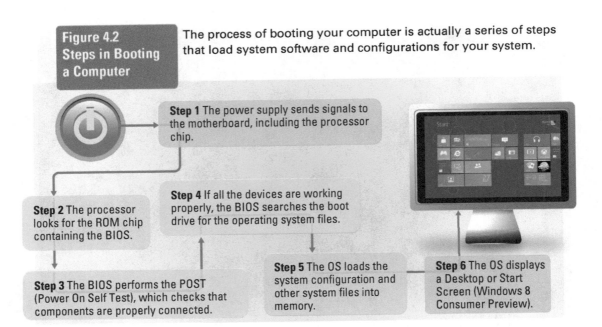

Figure 4.2 Steps in Booting a Computer The process of booting your computer is actually a series of steps that load system software and configurations for your system.

Step 1 The power supply sends signals to the motherboard, including the processor chip.

Step 2 The processor looks for the ROM chip containing the BIOS.

Step 3 The BIOS performs the POST (Power On Self Test), which checks that components are properly connected.

Step 4 If all the devices are working properly, the BIOS searches the boot drive for the operating system files.

Step 5 The OS loads the system configuration and other system files into memory.

Step 6 The OS displays a Desktop or Start Screen (Windows 8 Consumer Preview).

Taking a Look at the Operating System Package

An **operating system package** such as Windows or Linux includes system software that runs and manages your computer's hardware and software resources; organizes files and folders containing your documents, images, and other kinds of content; and helps you perform maintenance and repairs when your computer has problems. Operating system packages also offer security features such as password protection to keep others from using your computer and a firewall, which can prevent someone from remotely accessing your computer.

Operating system packages also include small applications you can use to get your work done or be entertained, such as very basic word processing programs like WordPad; games like Spider Solitaire; media players such as QuickTime Player to play music or videos; and tools such as a calculator, a calendar or address book, and an Internet browser.

A (Brief!) History of Operating Systems

There was a time when computers had no operating system. In this pre-OS time, every program had to have all the required **drivers** (software that allows an operating system to interface with hardware) and specifications needed to connect to hardware such as printers. In the early days of computing, functions in software were simple enough that this system worked. As programs became more sophisticated and hardware grew more complex, something was needed to orchestrate the interaction between software and hardware.

online **Take a Survey**

What experience do you have with operating systems?

Mainframe computers—the pre-consumer computers that were often the size of a large desk or van—typically used an operating system created for them by their manufacturer. UNIVAC I, the first commercial computer produced in the United States, is an example. In the pre-personal computer period, names of the operating systems were not significant because the hardware drove the purchase decision.

UNIX, developed by AT&T Bell Laboratories in the 1970s, was an OS written with the C programming language, which became popular with corporations for running their workstations. It was usable across a variety of hardware and could be customized by the companies who licensed it. UNIX continues to be widely used by larger organizations today, and there are several versions of this OS.

With the development of microprocessors, small personal computers began to catch on, and by the 1980s it was clear a more standardized OS was needed. Microsoft produced its first OS, MS-DOS, which eventually became known simply as **DOS** (an acronym for disk operating system). This and other early operating systems were **command-line interfaces**, meaning that you typed commands as text, but they were not in plain English—and not very intuitive.

A huge breakthrough in operating system development came in the 1980s and 1990s when the **graphical user interface (GUI)** was introduced to the public by Apple and then by Microsoft. A graphical user interface added a much more user-friendly way to work

The Remington Rand Corporation introduced the first commercial computer produced in the United States, the UNIVAC I, in 1951.

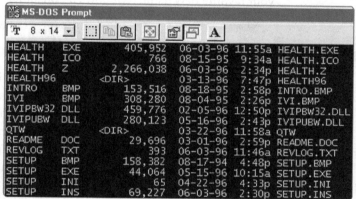

DOS sported white letters on a black background and required that you memorize commands to use the OS.

with a computer because you could click icons and choose options from menus and dialog boxes, rather than typing commands. With Windows 8 Microsoft is adding touchscreen functionality to its operating system, a significant shift in how users provide input to their computing devices modeled after mobile device operating systems.

Take the Next Step *online*

Activity 4.1.1
Flash Movie
How has Windows evolved into the feature-rich program of today?

Activity 4.1.2
Research
What is the origin of the term "booting"?

Operating systems make your computer work, but they also offer access to small applications and games to entertain you. For example, the Windows Store app is where you can download your favorite new game (Windows 8 Consumer Preview). This app offers new content often.

4.2 Perusing the Popular Operating System Packages

The major operating systems used by individual consumers in the world today are Windows, for PCs (or personal computers); the Mac OS X, for Apple computers; and Linux, an open source operating system available in different versions. (Open source means that the software was built with contributions by users and its source code is free to anybody to modify and use.) Newer consumer-oriented operating systems are geared toward mobile devices and computing "in the cloud."

Understanding Platforms and Platform Dependency

The term **platform** is used to describe the combination of hardware architecture and software used to run applications. The platform's OS may be dependent on the hardware. For example, a Mac operating system isn't designed to run on a Windows computer. This is called **platform dependency**. Table 4.1 lists four common operating system platforms.

Table 4.1 Operating System Platforms

Platform	Operating Systems
PC/Windows	Windows 8, Windows 7, Windows Vista, Windows XP, Windows 2000
Mac/Mac OS	OS X in various versions: Lion, Snow Leopard, Leopard, Tiger, Panther, OS 9
Netbooks/Tablets & iPads	Windows 8, Windows 7, Android, Chrome OS, iOS
PC to Mainframe/UNIX	New versions of UNIX are now released as open source software through the Open Solaris project, including SchillX, Belenix, and AIX
PC to Mainframe/Linux	Linux, being freely distributable, comes in many different distribution "flavors" such as Red Hat, SUSE, and Ubuntu, as well as a wealth of versions for specific languages such as Chinese (Sunwah Linux) and Norwegian (Skolelinux).

Our Digital World

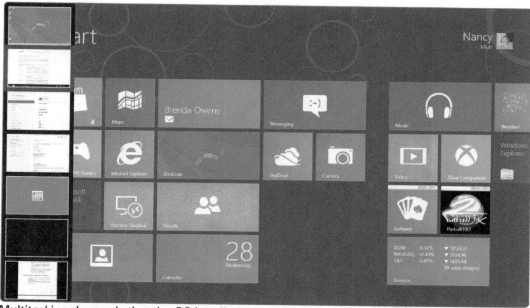

Multitasking demands that the OS handle several functions at once (Windows 8 Consumer Preview).

However, platform dependency is becoming less and less important as consumers demand cross-functionality when they buy computers and software. Today, software such as Boot Camp, included with the Mac OS X, allows you to run Windows on a Mac. Though there are still different versions of productivity software such as Word for PCs, Word for Mac, and Open Office's Writer, you can typically save files in each version that are compatible with (able to be used by) the other platform.

Still, when you purchase application software such as a computer game or word processor, you should make sure that you buy applications that will work with the platform your computer is based on. If you are using software in the cloud, the hosting site usually makes sure you have the latest or most compatible version for your computer.

Windows **Microsoft Windows** was initially a graphical interface layered on top of the DOS operating system. Eventually, it became a true GUI OS with a very robust feature set. Windows is the most widely used operating system in the world today. It can be used on computers from a variety of manufacturers and there are thousands of software products available to run on Windows.

The latest Windows OS is Windows 8, which moves towards a mobile computing look and feel similar to the Windows Phone platform. Users can interact with their desktop, laptop, or tablet computer using a touchscreen and on the new Start Screen live tiles that represent apps such as Weather, People, or Finance update on the fly. Whichever version you use, the widespread adoption of Windows by millions of users with a variety of computers and configurations requires that regular updates to the operating system be done to fix bugs or flaws as they arise.

> " It does not matter which browser, operating system, program or service you use — it falls down to whether the job can be done or not. If it can, then continue. If not, by all means move on. "
>
> ▶▶ Zack Whittaker, ZDNet

Today's popular graphical operating systems: Windows 8 (Consumer Preview), Mac Lion OS, and Linux.

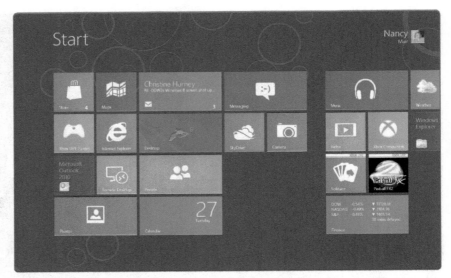

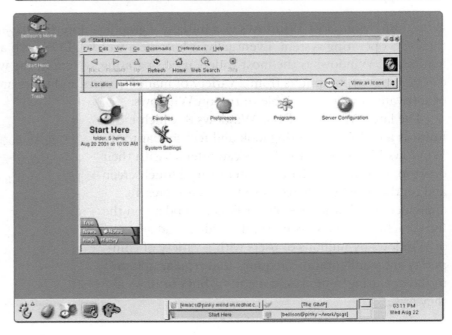

Our Digital World

Ethical Choices in Device Manufacturing

It seems like whenever there's a new technology, from videotapes to cell phones to computers, companies scramble to produce the winning version and consumers end up the losers, lost in a sea of incompatible technologies. Should device manufacturers be forced to work together to establish common standards for new technologies? Is that possible in a free market?

Mac Those who swear by Macs and the **Mac OS X** have several reasons to do so. Macs have very sophisticated graphics-handling capabilities and clear, crisp screens. Their computer designs are unique, as with the iMac that incorporates the CPU in the monitor and the sleek MacBook notebook computer.

Mac computers were very strongly marketed to the educational world in their early days, though PCs have made significant inroads in that environment. Other strong Mac markets historically have included creative industries such as graphic design and photo imaging because of Mac's sophisticated graphics-handling capabilities. Today, growing popularity of iPods, the iPhone, iPads, and the iTunes online store have convinced many more people to adopt Apple's hardware, software, and services. Mac OS X Lion even includes enhancements that mirror features found on iPhones and iPads, such as new trackpad gestures like pinching to zoom and swiping to navigate, access to a Mac App store with free and paid apps (programs) available for download, and a Launchpad for accessing all your apps.

The Mac's new popularity brings a downside, however. Once thought a less virus-prone system, the Mac OS has been receiving more attention from programmers of malicious software. In one incident in early 2011, a bogus program designed to look like a protection system infected computers and duped some users into providing credit card information. Luckily, antivirus programs can combat malicious software on both Mac and Windows systems.

> " How cool would it be if you could just buy a state-of-the-art smartphone, plug in a monitor, mouse and keyboard, and never have to buy a laptop or desktop computer again? "
>
> ▶▶ Liliputing.com

UNIX **UNIX** is a server operating system. There are several other server operating systems, such as Open Enterprise Server, and other specialized server operating systems, such as those used to run web applications and email.

Created by a handful of AT&T Bell Labs employees, UNIX was designed to run servers that supported many users. UNIX uses a command-line interface and because it's written with the C programming language, it is more portable across platforms—meaning that it can run on all types of computers including PCs and Macs. UNIX is a popular choice for web servers that support thousands or millions of users.

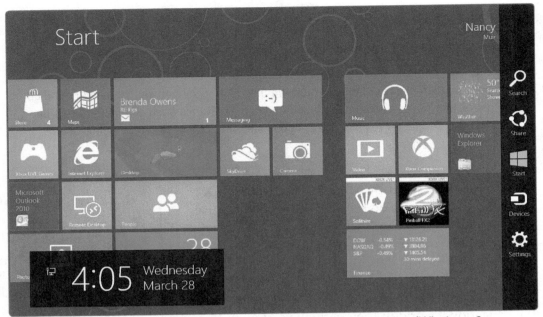

The Windows 8 Start Screen with apps available through graphical tiles (Windows 8 Consumer Preview).

An OS controls the interface you see, as with the Mac OS X desktop shown here.

Linux **Linux**, first developed by Linus Torvalds in 1991, is, to a great extent, based on UNIX; some people believe it may eventually take over UNIX's market. Linux can be used as either a network operating system or a personal computing OS. Linux is an **open source operating system**, meaning that the source code for it is freely available and many people can use it and modify it. Modifications contributed over the years have resulted in various distributions or versions of Linux, such as Red Hat, Ubuntu, Mandriva, and SUSE.

Linux can run on multiple platforms and users of Linux state that the OS is highly stable and flexible. When it first appeared, Linux was seen as the rebel's OS and was supported by lots of people who were against Microsoft and the general dependency on their products. Though Linux hasn't toppled Windows, it has definitely found its place in the OS world.

The Linux logo is a penguin, which has been known to appear in many costumes and versions.

The Future of the OS

It is possible that operating system packages could become less important, or at least, less visible to the average user in the not too distant future.

Google's **Chrome OS** is a Linux-based operating system that will appeal to people who work primarily in web-based applications. In June 2011 Chromebooks manufactured by Samsung and Acer were released. Chromebooks boast an 8-second startup with all settings, applications, and documents stored in the cloud. Using the Web to deliver the majority of the user experience makes Google Chrome an OS that is cross-platform, because it works on any computer that supports browsers (which is essentially all computing devices in use today, including mobile phones).

While the Chrome OS is currently only available on the Chromebook (netbook-like) platform, new consumer-oriented operating systems give you choices that span other platforms. While primarily an operating system for mobile phones (currently laying claim to 50% or more of that market), Google's **Android** is also offered as an operating system on tablets and some netbook models. Similarly, the **iOS** operating system from Apple powers some iPod models, iPhones, and iPad tablets.

All three of these operating systems in a sense function as web operating systems, providing access to services online. Android and iOS also allow users to customize their experience by downloading and installing apps on a device, while Chrome OS offers web apps. These modern operating systems allow consumers to take advantage of a variety of mobile computing platforms, and customize them to work wherever and whenever needed. Microsoft is betting with its Windows 8 OS that a more mobile OS interface depending heavily on a touchscreen approach to input will be the wave of the future.

Google's Chrome OS provides a web-based experience.

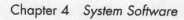

Take the Next Step *online*

Activity 4.2.1
Video

What types of tasks does network operating software handle?

CORE CONTENT

Activity 4.2.2
Research

Are Windows and the Mac OS X all that different?

Activity 4.2.3
Team Research

What does it take to run the Mac OS X on Windows (and vice versa)?

Activity 4.2.4
Flash Movie

How has Linux (an open source operating system) evolved over time?

Activity 4.2.5
Team Presentation

Will Chromebooks succeed?

4.3 The Tasks of the Operating System Package

Although there are different operating system packages out there, they have similar basic functions in common. Here's a rundown of those functions and what they help you do with your computer.

Providing a User Interface

A **user interface** is what you see when you look at your computer screen. Most operating systems provide a graphical user interface; this means that icons and pictures take the place of the text-based operating systems of the past.

Your computer's **desktop** is like home base for your computer, from which you use a text or graphical menu to run applications and work with files. As illustrated in Figure 4.3, GUIs use graphical buttons and windows that display operating system settings or open documents. You can open more than one window at a time; for example, one window may show your web browser open to surf the Internet at the same time that another window displays a photo editing program. You can also customize your desktop to use a different background image or color, or change the color scheme for all your desktop elements, including window borders and title bars.

Configuring Hardware

As previously defined, a driver is a small software program that your computer needs to communicate with a piece of hardware, such as a printer or keyboard. The driver provides the instructions the OS needs to communicate with the device. You may notice when you first plug in a new device, such as a wireless mouse toggle that you plug into a USB drive, that the OS first has to find the driver before you can use the mouse. If your system has the wrong driver for a

Figure 4.3
Some Customizable
Settings for Windows PCs

Operating systems allow you to customize their desktops with different backgrounds, resolution settings, and tools (Windows 8 Consumer Preview).

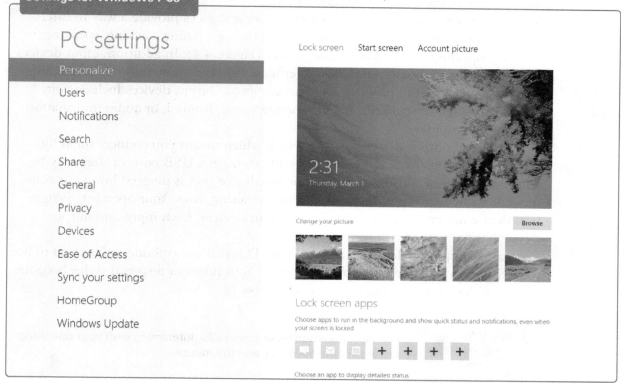

device, you may have problems; for example, a printer may print garbage text if you're not using the correct driver.

When you buy hardware and take it home, there will usually be a CD-ROM in the package that contains the necessary device driver software. In addition, most operating systems today come packaged with many common device drivers, or offer a way for you to download a driver from the Web. Most devices today work with **Plug and Play**, a feature that recognizes devices you plug into your computer, for example into a USB (universal serial bus) port. Once the Plug and Play feature identifies the hardware, the OS can install the necessary driver if the driver is available.

You may have to update drivers now and then—especially if you upgrade the OS. Your OS may be set up to perform regular updates to your system that download and install newer drivers for hardware automatically and your manufacturer may alert you to updated drivers if you have registered your computer.

Today most operating systems don't require a CD to install drivers, but it's a good idea to keep it around in case of problems.

Controlling Input and Output Devices

Your operating system also controls input and output devices. Commonly used input devices include your keyboard, mouse, microphone, finger or stylus on a touchscreen, or joystick (used for gaming). These devices provide a way to interact with your computer, telling it what to do through typing, clicking, speaking, or selecting options in menus and dialog boxes (Figure 4.4). In addition, input devices (typically your keyboard) allow you to enter text into documents you create using programs such as word processors or spreadsheets. Output devices include your monitor, printer, or speakers. These generate visual, printed, or audio information from your computer.

Input and output devices may be wired, which means you connect them by plugging them into your computer, typically through a USB port; or they may be wireless and connect through a transmission device that is plugged into your computer, leaving your input device free from restricting wires. Your operating system uses device drivers to set up and control input devices. Each input and output device has a unique driver.

Some computing devices, such as Tablet PCs and smartphones, allow you to use a touch screen to communicate with the OS. Your finger or a special stylus becomes the input device, rather than a mouse or keyboard.

Figure 4.4 Microsoft Word Input Options The most common input devices for interacting with your operating system are the keyboard and the mouse.

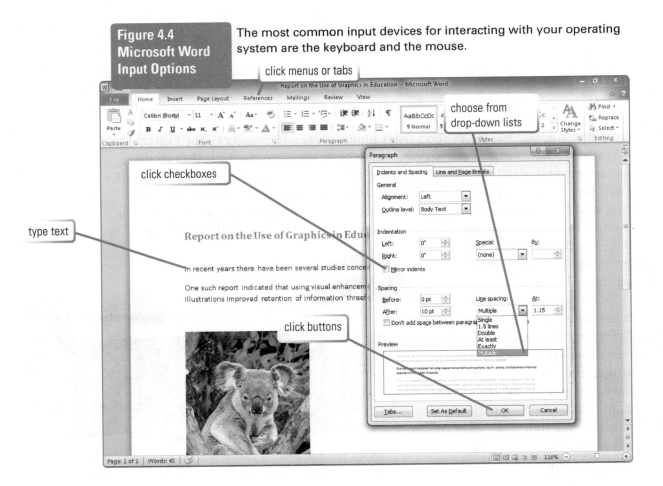

Managing System Performance and Memory

The speed with which your computer functions, called its **performance**, is largely determined by the computer processor, available cache, bus, and the amount of memory installed in the computer. All of these are orchestrated by system software.

Utilities in your operating system package monitor system performance and provide information about system resources. This allows you to troubleshoot performance and adjust settings, change which programs the OS loads when you start up, and so on.

Here's a brief rundown of the four most significant factors controlling system performance.

Memory Memory refers to the capacity for storage in a computer. One kind of memory is permanent, as with read-only memory (ROM), which holds information such as the BIOS and start-up instructions for the operating system. Another kind of memory is temporary, as with random access memory (RAM), which stores data while your computer is operating, but loses that data when you shut down your computer). **Virtual memory** is part of your operating system that handles data that cannot fit into RAM when you are running several programs at once. Figure 4.5 shows how, when RAM is used up, data is stored or "swapped" into virtual memory (the file moved into virtual memory is called a **swap file**). As each program is loaded, and data fills RAM's "bucket," it spills over into virtual memory.

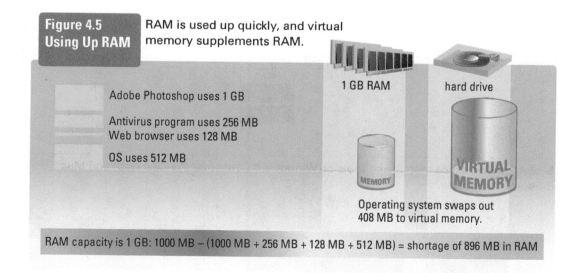

Figure 4.5 Using Up RAM RAM is used up quickly, and virtual memory supplements RAM.

Adobe Photoshop uses 1 GB

Antivirus program uses 256 MB
Web browser uses 128 MB

OS uses 512 MB

1 GB RAM

hard drive

MEMORY

VIRTUAL MEMORY

Operating system swaps out 408 MB to virtual memory.

RAM capacity is 1 GB: 1000 MB – (1000 MB + 256 MB + 128 MB + 512 MB) = shortage of 896 MB in RAM

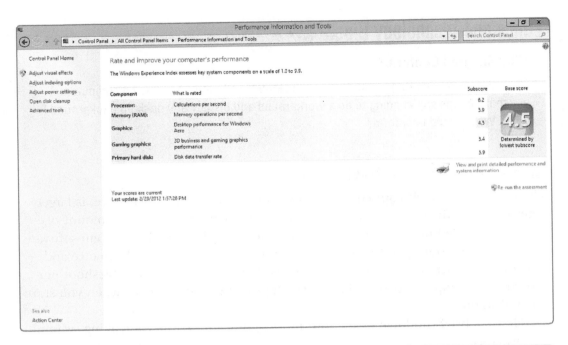

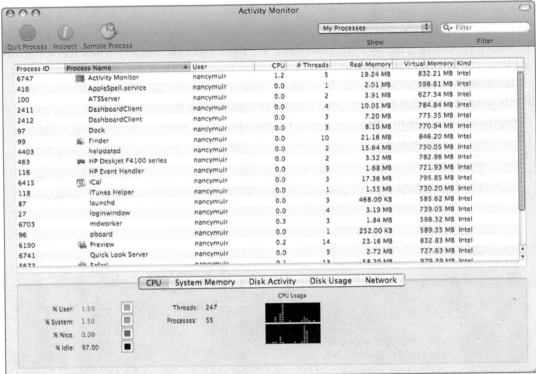

System performance monitoring tools on Windows 8 Consumer Preview (top) and Mac (bottom) computers.

Cache Cache memory is a dedicated holding area in which the data and instructions most recently called from RAM by the processor are temporarily stored. The process of caching allows your computer to hold a small amount of recently used data in memory so that, when you ask for something again, the OS doesn't have to run around in RAM looking for it. This is similar to the function of RAM. However, because the cache sits on the microprocessor, it can be accessed more quickly than RAM, which is stored on another chip. The larger the cache size, the more data can be held and quickly retrieved, though cache always has a maximum size to keep the searching of the cache itself efficient.

Processor The CPU, sometimes referred to as the computer's processor, is an electronic circuit that runs your computer's hardware and software. The OS coordinates the use of a processor's resources by scheduling and prioritizing tasks. In systems with more than one processor core (dual or quad core systems as shown in Figure 4.6), the OS manages tasks between/among processors.

Bus A bus is a subsystem that moves instructions and data around between the components in your computer (for example, between RAM and the processor and between the processor and the cache). The faster the bus, the faster the computer. One measurement of bus speed is how much data can move at one time. Another is the speed at which the data can travel. A bus with a larger capacity to move data and a faster speed helps your computer complete tasks faster.

Routing Data between Applications and Devices

It's midnight, and you've just finished a lengthy homework assignment and want to print a copy to submit to your instructor the next morning. You click the Print button in your word processor program and grab the pages as they come out of the printer. Ever wonder what your operating system is doing in the background?

Figure 4.7 (on page 116) shows how this routing of data between an application and a printer works and what role your operating system plays. Your OS may also route data to your network, or to other devices such as a fax.

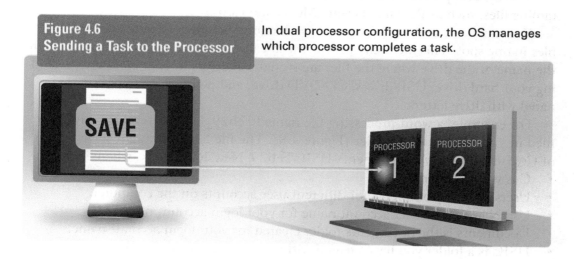

Figure 4.6
Sending a Task to the Processor

In dual processor configuration, the OS manages which processor completes a task.

SAVE

PROCESSOR 1   PROCESSOR 2

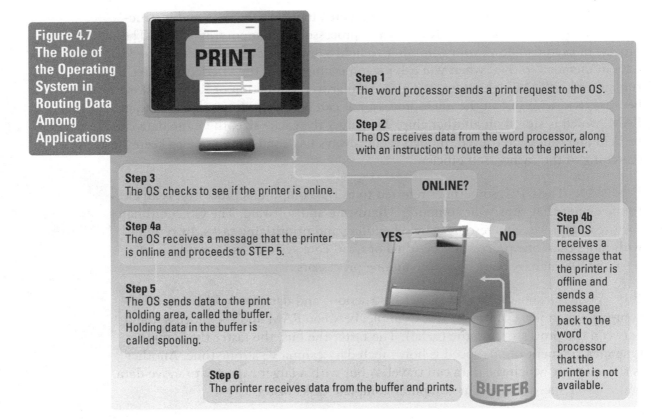

Figure 4.7 The Role of the Operating System in Routing Data Among Applications

PRINT

Step 1
The word processor sends a print request to the OS.

Step 2
The OS receives data from the word processor, along with an instruction to route the data to the printer.

Step 3
The OS checks to see if the printer is online.

ONLINE?

Step 4a
The OS receives a message that the printer is online and proceeds to STEP 5.

YES

NO

Step 4b
The OS receives a message that the printer is offline and sends a message back to the word processor that the printer is not available.

Step 5
The OS sends data to the print holding area, called the buffer. Holding data in the buffer is called spooling.

Step 6
The printer receives data from the buffer and prints.

BUFFER

Managing File Systems

It's the operating system that provides features used for storing and retrieving files. The OS has to keep track of the physical location where a document is saved on your hard disk; to do this, it maintains the **file allocation table (FAT)**. Because the bits that make up a file may be stored all around your hard disk, not in a contiguous group, this table provides an index of data locations the OS can reference, which speeds up the time it takes to open a file.

The OS also provides the commands you use for naming, organizing, and maintaining files, such as Rename, Delete, Move, and Copy.

You can create and organize your own hierarchy of file folders to store related files in one spot. This hierarchy provides a so-called **path** to the file that starts with the name of the drive where the files are stored. All drives in your computer, including your hard drive, USB drives, CD/DVD drive, and network drives, are designated with drive letters.

For example, a word processing file named Feb29_Newsletter.docx might be filed in your Documents folder (Figure 4.8). The file location might have a path of C:\Users*UserName*\Documents\HSJC/Feb29_Newsletter.docx, where

- C is your hard drive.
- Users is the set of folders for different user accounts on the computer.
- UserName is the user account name for your login account name.
- Documents is the documents folder created for your login account name.
- HSJC is a folder you have created within your documents folder.
- Feb29_Newsletter.docx is the file name.

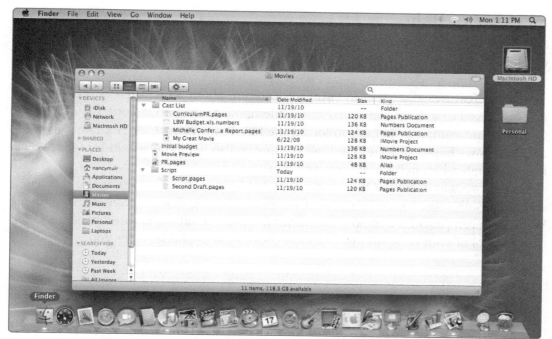

The Mac Finder window helps you locate files in a hierarchy of folders.

document path

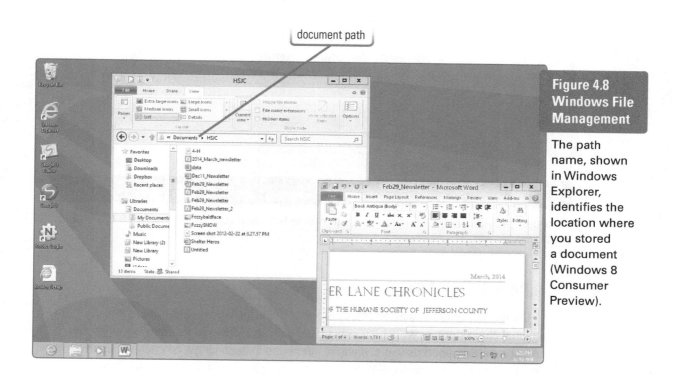

**Figure 4.8
Windows File
Management**

The path name, shown in Windows Explorer, identifies the location where you stored a document (Windows 8 Consumer Preview).

Search and Help

Operating systems all provide a method of searching your computer for the files you need, and a help system you can use to look for information about how to use your computer.

Search features allow you to enter information about a file, such as the date it was last saved or a word contained in the file name or the actual contents of the file, and your computer helps you locate the file. Features such as Finder on a Mac and Windows Explorer on a Windows computer also help you search for what you need through a hierarchy of folders and files.

A help system in every OS provides searchable support information and troubleshooting tools, some located on your computer and some that you can access online. Windows even provides a remote assistance feature that allows another person to take control of your computer to pinpoint your problem and fix it for you.

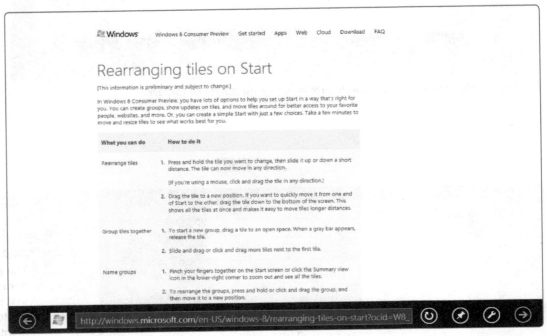

Windows provides help files and access to online help and support (Windows 8 Consumer Preview).

Computers in Your Career

Computer support specialists may work in a small, local computer repair store or national chain store, or work from a technical call center for a large software or hardware corporation to support its users. If you're interested in becoming a computer support specialist you must have a solid grounding in a computer-related field (at least an associate's degree) and be able to communicate well and deal with the public. Because many computer problems require troubleshooting within the OS, being comfortable with operating system settings, configurations, and utilities will help you succeed in your work.

Maintenance Features in an Operating System Package

System maintenance is an important task for system software, similar to taking your car into the shop on a regular basis for tune-ups so you keep it running efficiently. There are several utility programs included in your operating system package that you can use to perform system maintenance tasks, scan drives and files for problems, or otherwise help protect your system and troubleshoot problems. Typical utility program functions include those listed in Table 4.2.

Sending the Computer to Sleep or Shutting It Off

The operating system is in charge of shutting down your computer. The way you shut down your computer is important, because the proper procedure avoids losing unsaved data and properly saves system settings. In addition to shutting down your computer, you can use features with names such as Sleep or Hibernate to save computer power but still be able to return to your desktop and any running programs quickly without having to reboot.

Table 4.2 Utility Program Features

Function	Windows Feature Name	Macintosh Feature Name
Backing up or restoring damaged files	Backup Files	Time Machine
Performing automatic updates to get updated drivers or definitions	Windows Update	Software Update
Cleaning up your hard drive to get rid of files you haven't used for a long time or temporary files	Disk Cleanup	Repair Disk
Defragmenting your hard drive so that scattered bits of files are reorganized for efficiency in retrieving data	Disk Defragmenter	Disk Utility
Restoring your system to an earlier date to remove new settings that may have caused problems	System Restore	Time Machine
Scheduling regular maintenance tasks such as backing up and downloading updates	Task Scheduler	Time Machine
Uninstalling unwanted programs	Uninstall or Change a Program	Uninstaller
Providing security features such as a firewall or spyware protection	Windows Firewall and Windows Defender	Security

Take the Next Step *online*

Activity 4.3.1 Flash Movie	*What features does the latest version of Windows offer?*	CORE CONTENT
Activity 4.3.2 Research	*How do you put your computer to sleep?*	
Activity 4.3.3 Hands-on	*In what ways can you customize your OS?*	
Activity 4.3.4 In-Class or Blog Discussion	*What happens if your mouse and keyboard go away?*	

4.4 Going on the Road with Mobile Operating Systems

A **mobile operating system** (also known as a mobile OS or mobile platform) is the brains behind mobile smartphones (such as the iPhone, Blackberry, and the Palm Pre). These are devices with a rich feature set that essentially makes them into very small computers.

What Makes a Mobile OS Different?

A mobile OS, which is stored in ROM, is not nearly as robust as a personal computer operating system because a phone simply doesn't have a great deal of memory and most users don't need as much functionality from their phone.

A mobile OS also uses/accesses smaller resources so it can run quickly and efficiently. In some phones, the OS has to manage touch screen functionality and wireless broadband connections.

A Wealth of Mobile OS Choices

Stroll down the aisle of an electronics store and you'll notice dozens of mobile phone models, including **smartphones** that include an operating system. Different phone manufacturers adopt different operating systems for their various smartphones. Several smartphone companies are now opening online stores where users can download applications for their mobile phones, such as GPS navigation systems or games.

Applications that users download to their phones typically only work with that phone's OS. If you buy a new phone with a different operating system, you need to buy new apps.

Leading mobile operating systems include the one made by Research in Motion, used in BlackBerry devices, and the open source OS Symbian. Microsoft's Windows Phone operating system appears on several smartphone models. With its Palm Pre,

Table 4.3 Common Mobile Operating Systems

OS	Description
Android	An open source, cross-platform OS supported by Google.
BlackBerry OS	OS for BlackBerry phones.
BlackBerry Tablet OS	OS for BlackBerry Playbook.
iOS	Apple-developed iPhone and iPad OS based on Mac OS X.
J2ME	Java-based OS that comes in several "flavors."
webOS	Used in some HP and Palm smartphones such as Treo.
Symbian OS	Big in Europe where there are more Symbian-based devices.
Windows Phone	Microsoft's mobile OS.

Palm (acquired by Hewlett-Packard in 2010) began offering an operating system called webOS, Ericsson has its own entry, and search engine giant Google backs a platform called Android, which it claims is the only truly open platform that can handle multiple manufacturer's phones. Table 4.3 lists the most common systems.

There are a large number of mobile operating systems available. This wealth of options can be inconvenient for people buying and using phones, and difficult for wireless companies who have to support a complex set of systems and features.

> " If you're a fan of the stripped down mobile operating systems that power the pocket computers we call smartphones, the next generation Windows and Apple operating systems may make you very happy. "
>
> ▶▶ Alexis Madrigal
> Senior Editor, *The Atlantic*

A wealth of mobile operating systems run on phones from different phone manufacturers.

online Spotlight on the Future
P DCAST

Cloud Operating Systems

Operating systems—software that controls the essential functions of computers—are stored on hard drives. That could change in future, as some companies are pushing for operating systems that live on the Internet instead.

But at this point the future of cloud operating systems is a little cloudy, according to technology writer Dwight Silverman. He thinks the current model, in which operating systems live on the computers they command, will last for quite some time.

It gets down to peoples' desire to exert mastery over their machines, Silverman says.

"People will always need to be able to be able to store copies of their data on systems they control," he says.

Listen to the Chapter 4 Spotlight on the Future Podcast with Dwight Silverman, and be prepared to answer the following questions.

Talk about It

1. How does Silverman define a cloud operating system?
2. What's Silverman's opinion about how long operating systems will be housed on computer hard drives instead of "in the cloud"?
3. What would have to happen before a true cloud OS can develop?
4. What companies are promoting cloud operating systems?
5. Why are some companies interested in cloud operating systems?

Take the Next Step *online*

| Activity 4.4.1 | *What is 4G?* |
| Flash Movie | |

CORE CONTENT

| Activity 4.4.2 | *What's the best deal for a* |
| Team Presentation | *4G smartphone?* |

Computers in Your Career

When new versions of an operating system or applications appear and companies upgrade there are a few key jobs to be handled. If you provide network support in a corporation you will help to *roll out* new versions of software to all your users by installing and customizing the software. If you are a trainer, you may be called upon to provide instruction in the new software features. Other IT (information technology) workers may run a help desk, answering technical questions and troubleshooting problems that come up in the first few weeks or months of use.

Summing Up

What Controls Your Computer?

System software contains an **operating system (OS)**, which you use to interact with hardware and software, and **utility software** to maintain your computer and its performance. An operating system package—for example, Windows 8—contains the operating system plus certain utilities.

Starting your computer, called **booting**, is carried out by instructions located on a chip on your computer's motherboard. If you start by turning the power on, you're performing a **cold boot**. If you restart the computer (shut it down and then turn it on again without turning the power off), that's called a **warm boot**.

Early computer manufacturers used their own operating systems. Microsoft's first OS, MS-DOS, which eventually became known simply as **DOS**, was a **command-line interface**, meaning that you typed in text commands.

A huge breakthrough in operating systems happened in the 1980s when the **graphical user interface (GUI)** was introduced by Apple.

Perusing the Popular Operating System Packages

The major operating systems used by individual consumers today are **Microsoft Windows**, for PCs; the **Mac OS X**, for Apple computers; and various versions of **Linux**, an **open source operating system**. **UNIX** is an OS used by larger organizations to run their networks. Other operating systems such as Google's Chrome OS, Android, and iOS allow for computing on smaller devices such as tablets and smartphones, and enable the user to buy apps, either online through a browser or by downloading to the device.

The term **platform** identifies the architecture of a computer and the OS intended to run on it. **Platform dependency** is becoming less and less important as consumers demand cross-functionality when they buy computers and software.

The Tasks of the Operating System Package

Operating system packages have certain basic functions in common:
- Providing a **user interface**, including a **desktop**.
- Configuring hardware using device **drivers**.
- Controlling input and output devices.
- Determining the speed with which your computer functions (its **performance**), which involves the processor, available cache, bus, and the amount of memory.
- Providing information about system resources to enable you to troubleshoot performance, adjust settings, change which programs the OS loads when you start up, and so on.
- Routing data between applications and devices, as when you send a document to a printer or scan an image from hard copy using a scanner.
- Managing folder and file systems to store and retrieve information.

- Providing search capabilities for locating files and a help system for information about how to use your computer.
- Performing system maintenance tasks through utility software included in your operating system package.

Going on the Road with Mobile Operating Systems

Mobile operating systems are used to power some mobile **smartphones** (phones with a rich feature set that emulate some of the power of computers) and tablets. A mobile OS is stored in ROM and has to be able to use/access smaller resources and run quickly and efficiently.

Terms to Know

Concepts Check

Concepts Check 4.1   Multiple Choice

Take this quiz to test your understanding of key concepts in this chapter.

Concepts Check 4.2   Word Puzzle

Complete this puzzle to test your knowledge of key terms in this chapter.

Concepts Check 4.3   Matching

Test your understanding of terms and concepts presented in this chapter.

Concepts Check 4.4   Label It

Use the interactive tool to identify the standard components found in a Windows 8 desktop or documents window.

Concepts Check 4.5   Label It

Use the interactive tool to identify the standard components found in a Mac OS X Window.

Concepts Check 4.6   Arrange It

Use the interactive tool to complete the steps in the booting process

Projects

Check with your instructor for the preferred method to submit completed project work.

Project 4.1   To Upgrade or Not to Upgrade

Project 4.1.1   Individual

You work as an intern at a small restaurant consulting business. The owner employs five restaurant consultants who each have a desktop computer that is not networked and that uses the Windows 7 operating system. The consultants primarily use their computers for the following tasks:
- Track time and expenses
- Prepare new menu proposals for clients
- Cost food inputs for menu recipes
- Design new restaurant layouts using a CAD/CAM program

The owner is considering an upgrade from Windows 7 to Windows 8. To help the owner make the best decision for her business, research and compare the features of Windows 7 and Windows 8. Before you begin your investigation, prepare a list of questions you would ask or facts you would gather to analyze whether the owner should upgrade or not. Next to each question or fact, explain why you need to investigate the item. Based on your research, prepare a brief summary of the main points that the owner would be interested in knowing about Windows 8. Be sure to include a list of references for your information.

Project 4.1.2   Team

The owner of the restaurant consulting business has agreed to listen to a ten-minute sales presentation on converting her business PCs to Macs. As a team, prepare a slide presentation that highlights the features and functions of Macs and their applications to the needs of the business owner. In addition to presenting your arguments, your slide presentation should address usability, reliability, compatibility, and cost issues.

Project 4.2   Mobile Mania

Project 4.2.1   Individual

Your school's alumni committee has assigned you the task of purchasing a smartphone complete with a one-year service contract for a door prize at the alumni dinner. You have narrowed down the choices to an iPhone or a Black-Berry. Research these smartphones on the Internet, and prepare a table listing the pros and cons of each phone. Aside from the benefits and drawbacks, consider the costs associated with purchasing the phone along with the one-year contract. After a careful review of all factors, write a summary of your research including your recommendation for the door prize.

Project 4.2.2   Team

The manager of the school's alumni office has asked your team to research and recommend a wireless scanner that could be used to streamline the entry process into alumni venues. Currently, each person presents a ticket to an usher who must read the ticket to verify its validity. This manual check-in system bogs down the entry process, resulting in long lines. To provide a solution to this problem, research wireless scanners and the operating systems that are used on the devices. Then prepare a brief presentation for the alumni office manager with your team's recommendation.

Project 4.3   Housekeeping 101

Project 4.3.1   Individual

Using utility programs to perform system maintenance tasks is important to the efficient operation of a computer. To determine if computer maintenance is a priority among the computer users you know, choose a representative sampling of ten friends and/or relatives who use the computer for a variety of functions. Provide them with a survey checklist of tasks performed by utility software programs, and ask them to check the tasks that they execute on a regular basis. These tasks may include backing up of data files, running disk cleanup, defragmenting the disk, running antiviral programs, and so on.

Include a note with your survey checklist reminding participants that if they use a multipurpose utility program, such as Norton 360, they should check all of the applicable tasks that the program performs. Prepare a spreadsheet that displays the survey data, and write a summary of the survey's results. In your summary, draw a conclusion as to the importance of computer maintenance among your survey participants. Provide an explanation as to whether the survey is or is not reasonably representative of the general population of computer users.

Project 4.3.2   Team

Read the article at www.emcp.net/ComputerChecklist for a list of 29 tasks a technical support technician performs to keep a computer running smoothly. (As you are reading, keep in mind that this list is geared toward computer maintenance in a corporate setting by a dedicated IT staff.) Then, within your team, discuss the tasks on this list that would be useful for home computer users, and select the 10 most important tasks. As a group, design a Top 10 Maintenance Task Checklist that could be printed and distributed to home computer users. For each task on the checklist, note the frequency with which the task should be performed—for example, weekly, monthly, or annually. Also, be sure to include a tip for each task that provides users with the location of the system tools needed within the operating system software.

Project 4.4   Accessibility Options

Project 4.4.1   Individual

You work as a volunteer with senior citizens at a local community center. These individuals have asked for your assistance with customizing their desktop computer's settings to make their computers more user-friendly. Specifically, they have mentioned difficulties with reading small type and hearing system sounds during certain activities. Research the Ease of Access Center options in Windows. Experiment with various settings until you find a group of customization options that you think will address their needs. Prepare a handout with instructions on how to set up the Ease of Access options you have decided to recommend. Include screenshots where appropriate.

Project 4.4.2   Team

Many senior citizens at the community center have arthritis, making it difficult for them to type on a computer. To help them with this task, you would like to set up speech recognition on their computers. Research the speech recognition technology that is included with the operating system. Determine the key features of the program and whether any special hardware is needed for the program to work. Also, find out if the speech recognition feature has support for Spanish, the first language of several of the senior citizens. Prepare a presentation that summarizes the results of your research and evaluates the adequacy of the program for the needs of these individuals.

Project 4.5　Wiki — File Management Tips and Tricks

Project 4.5.1　Individual or Team

You or your team will be assigned to address one or more of the file management questions listed below:

- What are some naming convention guidelines to follow when setting up files and folders?
- What is the distinction between a file and a folder? How is each one visually represented?
- What are the default folders provided with the operating system?
- What is a file extension? Should file extensions be displayed?
- How do I browse the folders on my computer or other storage device?
- How can I search for a file?
- How do I perform common file management tasks?
- What can I do with deleted files that have been sent to the Recycle Bin (Windows) or Trash (Mac)?

Prepare a posting to the course wiki site for your assigned topic. Write the posting as if it were going to be used as a help document for people unfamiliar with file management.

Project 4.5.2　Individual or Team

You or your team will be assigned to edit and verify the content posted on the wiki site from Project 4.5.1. If you add or edit any content, make sure you include a notation within the page that includes your name or team members' names and the date you edited the content—for example, "Edited by [student name or team members' names] on [date]." Keep a list of references that you used to verify your content changes. When you are finished with your verification, include a notation at the end of the entry—for example, "Verified by [student name or team members' names] on [date]."

Project 4.6　Wiki — Troubleshooting Tips

Project 4.6.1　Individual or Team

You or your team will be assigned to one or more of the following topics related to troubleshooting computer problems:

- Help! My printer is not working.
- Help! My Internet is not working.
- Help! My file will not open.
- Help! My computer keeps freezing up.
- Help! My computer is running very slowly.
- Help! My DVD won't play.
- Help! No sound is coming out of the speakers.
- Help! My email won't send or receive messages.
- Help! The taskbar is gone.
- Help! I can't upload the pictures from my camera.

Prepare a posting to the course wiki site for your assigned topic. The goal is to provide the average computer user with simple, precise instructions to follow to resolve the problem without calling in an expert. When writing your instructions, use clear, concise language and avoid technical jargon that might confuse your audience.

Project 4.6.2   Individual or Team

You or your team will be assigned to edit and verify the content posted on the wiki site from Project 4.6.1. If you add or edit any content, make sure you include a notation within the page that includes your name or team members' names and the date you edited the content—for example, "Edited by [student name or team members' names] on [date]." Keep a list of references that you used to verify your content changes. When you are finished with your verification, include a notation at the end of the entry—for example, "Verified by [student name or team members' names] on [date]."

Class Conversations

Topic 4.1   Is Windows Activation and Validation Necessary?

Windows software license terms include a requirement that the software be activated (usually done just after installation) and validated (checks that the software has been activated and properly licensed). In the event that a validation check reveals that the software is not properly licensed, the functionality of the software may be affected. For example, some features may not work, or updates will no longer be provided. Activation is intended to prevent a form of software piracy known as *casual copying* or *softlifting*. If you were to load Windows 8 on your computer and then share your installation media with a second individual who then loads it on his or her computer, you would be guilty of casual copying. According to Microsoft's website, *"Casual copying accounts for a large portion of the economic losses due to piracy . . . reduced piracy means that the software industry can invest more in product development, quality and support. . . . Ultimately, customers will benefit from the economic impact of reduced piracy through increased job opportunities and higher wages."* Do you agree that mandatory activation and validation reduce casual copying? Why or why not? Do you agree that reducing casual copying leads to higher quality software, more job opportunities, and higher wages? Why or why not? Consider an alternative to activation and validation and provide a piracy reduction suggestion of your own.

Topic 4.2   Is Obsolescence Planned?

Many end users find operating systems are using processor, memory, and storage resources at such increasing rates that a person who wants to install a new version is usually faced with replacing his or her computer or paying for required hardware upgrades. For example, many computers that were successfully using Windows XP could not support the hardware demands of Windows Vista, nor its successor Windows 7. Some people have speculated that the software companies plan for this obsolescence to maintain sales at levels that support profits for shareholders. Others say that software companies have to keep upgrading their OS to keep up with developments made by hardware companies. Which do you believe is true—software has to develop to keep up with hardware, or vice versa? Provide a rationale for your position. Will web-based operating systems mean that obsolescence will no longer be an issue? Why or why not?

Topic 4.3   Creating a File Naming Standard

A large amount of the time that a user spends interacting with the OS involves file management tasks. Browsing the content of a CD, a USB drive, or a hard drive, looking for that elusive file that you created last week, the name of which you can no longer remember, is something that has happened to everyone. A file name that seemed clever and memorable last week will no longer be memorable three months down the road. The search ability of an OS has improved with each new release over the years but one can still spend an inordinate amount of time looking for a file. Assume you have been hired by a company to devise a standard file naming system for all employees to use when naming new files. Consider how you would go about developing such a standard. For example, what questions would you need to ask end users before you attempted to develop a set of "rules" to use when assigning new file names so they can be easily retrieved? How would the file folder hierarchy be developed so that each department has similar folders and subfolders? What challenges do you foresee in developing a file naming standard?

Application Software
The Key to Digital Productivity

What You'll Accomplish

When you finish this chapter, you'll be able to:

- Understand the role of application software.
- Provide examples of major categories of application software, including mobile applications.
- Explain how software products can use content created in other software products.
- Describe the software development life cycle.
- Understand how software is priced and delivered.
- Define cloud computing.

Why Should I Care?

Your computer exists largely to run application software, the software you use to get things done. In your personal life and on the job you will use software that helps you accomplish tasks, and you will learn new software to get your work done. Understanding the different types of software that exist and how they are used will help you take advantage of a wide variety of tools to be more productive.

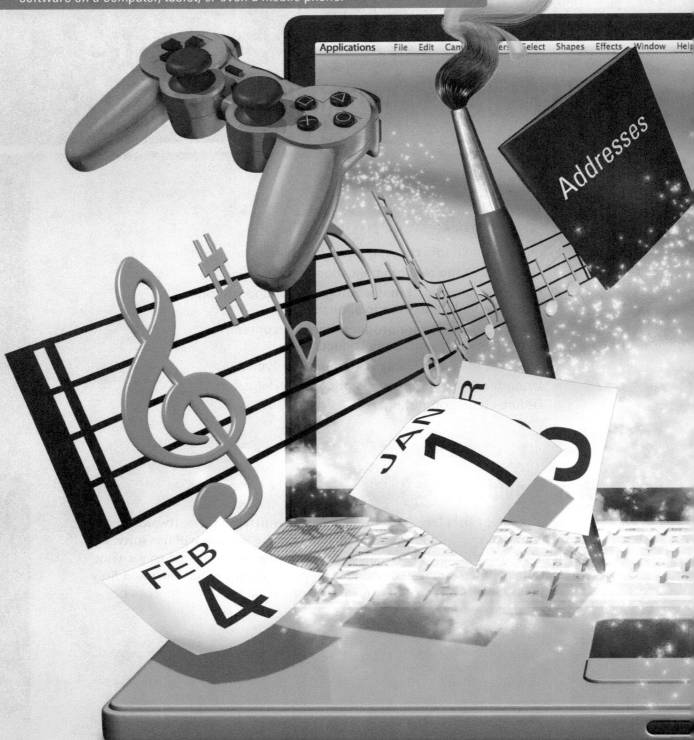

Chapter 5 Application Software: The Key to Digital Productivity

We use application software to get our work done, from writing and calculating to analyzing and presenting information. But we also use application software for fun to play games, listen to music, view photos, and read books. We can use software on a computer, tablet, or even a mobile phone.

System software, specifically the operating systems described in Chapter 4, enables your computer to function and run **application software**. You use application software to make your computer work for you. Application software helps you do many things such as get your work done, learn something new, communicate with others, create art, or play games.

Application software started out providing basic functions. Products such as VisiCalc, the first spreadsheet application for personal computers, were basically glorified calculators. Early word processors, such as WordStar, offered little more than the ability to enter text and edit text to create simple documents. When using these products you had to key command codes to enter or delete text, or even scroll (move up and down the page) through a document.

online ✓**Take a Survey**
How do you use software?

In the next section, you will discover what major categories of software exist today and how each is used.

With very simple interfaces and functionality, early software such as VisiCalc (right) and WordStar (below), provided the foundation for today's software applications.

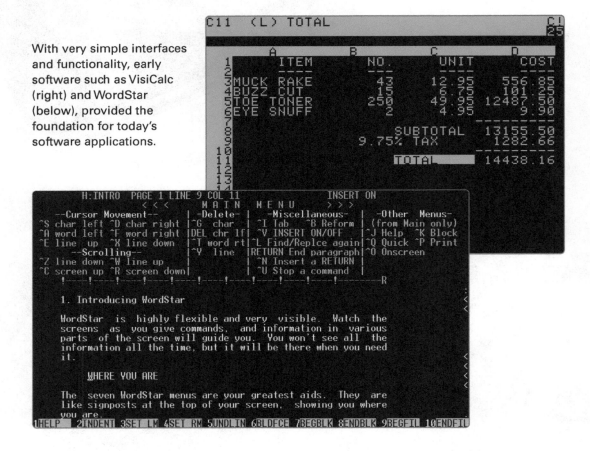

5.2 The Many Types of Application Software

From the early days of consumer software consisting of only basic business tools or simple games, software application development has exploded for both computers and all varieties of mobile devices. We now have available a huge number of categories of software applications, each with sophisticated feature sets. Using application software you might:

- Produce business documents such as reports, memos, budgets, charts, presentations, product catalogs, and customer lists.
- Manage massive amounts of data for student records, patient records, or employment records.
- Complete a learning exercise, a course, or even an entire degree without ever entering a classroom.
- Create works of art, including photos, drawings, animations, videos, and music.
- Organize content such as photos, appointments, contacts, home inventories, or music playlists.
- Manage your personal finances, handle your tax reporting, or generate legal documents.
- Play games or pursue hobbies such as sports or interior design.
- Stream music or video for entertainment.
- Communicate with others individually or in large online conferences.
- Perform maintenance or security tasks that help keep your computer functioning and your data secure.

In fact, software is so much a part of our lives that it's difficult to categorize application software products today by work or personal use. For instance, word processors aren't just used for business and design software isn't just used by artists. Financial software is used for creating department budgets and invoices as well as to track personal finances.

In this section we have categorized software applications by what they help you do. As you read through the following sections, consider how many categories of software you use.

Productivity Software: Getting Work Done

Productivity software includes software that people typically use to get work done, such as a word processor (working with words), spreadsheet (working with data, numbers, calculations, and charting), database (organizing and retrieving data records), or presentation program (creating slideshows with text and graphics). Software suites such as Microsoft Office and Apple iWork combine productivity applications, because many people use two or more of these products to get their work done. Software suites often include a word processor, a spreadsheet application, presentation software, and database management software. Suites also allow users to integrate content from one program into another, such as including a spreadsheet chart in a report created with a word processor. Now productivity software and suites are available for many smartphones and other mobile devices so you can be productive while away. Productivity suites available in the cloud—notably Office Web Apps and Google Docs—also enable you to work wherever you have Internet connectivity.

Word Processor Software **Word processor software** certainly does "process" words, but today it does a great deal more. With a word processor you can create documents that include sophisticated formatting; change text fonts (styles applied to text); add effects such as bold, italics, and underlining; add shadows, background colors, and other effects to text and objects; and include tables, photos, drawings, and links to online content. You can also use templates (pre-designed documents with formatting and graphics already in place for you to fill in) to design web pages, newsletters, and more. A mail merge feature makes it easy to take a list of names and addresses and print personalized letters and envelopes or labels. Figure 5.1 shows the application of some of the word processing features and tools Microsoft Word offers.

Spreadsheet Software **Spreadsheet software**, such as Microsoft Excel, is an application where numbers rule. Using spreadsheet software you can perform calculations that range from simple (adding, averaging, multiplying) to complex (estimating standard deviations based on a range of numbers, for example). In addition, spreadsheet software offers sophisticated charting capabilities. Formatting tools help you create polished looking documents such as budgets, invoices, schedules, attendance records, and purchase orders. With spreadsheet software such as Microsoft Excel, Numbers for the Mac, Calc (part of OpenOffice), and Quattro Pro (part of Corel's WordPerfect Office suite), you can also keep track of data such as your holiday card list and sort that list or search for specific names or other data. Figure 5.2 shows a typical spreadsheet making use of several key features.

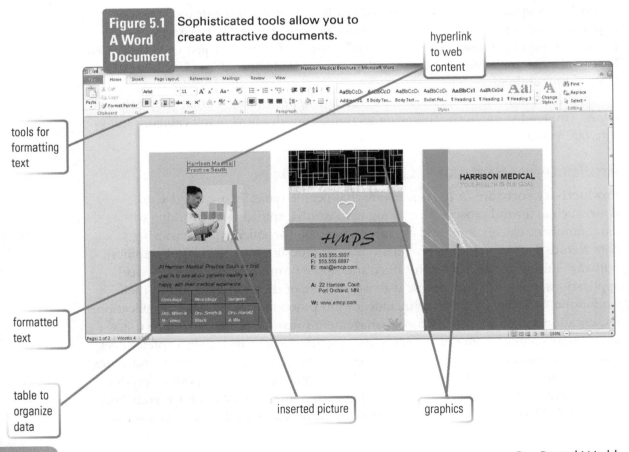

Figure 5.1 A Word Document Sophisticated tools allow you to create attractive documents.

hyperlink to web content

tools for formatting text

formatted text

table to organize data

inserted picture

graphics

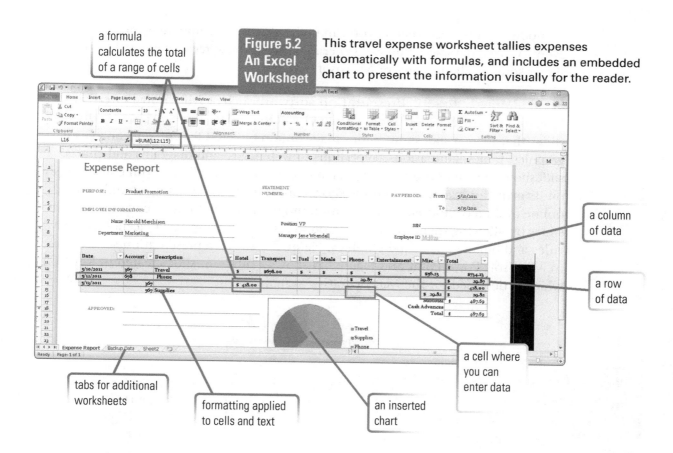

a formula calculates the total of a range of cells

Figure 5.2 An Excel Worksheet This travel expense worksheet tallies expenses automatically with formulas, and includes an embedded chart to present the information visually for the reader.

a column of data

a row of data

a cell where you can enter data

tabs for additional worksheets

formatting applied to cells and text

an inserted chart

Computers in Your Career

Spreadsheet software isn't just used by accountants. Managers use spreadsheets to compile and track department and project budgets. Statisticians and people working in marketing use the charting features of spreadsheets to map trends and summarize survey findings. Salespeople may use a spreadsheet to keep track of sales by customer or region. The calculation, analysis, and charting features of spreadsheet software can be useful in many, many occupations.

Database Software **Database software** can manage large quantities of data. The software provides functions for organizing the data into related lists and retrieving useful information from these lists. For example, imagine that you are a salesperson who wants to create a list of customers. Of course you want to include the name, address, and company name for each person. However, you might also want each customer record to include the customer's birthday, spouse's name, and favorite hobby as well as a record of purchases in the past year. You can also set up fields to look up data such as city names based on a ZIP code, saving you time reentering data. Once that data is entered into a table you can view information in a spreadsheet-like list or as individual customer record forms. You can create queries that let you find specific data sets. For example, say you want to find every customer with a birthday in June who is interested in sports and has purchased at least $2,000 of products in the last year so you can invite them to a company-sponsored sports event. With a database, you can generate a list of those records easily. Figure 5.3 shows some of the features of Microsoft Access.

Presentation Software **Presentation software** such as Microsoft PowerPoint, KeyNote for the Mac, or Impress from OpenOffice, uses the concept of individual slides that form a slideshow. Slides may contain bulleted lists of key concepts, graphics, tables, animations, hyperlinks to web pages, and diagrams and charts. A slideshow can support a presenter's comments during a talk, can run continuously on its own (for example at a trade show booth), or be browsed by an individual online or on a computer. A presentation program may help users create attractive slides by allowing them to use background art from a template, placeholders for titles and bulleted lists, and graphics. Figure 5.4 shows a presentation slide created in Microsoft PowerPoint and Figure 5.5 shows a different slide created in KeyNote, which is designed for the Mac operating system.

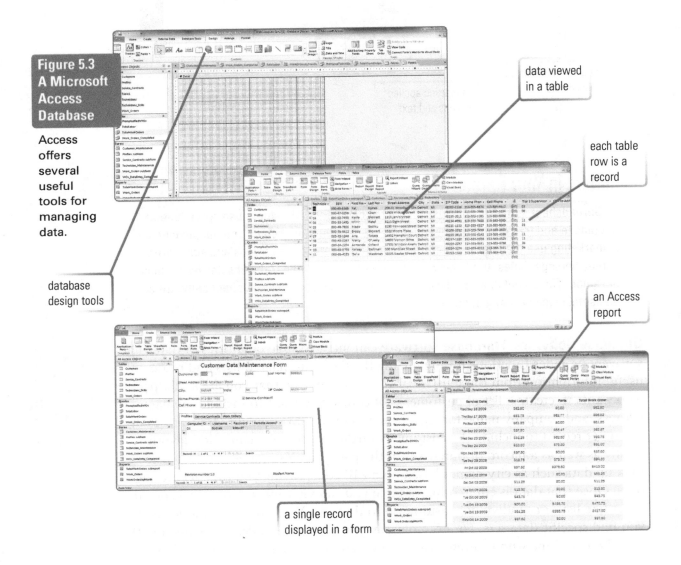

**Figure 5.3
A Microsoft
Access
Database**

Access offers several useful tools for managing data.

database design tools

data viewed in a table

each table row is a record

an Access report

a single record displayed in a form

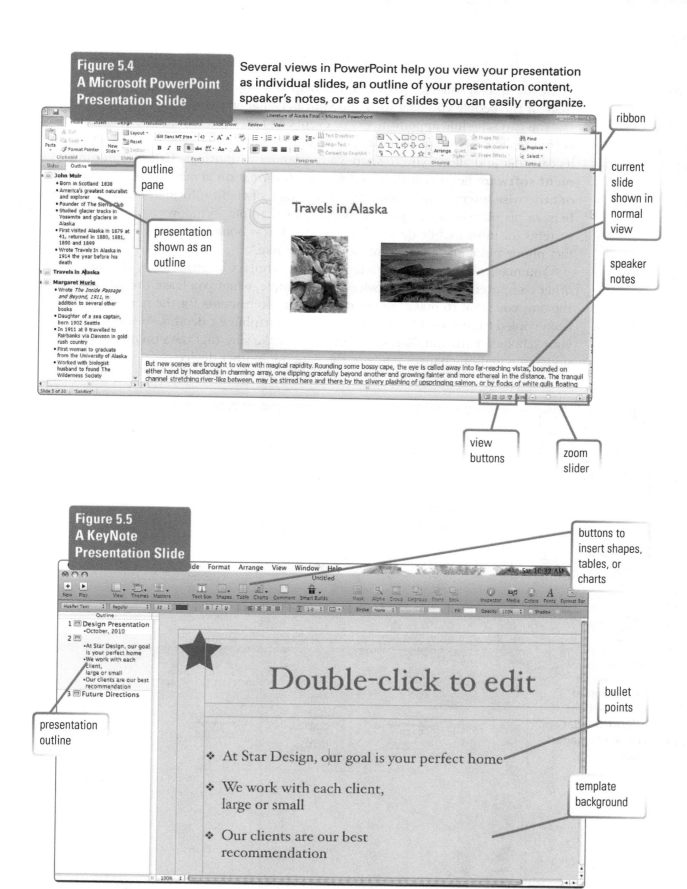

Figure 5.4 A Microsoft PowerPoint Presentation Slide

Several views in PowerPoint help you view your presentation as individual slides, an outline of your presentation content, speaker's notes, or as a set of slides you can easily reorganize.

Figure 5.5 A KeyNote Presentation Slide

Calendar, Organizer, and Contact Management Software

There are several software products that help you organize your life by keeping track of the people you deal with and your personal and work schedules.

You can schedule appointments or events and set up reminders in **calendar software**. The web-based Google Calendar, for example, lets you schedule events in its calendar and allows you to share your calendar with others. **Contact management software** helps you store and manage information about the people you work or otherwise interact with. You might keep track of client information, family members, or people who are in your book club, for example. Windows and the operating systems for most mobile devices include an address book function for storing contact phone numbers, email addresses, and the like.

You may want to share calendar event and contact information with your other computers and mobile devices. For example, when you leave the office for the day, you want to make sure that all your appointments for the next day have been copied from your PC calendar to your smartphone calendar, so you'll have your schedule with you. You **sync** devices to make sure that data on one device is updated based on changes made to the data on another device.

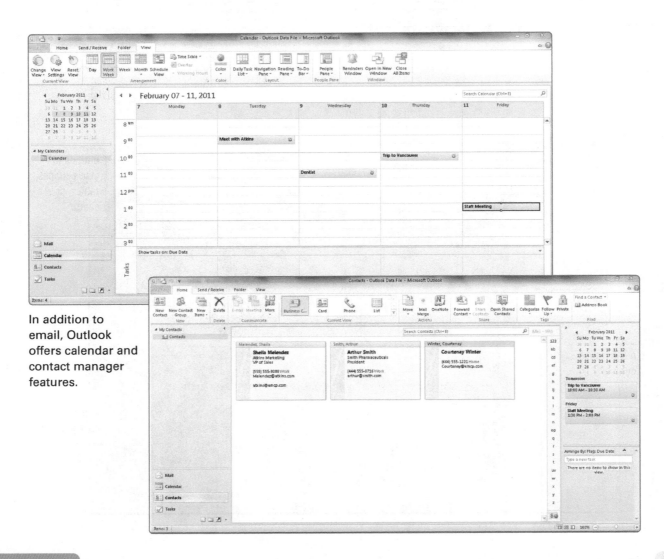

In addition to email, Outlook offers calendar and contact manager features.

Some **organizer software** includes multiple features. Microsoft Outlook, for example, combines schedule, contact, and email management in one package. Windows Live, a web-based service, includes a calendar feature plus email and SkyDrive for document storage and sharing.

Still other applications and services, such as SalesForce.com or ACT!, expand on contact management and function as **customer relationship management (CRM) software**. CRM is a suite of software or online services used to store and organize client and sales prospect information, as well as automating and synchronizing other customer-facing business functions such as marketing, customer service, and technical support. This type of software can be very useful for those who have to keep track of many customers or a lengthy sales or product implementation process.

Graphics, Multimedia, and Web Pages

If you like to work with drawings, photos, or other kinds of images, you may have used **graphics software**, which is software that allows you to create, edit, or manipulate images (drawings, photos). Though most productivity software such as word processors and presentation software includes several graphics features, design professionals work with products that are much more feature-rich, such as:

- **Desktop publishing (DTP) software**, which is used by design professionals to lay out pages for books, magazines, brochures, product packaging, and other print materials. Adobe InDesign, Corel Draw, and QuarkXPress are three of the most popular DTP products. These software applications allow a great deal of precision and control over the placement of objects and text on a page by using grids and columns, a large variety of fonts and text formatting tools, and the ability to insert and work with images.

- **Photo editing software**, which is used by design professionals to enhance photo quality or apply special effects such as blurring elements or feathering the edges of a photo. Photo editing software such as Adobe Photoshop can also be used to edit content out of a picture or combine photo content in a more comprehensive composition.

- **Screen capture software** is useful for those writing software documentation or books about software, programming, or other technology. With this software you can capture the contents of the entire computer screen or only a portion, and the resulting image can be helpful in showing people how to use a particular software feature. Recent Windows versions include a basic screen capture application called Snipping Tool. However, if you need more advanced capabilities such as the ability to change the image resolution or add annotations and make other edits to screen capture images, then an inexpensive third-party program such as Snagit or HyperSnap-DX might be a better choice.

Design professionals have a variety of very sophisticated software products to choose from.

Computers in Your Career

Even if you don't intend to become a professional designer, you are still likely to use design software in your personal or work life. Simpler desktop publishing software, such as Microsoft Publisher, is very useful for designing flyers to advertise that used refrigerator, find a lost pet, or create a home business brochure or business card. Windows Movie Maker is an entry-level video editing software program that is simple to learn and might be useful in creating a video promoting your company's newest product on YouTube, for example. Many jobs, including teaching and sales, require that you give presentations, which can be enhanced by adding animations or music. No matter what your career path, consider exploring graphics and multimedia products to keep your work creative.

Still images aren't the only medium you can work with from your computer. **Multimedia software** enables you to work with media, such as animations, audio, and video. Here are a few popular categories of multimedia software:

- **Animation software** such as Adobe Flash enables you to animate objects and create interactive content (content the viewer can manipulate and control). Animations are sometimes combined with music or narration. Animations are like sophisticated cartoons that can be used in presentations and on the Web to educate, advertise products, or entertain.
- **Audio software** such as Audacity or Sony Creative helps you work with music files and record and edit audio used for **podcasts** (short audio presentations that can be posted online) or as audio files to be shared with others.
- **Video editing software** such as Adobe Premiere Elements, Pinnacle Studio, and Movie Maker (part of the free Windows Live Essentials Suite) are entry-level programs used to create and edit videos. Videos might include an audio track with voice or music, or a variety of special effects. Another product, Camtasia Studio, can record video of activity on your computer screen, which is useful for creating training videos for users. Professional level video editing programs can cost more than $1,000 and take significant time and training to master.

Another popular type of application software for personal and business use is **web authoring software**. Programs such as Microsoft Expression Web and Adobe Dreamweaver provide advanced tools for creating web pages. Some of these products require knowledge of HTML (hypertext markup language) and advanced scripting technologies; others allow you to use a word processor–like interface to create text and add links, animations, and graphics on web pages. The current generation of Web authoring programs are designed to adhere to or follow current standards for implementing HTML. These standards, established by the World Wide Web Consortium (W3C), define how to create pages that will display correctly in most Web browsers. Rather than forcing you to work in code, most web authoring tools offer a **WYSIWYG (what you see is what you get)** interface. Wiz-e-wig simply means that while you are designing the page in the software, the contents should look exactly as they will in a browser or when printed.

Major multimedia program suites often include a web authoring program. For example, Adobe's Creative Suite, depending on which version you use, can include more than ten programs for working in print, interactive, audio, video, and web media.

Entertainment and Personal Use

Software isn't limited to the workplace. There are huge industries built around entertainment, gaming, and personal use software products.

Entertainment software is a category of software that includes computer games you play on your computer or game console. According to the Entertainment Software Association's 2011 Essential Facts about the Computer and Video Game Industry, 72 percent of U.S. households play computer and video games. The average age of gamers is 37, with more than 42 percent of gamers being female. Twenty-nine percent of game players are over the age of 50, an increase from nine percent in 1999. But gaming software isn't just for fun; it's also used in educational settings, to improve physical fitness (as with Nintendo's Wii Fit), and to communicate about social causes (as with Food Force from the United Nations World Food Programme).

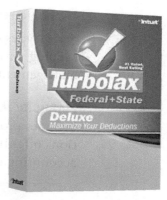

Products such as TurboTax help individuals and small businesses prepare yearly tax returns.

Hobby-related software covers almost any kind of interest, such as genealogy, scrapbooking, sports, home design, or gardening. In some cases, what is a hobby to one person is a job to another, so you may end up using one or more of these products in your work.

If you want to organize your legal affairs or finances, there are many software products to help you. You can use specialized software to create your own legal documents such as wills, living trusts, or real estate leases. You can use tax software such as TurboTax to help you prepare your taxes. Personal financial packages such as Quicken allow you to track checking account activity, create and print checks, download a checking account statement from your bank's website, reconcile your balance, and export information to tax software. In addition, you can track credit card accounts and investments.

You can help to address a major crisis and feed millions of hungry people with Food Force from the United Nations World Food Programme.

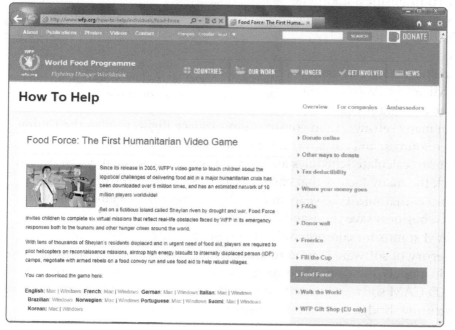

Playing It Safe

If you download software such as games or media players, be sure you get them from a trusted source or you could be downloading viruses or spyware along with your game. Use an antivirus and antispyware software such as McAfee or Norton, or a free product such as Microsoft Security Essentials or Avast Free Antivirus. Run updates and scans often.

Software Gets Professional

Some types of application software address specific business needs, such as bookkeeping, project management, or the processes used in industries such as hotel management or banking.

Financial Applications Financial software used by accounting professionals includes programs such as QuickBooks and Peachtree. These accounting applications offer business-oriented features such as payroll, general ledger (the main accounting method for a business), invoicing, and reporting.

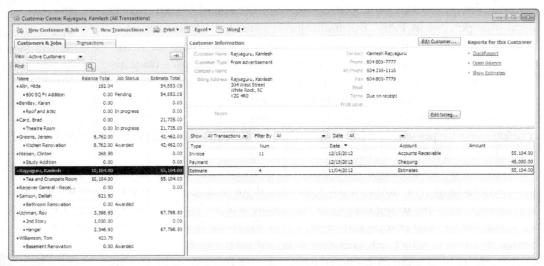

QuickBooks is an example of financial software used by accounting professionals. Financial software is used to keep track of information about a company's customers and the transactions that take place with those customers.

Business Processes Some software applications used in business address specific processes that are useful in a variety of industries. Here are a few such products:

Microsoft Project is used in various industries to plan, track, and report on projects.

- Project management software such as Microsoft Project or the open source program OpenProj is used in many settings, from construction to space flight, to plan the timing of tasks, resources, and costs. With very sophisticated tools and the use of algorithms to calculate schedules and costs, project management software can help track the many factors that can cause delays or cost overruns. In very large projects that may take years to complete, project management software can help a business save thousands of dollars.
- CAD/CAM stands for computer-aided design/computer-aided manufacturing. This category of software is used to create complex engineering drawings and geometric models and to provide specifications for the manufacture of products. CAD/CAM software is used extensively in industries such as automotive manufacturing, bridge and factory construction, and architecture.

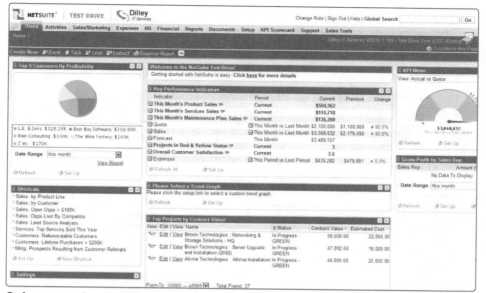

Software can be used to keep track of the various phases of a business process.

- Purchasing software is used by people in any industry where a sophisticated purchasing process must be managed. That process begins when a purchasing agent seeks quotes for a particular item, generates a purchase order, tracks that the item has been received, and submits an invoice to accounting for payment. Purchasing software is also used to track inventory and place new orders so a company's supply of a vital part or material never runs out.

- Document management software and systems enable a business to better store and manage critical business information including electronic or scanned documents such as contracts, images, email messages, and other forms of data. These systems not only replace bulky physical storage such as filing cabinets, but also enable people to retrieve and search documents without regard to physical or geographic location. When these systems reduce paper usage, they are also more green than traditional filing systems.

Industry-Specific Software Many industries have very specific software needs. For example, hotels, medical offices, travel businesses, real estate offices, and banks have different functions that might require a specialized software package.

If you ran a large hotel, for example, you would need software such as Guest Tracker that handles guest registrations, tracks charges such as room service and movies viewed, and generates a final bill. In the medical industry, specialized software handles insurance forms and billing, drug prescriptions for

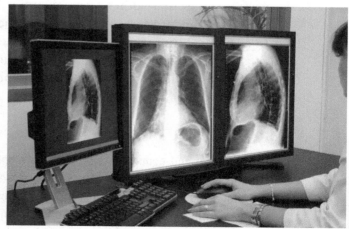

Many industries have their own unique computing needs that industry-specific software can accommodate.

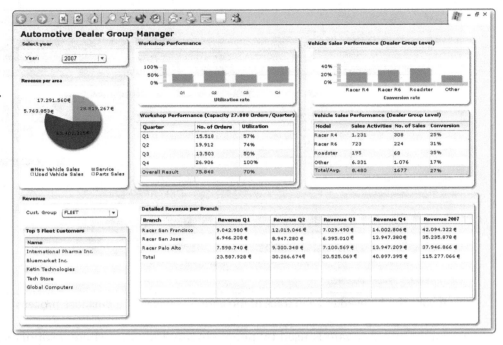

SAP enterprise products help track business activity and generate sophisticated analyses and reports.

pharmacies, and electronic health record (EHR) management. Real estate professionals use property management software to keep track of rental properties and real estate sales software to analyze property values and track listings.

Custom and Enterprise Software Larger companies (often referred to as enterprises) sometimes create their own software to handle the very specific processes of their businesses. However, custom software is expensive to create and maintain, so many large companies adopt enterprise software such as SAP ERP, which addresses common business processes, but is highly customizable. ERP stands for enterprise resource planning. It is a category of software that deals with standard business processes such as managing customer information, product inventories, and employee records and benefits systems.

A company such as German-based SAP or the U.S.-based Oracle produces software modules that address these common business functions, building in best-practices and standard forms and features. They then work with individual companies to customize those product features to the organization's specific procedures.

In recent years enterprise software companies have broadened their offerings to include small and mid-sized business products, but depending on the degree of

Computers in Your Career

An up-and-coming career option is computer forensics used by law enforcement. In this field, you solve mysteries as you find hidden or deleted information on computers that helps law enforcement solve crimes. You might specialize in cryptography, which uses software to decode information hidden in pictures or text. Some computer forensics specialists use utility software to recover deleted files that can be used as evidence in crimes from child pornography rings to embezzlement.

customization and training required, implementing an enterprise software product or suite of products at a company can be a very costly proposition. Still, when such products streamline and improve company procedures, the payoff in productivity and profit can be huge.

Mobile Applications

Today everybody is mobile, so applications have come to your cell phone or smartphone in a big way. Mobile applications were typically not as full-featured as their non-mobile counterparts because of the limitations of memory and screen size, but today's smartphones and tablets feature much more power and storage than earlier hardware. As a result, there are more applications being created for mobile devices all the time, allowing you to perform a variety of activities.

For example, some productivity software is available in simpler versions for use on smartphones, such as Word, Excel, and PowerPoint Mobile. Many organizers also come in versions that work on your mobile phone. Google has an entire suite of applications that include calendar, mapping, and news/weather software for mobile phones.

Other mobile software options include:

- Games
- Tools such as calculators, currency convertors, and music players
- Mobile banking
- WikiMobile (Wikipedia's mobile app)
- Browsers
- Search engines
- Instant messaging
- GPS navigation applications

In addition, you can access and upload content to sites such as Facebook and YouTube from your phone by installing a mobile application. The list of mobile applications is huge and growing all the time.

Take the Next Step *online*

Activity 5.2.1 Flash Movie	*How can software help you learn?*	CORE CONTENT
Activity 5.2.2 Hands-on	*Can you identify different types of software applications?*	
Activity 5.2.3 Research	*What software will you use in your career?*	
Activity 5.2.4 Research	*What software is available that can be shared by Macs and PCs?*	
Activity 5.2.5 Research	*What makes an effective slideshow presentation?*	

The way that software is developed and delivered to you has changed dramatically over the last several years, mainly due to the Internet and the ability to download software applications quickly to your computer or allow you to use software hosted on the Web. Other changes such as the development of open source and shareware applications have also had an impact on the cost of software for the consumer.

Developing Software

Through the years some software products have become incredibly sophisticated as new features are added in each version. The **software development life cycle (SDLC)** has evolved over time. This procedure dictates the general flow of creating a new software product. As illustrated in Figure 5.6, the SDLC involves:

- Performing market research to ensure there is a need or demand for the product.
- Completing a business analysis to match the solution to the need.
- Creating a plan for implementing the software which involves creating a budget and schedule for the project.
- Writing the software, which is the phase where software engineers and programmers write the actual program code.
- Testing the software, which involves having users test the **alpha version** (the first stage of testing of the software) and then one or more **beta versions** (the second stage of testing of a software product). Once all tests are complete and the product seems stable, a final **release to manufacturing (RTM) version** is produced.
- Deploying it to the public, either by selling the product in a package or online, or installing it on a company network or workstations if it is a custom software product.
- Performing maintenance and bug fixes (a **bug** is a problem or malfunction in a program) to keep the product functioning optimally. During this phase updates to this version of the software may be released to resolve several issues at once.

In subsequent years new versions of the product will occasionally be released and users can make the choice to upgrade to that new version or not.

> " Software undergoes beta testing shortly before it's released. Beta is Latin for 'still doesn't work.' "
>
> ▶▶| Author Unknown

Ethics and Technology Blog *online*

When Is It OK to Use Trial Software?

I recently needed to use a desktop publishing product to create a flyer for a fundraiser for my music club trip to England. I was only going to use it once, so I downloaded a trial version, made the flyer, and then deleted the software. Is there anything wrong with that?

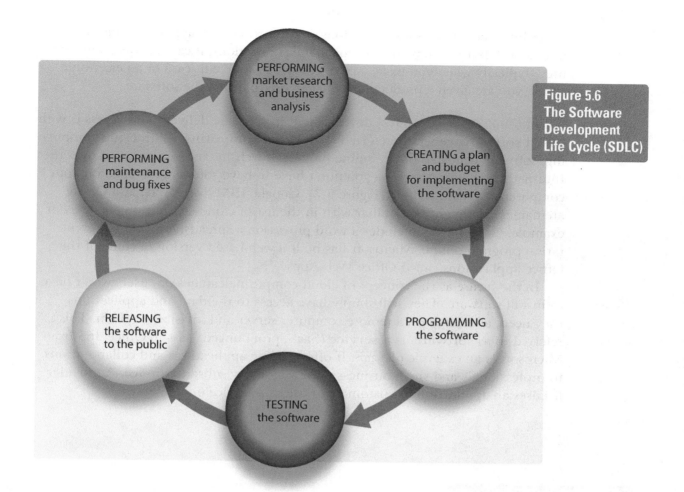

Figure 5.6
The Software
Development
Life Cycle (SDLC)

How Software Is Delivered to You

There was a time when software only came in boxes which contained several floppy disks (thin plastic disks five inches or so in diameter) and large, printed manuals. You might have been required to insert almost a dozen floppy disks into your computer floppy drive to install a large application such as an operating system. Free technical support came with most products to help users install and troubleshoot when problems arose.

Packaged and Downloaded Software Today, **packaged software** (software in boxes) still exists but the software often is contained on a single DVD, and the printed documentation has virtually disappeared. Instead, help files in the product itself or on the manufacturer's website are available, and free technical support has been replaced with manufacturer-provided and user-sponsored tutorials and blogs.

Software products can be purchased individually, or you can buy some in a **software suite**, which bundles several products together. Key benefits of suites include a common user interface, the ability to share data between the products easily, and shared features that make functionality such as graphing available to all the products.

Another significant development in recent years is the ability to buy and download software online, from either the manufacturer or an online retailer. Before faster Internet connections came along, transmitting huge application files was impractical, but today, with fast broadband connections, it can take just a few minutes. Typically when you make a payment with your credit card or an electronic check, you are given a product key you can use to install the software.

Cloud Computing   The latest development in software delivery and access is **web-based software**, generally referred to as **cloud computing**. With cloud computing, software is hosted on an online provider's website and you access it over the Internet using your browser—you don't have to have software installed on your computer to get work done (Figure 5.7). Google, IBM, Microsoft, and Oracle are names you might be familiar with in the list of cloud computing players. For example, Google Docs includes a word processor, a spreadsheet, and a presentation program online. Microsoft has built a web-based version of some of the Office applications called Office Web Apps.

In the future as the concept of cloud computing catches on, users won't have to install software. They will simply have access to the data and applications they need, all hosted on a remote computer server and invisible to them. This is referred to as **software as a service** (SaaS, pronounced "sass"). Office 365 from Microsoft is an example of SaaS. If offers online applications and collaborations to professionals and small businesses for a monthly subscription fee. A provider licenses an application to customers to use as a service on demand.

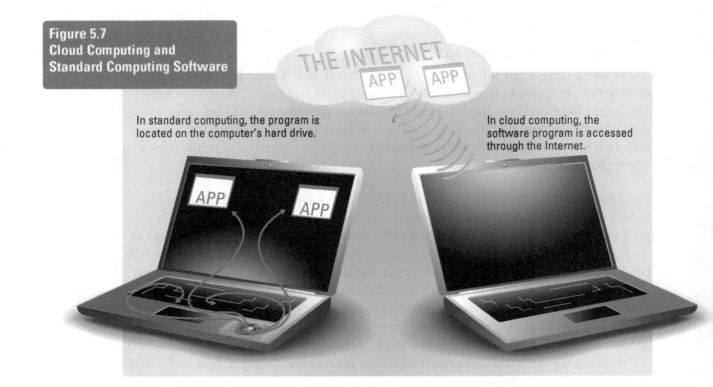

**Figure 5.7
Cloud Computing and
Standard Computing Software**

THE INTERNET
APP   APP

In standard computing, the program is located on the computer's hard drive.

In cloud computing, the software program is accessed through the Internet.

APP   APP

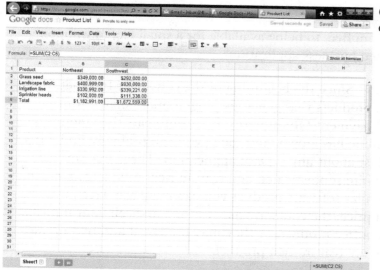
Google Docs is an example of web-based software.

The cloud computing model has several advantages:
- There is no need to download a large application or take up room on your hard drive.
- Updates to the software product can be made frequently by the provider and are transparent (invisible) to the user.
- There is less danger of a conflict with another software product or driver on your computer.
- Some applications are free.

Table 5.1 lists several web-based software products you can try out today.

Playing It Safe

Many web-based software applications allow you to store documents and data online. Before you sign up for such a service, it's vital that you make sure it is reputable. You don't want to upload your sensitive financial or medical information to a service that is not committed to protecting it from hackers or other abuses.

Table 5.1 Web-Based Productivity Software

Product	Function
30 Boxes	Online calendar and organization
37signals	Contact, projects, and information management
Central Desktop	Collaboration and project management
Glide OS	Word processor, spreadsheet, presentation, calendar, address book, website building, email, photo editing, and music player applications
Google Docs	Word processor, spreadsheet, presentation, form, and drawing programs plus document sharing
Gliffy	Diagramming
Google Calendar	Calendar and sharing
HipCal	Calendar, to-do list, and address book
iRows	Online spreadsheets
Num Sum	Shareable web spreadsheets
Office 365	Subscription-based Office Web Apps, webmail, and collaboration features such as SharePoint and Instant Messaging
Office Web Apps	Free online versions of Word, Excel, PowerPoint, and OneNote, with document sharing
ThinkFree	Document sharing
Trumba	Customizable calendar and event aggregator

Software Pricing

Software pricing ranges from free, to being available for a small fee, to whopping costs for some sophisticated business applications.

Freeware and Shareware Since the beginning of the consumer Internet, there have been some software products that generous programmers shared for free (**freeware**) or for a small payment (**shareware**). In recent years the amount of free software available online has grown, and today you can probably find a free or shareware version of just about any type of application. These free software products are sometimes quite sophisticated and feature-rich; others are a much simplified version of a similar software product you can purchase. Free products may come with a hidden price; the company may capture and sell your information when you download a free product, or they may use email and pop-up messages to upsell you to a more feature-rich product.

Open Source Software The open source movement makes **source code** (the programming code used to build the software) available to everyone in an effort to continue to build **open source software** and improve on functionality. The open source movement has produced some applications that are contributed to by individuals and are free to all. For example, the White House now uses Drupal, an open source web development system. In certain instances, companies have used that open source code to develop software products and charge for them.

Getting a License When you pay for a software product, you will find a wide range of pricing, from a lower-cost price for upgrading to a new version, to competitive pricing for the full product at retail sites, auction sites, and manufacturers' sites.

Popular shareware site Tucows.com has been around for many years, offering a wide assortment of shareware and freeware.

Our Digital World

Companies that wish to buy software for many employees enter into software licensing agreements that allow them to install a product on multiple workstations, or install the product on their network for individual computer users to access.

The Cost of Software in the Cloud With the cloud computing model, vendors can charge a subscription fee. They host the application on their servers or download it to a device. They can then disable the service when the user's contract expires. In some cases use of the products is free, as with basic Google Docs, some Adobe products, and Zoho. Microsoft offers Office Web Apps free for personal use to anybody who signs up for a Windows Live account or by license to corporate customers.

Take the Next Step *online*

Activity 5.3.1 Video	*How do I access my software using cloud computing?*	CORE CONTENT
Activity 5.3.2 Video	*How did the open source movement evolve?*	CORE CONTENT
Activity 5.3.3 Flash Movie	*How does software work?*	CORE CONTENT
Activity 5.3.4 Research	*Do you get what you pay for when using free software?*	
Activity 5.3.5 Team Planning	*How do I schedule a team meeting using an online scheduler?*	
Activity 5.3.6 Team Presentation	*How can collaborating online make project planning more efficient?*	

Will App Stores Take Over Software Sales?

The way many of us buy computer software has changed dramatically in the past few years, a trend that will accelerate, according to technology journalist Dwight Silverman. The catalyst for the change has been the "App Store" for the iPhone, in which consumers download programs from a special online store—a store controlled entirely by Apple. Now Apple has opened an app store for Mac computers as well, which means consumers are less likely to buy physical copies of programs that come in a box. There are app stores for Android from both Google and Amazon, and Microsoft is likely to sell downloadable software for future versions of Windows as well. The app store trend carries some real benefits. "These app stores seem to be very appealing because they're simple and the software has been less expensive than traditional software," said Silverman. But there are downsides as well.

Listen to the Chapter 5 Spotlight on the Future podcast to learn more and then be prepared to answer the following questions.

Talk about It

1. What does Silverman mean by the "walled garden" model of software?
2. Which company is responsible for the move to app stores?
3. How do "walled gardens" improve computer security?
4. Why is software sold in app stores cheaper than buying programs in a store?
5. What is a downside of the "walled garden" approach?

5.4 Software Working Together

Today many applications can use content created in other applications by importing or embedding the content. In addition, some small, shared features allow suites of software products to share functionality such as diagramming or drawing.

Importing and Exporting

Many software applications allow you to **export** (send data to another application) and **import** (bring data in from another application) between applications. This works seamlessly in software suites such as Corel's WordPerfect Office suite and Microsoft Office. For example, PowerPoint includes an option to export a PowerPoint presentation to Word as handouts.

Other means of exporting and importing involve saving text in certain file types, such as **rich text format (RTF)**, which allows you to exchange data with many other applications. The RTF format reduces a document to a more rudimentary, commonly useable format that another software product is more likely to be able to open or import.

Another widely used file type for importing and exporting is the **comma-separated-values (CSV) format**, which separates each piece of data with a comma. Using this format you might, for example, export all of your contacts from an Excel spreadsheet into a contact management application.

Converting Handwritten Notes and Speech to Text

Using handwriting recognition software, you can take content such as notes you handwrite on a tablet PC screen and convert them to a text file. That text file can then be used by a word processor or other program. Some mobile devices have built in **handwriting recognition software** to turn notes written using a stylus into text. A more recent development is pen-like devices that recognize what you write on paper and convert it to text.

With **speech recognition software**, you speak into a microphone connected to or built into your computer. The software turns the sounds into text that you can then edit in a word processor. Speech recognition is built into Microsoft Windows, for example, and can be activated from within Microsoft Word.

Accuracy can be an issue with any handwriting and speech recognition system, as there are many variables in each person's handwriting and voice inflections and accents. Generally speaking, handwriting recognition has advanced more rapidly and can recognize nearly anyone's writing.

Tablet PCs are useful for handwriting notes when in a meeting or on the road.

Embedding and Linking Content

Microsoft Office products use a technology called **object linking and embedding (OLE)** that allows content to be treated as objects that can be inserted into different software documents even if they were not created using that software. For example, you can place a pie chart from Excel in a Word document. Using linking, you can even edit that pie chart using Excel tools from within Word. The object placed in a document using OLE is referred to as an **embedded object**.

Embedding may be familiar to you from using web pages, where a designer might embed a video or audio clip on a page. The embedded video was not created with the web authoring software, and in fact typically plays using a media player installed on your computer.

Using Shared Features

A **shared feature** is a small application that cannot run on its own, but can be used with other software products. Shared features contain a particular functionality, such as the ability to build diagrams, and sometimes libraries of images that are useful to several kinds of software products. By allowing multiple products to draw on the feature, you save space on your computer and have a consistent procedure for getting that work done.

WordArt is a popular text enhancement feature that can be shared by all Microsoft Office applications.

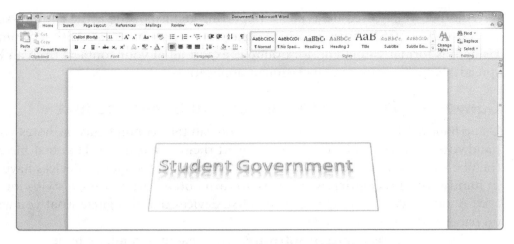

Some common shared features used by Microsoft Office products are:
- WordArt, which allows you to add shape, dimension, and color to text.
- SmartArt for diagramming processes and work flow.
- Chart to help you build charts and graphs.
- ClipArt, a library of artwork you can organize and insert into documents.
- AutoShapes, a collection of shapes you can draw in a document.

Take the Next Step *online*

Activity 5.4.1 Flash Movie	*How do I import from Word into PowerPoint and then from PowerPoint into Word?*	CORE CONTENT
Activity 5.4.2 Flash Movie	*How do you identify the format that a file is saved in?*	CORE CONTENT
Activity 5.4.3 Hands-on	*How do I share a file?*	
Activity 5.4.4 Team Research	*What are the latest advances in handwriting recognition software and speech recognition software?*	

Summing Up

Software's Role in the World of Computing

Application software includes the software you use to get things done, from producing reports for work to creating art or playing games.

The Many Types of Application Software

Productivity software typically includes software that people use to get work done such as a word processor, spreadsheet, database, or presentation software. This type of software is often compiled into suites of applications, such as Microsoft Office and Apple iWork. Some productivity software also is available in simpler versions for use on smartphones, such as Word, Excel, and PowerPoint Mobile. Four major categories of productivity software are:

- **Word processor software** with which you can create documents that include sophisticated text formatting, tables, photos, drawings, and links to online content. You can also use templates to design web pages, newsletters and more.
- **Spreadsheet software**, which allows you to perform calculations that range from simple (adding, averaging, multiplying) to complex (estimates of standard deviations based on a range of numbers, for example).
- **Database software** organizes data. Once that data is entered into relational tables you can view information in a spreadsheet-like list or as individual records using forms. You can then create queries that let you find specific data sets.
- **Presentation software** uses the concept of individual slides that form a slideshow. Slides may contain bulleted lists of key concepts, graphics, tables, animations, hyperlinks to web pages, or diagrams and charts. A slideshow can support a presenter's comments during a talk, can run continuously on its own (for example at a trade show booth), or be browsed by an individual online or on a computer.

Other categories of software include:

- **Organizer software** and **contact management software** that help you organize your time and professional or personal contacts, and **customer relationship management (CRM) software** that helps coordinate client-focused business functions.
- **Graphics software**, **authoring software**, and **multimedia software** including **desktop publishing (DTP) software**, **photo editing software**, and **animation software** used by many design professionals.
- **Entertainment software** includes games and special interest software such as genealogy or sports.
- Software is also available for managing your personal finances.

- Professional software includes software that handles professional financial or business tasks, software written for specific industry needs, and custom or enterprise software that packages business best practices and procedures in a customizable fashion.
- Software for mobile devices may be simpler versions of full featured computer software, but with the increasing power of smartphones and tablets, the variety and capabilities of mobile software continue to increase rapidly.

Developing and Delivering Software

Software delivery venues have changed dramatically over the last several years, mainly due to the Internet and its ability to download software applications to your computer or allow you to use web-based software.

Software has a life cycle, and the process of developing software is described as the **software development life cycle (SDLC)**. Software typically comes out in new versions every few years. During development by software engineers who write the source code, the new version goes through various development and testing phases—first an **alpha version** or very initial draft is released, and then one or more **beta versions**. When the software is in a final version, called the **release to manufacturing (RTM) version**, it is then duplicated and sold to the public.

Today, you can buy **packaged software**, which can be downloaded or purchased on storage media, typically DVD.

The latest development in software delivery is **web-based software**, generally referred to as **cloud computing**. With this model, software is hosted on an online provider's website and you access it over the Internet using your browser. Software updates are usually done in the background as you work, over the Internet.

In recent years the amount of free software available online has grown, and today you can probably find a **freeware** or **shareware** version of just about any type of application. The **open source software** movement has produced many applications that enable the users to study the source code of programs, change and improve their designs, and distribute their updates.

Companies that wish to buy software for many employees enter into software licensing agreements that allow them to install a product on multiple workstations.

Software Working Together

Many software applications allow you to **import** and **export** data to other software. This works seamlessly in software suites such as Corel WordPerfect Office and Microsoft Office. If you use certain formats of text such as **rich text format (RTF)** and **comma-separated-values (CSV)** format, you can exchange data with many other applications.

Using **handwriting recognition software**, you can take notes you handwrite and convert them to a text file that can then be used by word processors or other software. **Speech recognition software** turns words (sounds) spoken into a microphone into text that you can then edit.

Microsoft Office products and many other programs use a technology called **object linking and embedding (OLE)** to insert content into different software documents. Using linking, you can even edit an Excel pie chart from within Word.

Shared features are small applications that cannot run on their own, but can be used from within other software products. Allowing multiple products to draw on the shared feature saves storage space on your computer and provides a consistent procedure for getting that work done.

Terms to Know

Software's Role in the World of Computing
application software, 134

The Many Types of Application Software
productivity software, 135
word processor software, 136
spreadsheet software, 136
database software, 137
presentation software, 138
calendar software, 140
contact management software, 140
sync, 140
organizer software, 141
customer relationship management (CRM) software, 141
graphics software, 141
desktop publishing (DTP) software, 141

photo editing software, 141
screen capture software, 141
multimedia software, 142
animation software, 142
audio software, 142
podcast, 142
video editing software, 142
web authoring software, 142
WYSIWYG, 142
entertainment software, 143
edutainment, Activity 5.2.1
web-based training, Activity 5.2.1

Developing and Delivering Software
software development life cycle (SDLC), 148
alpha version, 148
beta version, 148
release to manufacturing (RTM) version, 148
bug, 148
packaged software, 149
software suite, 149
web-based software, 150

cloud computing, 150
software as a service (SaaS), 150
freeware, 152
shareware, 152
source code, 152
open source software, 152
software on demand, Activity 5.3.1
cloud storage, Activity 5.3.1
GNU General Public License, Activity 5.3.2

Software Working Together

Concepts Check

Concepts Check 5.1   Multiple Choice
Take this quiz to test your understanding of key concepts in this chapter.

Concepts Check 5.2   Word Puzzle
Complete this puzzle to test your knowledge of key terms in this chapter.

Concepts Check 5.3   Label It
Label the elements in a spreadsheet.

Concepts Check 5.4   Matching
Match the software application to the primary use of the software.

Concepts Check 5.5   Arrange It
Use the interactive tool to identify the steps in the software development life cycle.

Projects

Check with your instructor for the preferred method to submit completed work.

Project 5.1   Spreadsheet Analysis

Project 5.1.1   Individual

You have been assigned to create a spreadsheet that reflects the interests of your friends. Survey 10 friends and ask them to name their favorite food, sport, and movie. When you have finished collecting your information, set up the categories on a spreadsheet and enter your friends' responses. On the same spreadsheet, create a separate table that summarizes your data. Submit the spreadsheet to your instructor.

Project 5.1.2   Individual

Using the data from the spreadsheet you created in Project 5.1.1, create a bar chart that displays your survey results. To complete this task, use the charting tools to select the type of bar graph you want to design. Then format the chart and submit it to your instructor.

Project 5.2   Using Web-Based Tools

Project 5.2.1   Individual

Learning organizational and time management skills is important in today's busy society. As a student, you know firsthand the difficulties in balancing your classes, assignments, and possibly a job and family responsibilities. At times, you may forget assignments, appointments, or upcoming events. One tool that can help you stay organized is a Google Calendar. Create a school calendar to record all appointments, assignments, tests, and so on for the next two weeks. When you have finished scheduling your information, export the calendar and submit it to your instructor.

Project 5.2.2   Team

Your company's executive board is considering using Google tools such as Gmail, Google Docs, and Google Reader to organize their communications and documents. The board members have asked your IT team to prepare a slide presentation that outlines the advantages of using these Google tools. Using Google Docs, create a collaborative presentation that discusses these Google tools and their applications. When complete, share the presentation with your class.

Project 5.3   Graphics and Multimedia

Project 5.3.1   Individual or Team

You have been asked to create a podcast overview of software applications. Choose two applications and create a podcast describing the purpose, cost, useful features, and the types of documents the application produces. You will also include the rationale for purchasing the application. First, download Audacity from www.emcp.net/audacity and the Lame MP3 converter from www.emcp.net/lame to record and convert your podcast to an MP3 format. Then create an audio file and export it as an MP3 file. Finally, create an account on Podbean (www.podbean.com) where you can post your podcast. Share the link with your instructor and classmates.

Project 5.3.2   Team

The public relations director of your school has asked the students in your Introduction to Computers class to create a flyer promoting the course. With your teammates, select a software application, such as Publisher or Word, to design your flyer. As you develop the content for the flyer, consider the basic information your flyer should provide: a general course description, the time and location of the class, the cost of the course, any course prerequisites, and the instructor's name. In addition to this general information, provide specific course objectives, learning tools, student projects, and activities that might serve as incentives for students to register for the course. To add visual interest, incorporate graphics by using tools such as WordArt.

Project 5.3.3 Team

Use the free Gmail photo sharing tool, Picasa (http://picasa.google.com), to create a photo album scavenger hunt for your classmates. Have your team prepare a photo album of landmarks or sites in your local area. Ask each member of your team to contribute either an existing digital photo that they have or to go on location to take a new photo. Try to find photos that show enough detail to provide clues as to the photos' locations. Upload the individual photos to the team's Picasa album. When complete, share your team's album with the class. Ask other teams to post their responses as to the locations of the photos.

Project 5.4 Word Processor and Presentation Software

Project 5.4.1 Individual

You need to explain to a colleague how to change a font in Microsoft Word. In order to do this, you have decided to create a series of screen captures with callouts (descriptive labels). Use the software program Jing (available at www. emcp.net/jing) to create the screen captures. Then insert the screen captures in a text document and add callouts.

Project 5.4.2 Team

You are a college student and a part-time employee of the IT department of a local business. Your manager recognizes your knowledge of current technological advances and would like you to share your insights with other members of the department. In particular, your manager would like you to explain cloud computing, the latest development in software delivery and access. Working with a team of colleagues, create a PowerPoint presentation explaining cloud computing. Then post the presentation to Microsoft's Office Live Workspace or to a course website to share with your class and instructor.

Project 5.5 Wiki — Collaborative Use of Software

Project 5.5.1 Individual or Team

Businesses today prefer to use software applications that allow their employees to collaborate on the creation of documents. To model that practice, your class will create a document for the class wiki on the advantages and disadvantages of buying a PC or a Mac. The document's content should include an analysis of features and applications available for each platform, the costs of components and any upgrades, and so on. Your instructor will divide you into three teams. The first team will provide the written content and post it as a document on the class wiki. The second team will edit the content of the wiki document. The third team will format the wiki document and add visuals. The final version of this document will be viewed on the class wiki.

Project 5.5.2 Individual or Team

You or your team will be assigned to edit and verify the content posted on the wiki site from Project 5.5.1. If you add or edit any content, make sure you include a notation within the page that includes your name or team members' names and the date you edited the content—for example, "Edited by [student name or team members' names] on [date]." Keep a list of references that you used to verify your content changes. When you are finished with your verification, include a notation at the end of the entry—for example, "Verified by [student name or team members' names] on [date]."

Project 5.6 Learning about Application Software

Project 5.6.1 Individual

As a help desk employee of a large insurance company, you often receive calls about how to use a variety of software applications. You have begun to keep a list of the most frequently asked questions and have decided to prepare a reference guide for employees that you will post to the company intranet. To help you with this task, go to Microsoft Office Online Help and find the answers to the following questions:

1. I have a 2010 file that I need to send to my colleague who has 2003. How do I save the file in the 2003 format?
2. The data for my report is slightly confusing. I think that it would be better communicated in a table. How can I insert a table in Word to make my data more reader- friendly?
3. How do I create a chart for the 2011 sales data?
4. Is there a way to create a formula to total the values of the range A1:A7?
5. I have to give a PowerPoint presentation to the Board of Directors, and I need to know how to export my Excel spreadsheet and import it to my PowerPoint presentation. Is this possible?
6. I want to run a query in my Access database showing all my customers in the United States. How do I run an Access query?
7. I have two tables in Access, and I want to join the tables so that I can run a query with data from both tables. How do I join tables in Access?
8. All my colleagues use a variety of animations in their PowerPoint presentations. I have an object that I would like to animate. How do I apply a custom animation to an object?
9. One of my colleagues uses the Outline View to create PowerPoint presentations. I am unable to locate how to create a presentation in Outline View. Are there specific steps that need to be followed?
10. I have two new customers that I would like to add to my contact list in Outlook. Is there a way to add contacts?

Project 5.6.2 **Team**

You are a member of the IT department in a company about to adopt an enterprise software solution. The vice president of information systems has assigned your group to create a PowerPoint presentation for training customer service employees on enterprise customer relationship management (CRM) software. Research enterprise CRM software, and create a slide presentation that uses sound and animation. Submit the presentation along with a reference list of sources to your instructor.

Class Conversations

Topic 5.1   Software Plagiarism

You have recently purchased the newest version of a web authoring software application which costs over $700, but you feel it is well worth it because of all the great features. Your friend also wants to use the same software but can't afford it. Your friend asks you if he/she can borrow your discs to install the application on his/her computer. You check the software terms of use and find that this is illegal. What would you do?

Topic 5.2   Photo Manipulation

Photo editing dates back to the 1860s. Manipulating photos can be done to misrepresent products, sensationalize something in the press, or cause somebody embarrassment. There have been several controversial photos that have been edited and placed in magazines or newspapers, such as a 1982 National Geographic cover photo of the pyramids in Egypt and a 2008 picture of vice presidential candidate Sarah Palin. Do you think that manipulating photos is ethical? Why or why not?

Topic 5.3   Spell Check Dependency

Spell check is a feature available in many software applications. Most of you probably have grown up using spell check and grammar check. Are you dependent on spell check to proof your documents? Do you believe that features such as spell check and online calculators are causing our population to be overly dependent on them and unable to spell or calculate without those tools? What effect could this dependence have on the literacy of our society—or does it not matter how these things are checked, as long as the tools are available?

Communications and Network Technologies
Connecting Through Computers

What You'll Accomplish

When you finish this chapter, you'll be able to:

- Define computer networking and its uses at work and home.
- Describe a communications system and the process that enables a sender and receiver to exchange data.
- Distinguish the various types of transmission media for wired and wireless networks.
- Recognize the role that network standards and protocols play in communications.
- Describe and differentiate among various networking devices and software that enable you to send and receive data.
- Explain the importance of network security.

Why Should I Care?

Your computer and mobile device depend on a communications system to send and receive data over a network. Without such a system, you couldn't send emails and text messages, download music, or share a printer with other computers. Whether you're downloading a new app, sharing a file or a device with other computers in your home or office, or tapping into the resources on the worldwide network that is the Internet, understanding how to use the power of networks to share with others can make your work easier and your life more satisfying.

Chapter 6 Communications and Network Technologies: Connecting Through Computers

Computer networks allow people to connect to share work, devices, and information. Whether wired or wireless, networks use various technologies, hardware components, and software to make the connection.

http://

Our Digital World

6.1 How Does the World Use Networking?

A **computer network** consists of two or more computing or other devices connected by a communications medium, such as a wireless signal or a cable. A computer network provides a way to connect with others and share files and resources such as printers or an Internet connection.

In business settings, networks allow you to communicate with employees, suppliers, vendors, customers, and government agencies. Many companies have their own network, called an **intranet**, which is essentially a private Internet within the company's corporate "walls." Some companies also offer an extension of their internal network, called an **extranet**, to suppliers and customers. For example, a supplier might be allowed to access inventory information on a company's internal network to make sure the company does not run short of a vital part for its manufacturing process.

In your home, networks are useful for sharing resources among members of your family. For example, using a home network, you might share one printer or network storage among three or four computers.

The Internet is a global network made up of many networks linked together. If you consider all the applications, services, and tools the Internet allows you to access, as you discovered in Chapter 2, you can begin to understand the power of networking and how it opens up a new world of sharing and functionality.

> " As network administrator I can take down the network with one keystroke. It's just like being a doctor but without getting gooky stuff on my paws. "
>
> ▶▶ Scott Adams, Creator of "Dogbert"

online ✓ Take a Survey

How do networks fit into your life today?

6.2 Exploring Communications Systems

A computer network is one kind of **communications system**. This system includes sending and receiving hardware, transmission and relay systems, common sets of standards so all the equipment can "talk" to each other, and communications software.

You use such a networked communications system whenever you send/receive text or email messages, pay a bill online, shop at an Internet store, send a document to a shared printer at work or at home, or download music or videos. Figure 6.1 shows some of the common communications system components in use today.

The world of a computer network communications system is made up of:

- Transmission media upon which the data travels to/from its destination.
- A set of standards and **network protocols** (rules for how data is handled as it travels along a communications channel). Devices use these protocols to send and receive data to and from each other.
- Hardware and software to connect to a communications pathway from the sending and receiving ends.

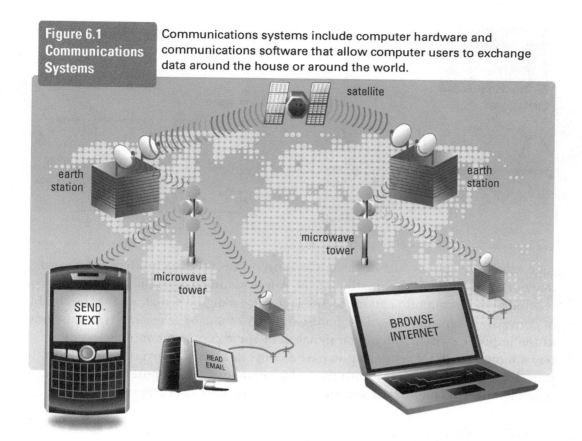

Figure 6.1 Communications Systems Communications systems include computer hardware and communications software that allow computer users to exchange data around the house or around the world.

The first step in understanding a communications system is to learn the basics about transmission signals and transmission speed when communicating over a network.

Types of Signals

There are two kinds of signals used in transmitting voices and other sounds over a computer network: analog and digital (Figure 6.2). An **analog signal** is formed by continuous sound waves that fluctuate from high to low. Your voice is transmitted as an analog signal over traditional telephone lines at a certain frequency. A **digital signal** uses a discrete signal that is either high or low. In computer terms, high represents the digital bit 1, and low represents the digital bit 0. These are the only two states for digital data.

Telephone lines carry your voice and other data using an analog signal. However, computers don't "speak" analog; rather, they use a binary system of 1s and 0s, also called digital signals or data. If you send data between computers using an analog medium such as a phone line, the signal has to be transformed from digital, to analog (modulated), and back again to digital (demodulated) to be understood by the computer on the receiving end. The piece of hardware that sends and receives data from a transmission source

Modems convert analog signals to digital signals and vice versa. Newer communications technologies use digital signals.

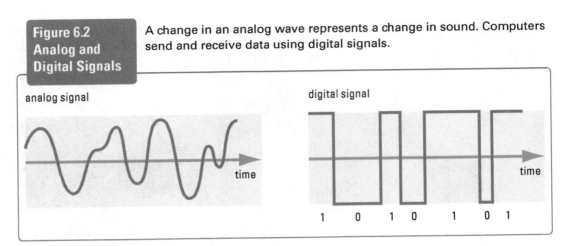

Figure 6.2 Analog and Digital Signals

A change in an analog wave represents a change in sound. Computers send and receive data using digital signals.

analog signal

digital signal

time

time

1   0   1   0   1   0   1

such as your telephone line or cable television connection is a **modem**. The word modem comes from a combination of the words *mo*dulate and *dem*odulate.

Today most communications technologies use a digital signal, saving the trouble of converting transmissions. The demise in 2009 of analog television transmissions as the industry switched to digital signals sent some people scrambling to either buy a more recent TV set or to purchase a converter box to convert digital transmissions back to analog to work with their older equipment. Computer networks use a pure digital signal method of sending and receiving data over a network.

Transmission Speed

If you've ever been frustrated with how long it takes to download a file from a website, you're familiar with the fact that, in a communications system, data moves from one computer to another at different speeds. The speed of transmission is determined by a few key factors.

The first factor is the speed at which a signal can change from high to low, which is called **frequency**. A signal sent at a faster frequency provides faster transmission (Figure 6.3).

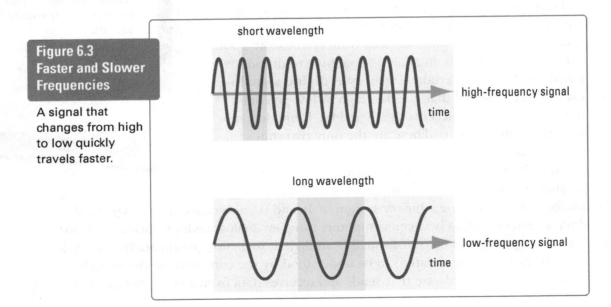

Figure 6.3 Faster and Slower Frequencies

A signal that changes from high to low quickly travels faster.

short wavelength

high-frequency signal

time

long wavelength

low-frequency signal

time

Our Digital World

The other factor contributing to the speed of data transmission is bandwidth. On a computer network the term **bandwidth** refers to the number of bits (pieces of data) per second that can be transmitted over a communications medium. Think of bandwidth as being like a highway. At rush hour, with the same amount of cars, a two-lane highway accommodates less traffic and everybody moves at a slower speed than on a four-lane highway, where much more traffic can travel at a faster speed. Table 6.1 lists communications bandwidth measurements.

If you have plenty of bandwidth and your data is transmitted at a high frequency, you get faster transmission speeds. Any communications medium that is capable of carrying a large amount of data at a fast speed is known as **broadband**.

Though transmission speeds at any moment in time may vary depending on network traffic and other factors, each of the common communications media has a typical speed. Table 6.2 lists typical transmission speeds. Providers continue to improve transmission speeds, and for some forms of connections, you can purchase plans offering much faster connections than those listed in Table 6.2. Some very high-powered connections being tested today provide transmission speeds of as much as 100 gigabits (one billion bits) per second, which allows you to download a high-definition movie in 2 seconds.

Table 6.1 Bandwidth Measurements

Term	Abbreviation	Meaning
1 kilobit per second	1 Kbps	1 thousand bits per second
1 megabit per second	1 Mbps	1 million bits per second
1 gigabit per second	1 Gbps	1 billion bits per second
1 terabit per second	1 Tbps	1 trillion bits per second
1 petabit per second	1 Pbps	1 quadrillion bits per second

Table 6.2 Comparison of Average Network Connection Speeds

Type of Connection	Typical Speed
56 K dial-up	56 Kbps
satellite	1.5 Mbps
DSL	7 Mbps
fiber-optic	25 Mbps
cable	50 Mbps

Of course, everybody wants high-speed Internet transmissions, but the higher the speed, the higher the cost. When you think about the type of connection you need for your computer, consider what you will send over the network. Do you send/receive a great many graphics or videos, which are typically very large files? Do you want to stream music or video, or play online games? In those instances, you need a broadband connection. On the other hand, if most of your transmissions are simply text messages or text documents, then a lower speed connection will probably work for you.

6.3 Transmission Systems

The signals that are sent in a communications system might be transmitted via a wired medium (a cable) or wirelessly, using radio waves.

Wired Transmissions

At one time all company networks were wired. Long strings of wire connected each workstation to the network. Though they have lost popularity in the age of wireless, wired network models are still in use.

Wired transmissions send a signal through various media, including (Figure 6.4):

- **Twisted-pair cable,** which is used for your wired telephone connection. This type of cable consists of two independently insulated wires wrapped around one another. Twisted-pair cable is used to transmit over short distances. It is used in many homes because signals can travel over the built-in telephone system. Cat 5 is an example of twisted-pair cable used in Ethernet networks.
- **Coaxial cable,** which is the same cable used to transmit cable television signals over an insulated wire at a fast speed—in this case, millions of bits per second.
- **Fiber-optic cable,** which uses a protected string of glass that transmits beams of light. Fiber-optic transmission is very fast, transmitting billions of bits per second.

Many businesses lease T-lines (such as T1 or T3), developed by long distance telephone companies, to carry multiple types of signals (voice and data) at very fast speeds.

Wireless Transmissions

There are several wireless transmission systems in use today, including cellular, microwaves, and satellite. All use radio waves to transmit data, but each system handles these transmissions in different ways, and the systems vary in signal strength and frequency.

A **cellular network,** like those used by your cell phone, transmits signals, called **cellular transmissions,** by using cell towers (Figure 6.5). Each cell tower has its own range (or cell) of coverage. Cellular systems are used to transmit both voice and data in every direction. There are several generations of cellular transmissions, from the first generation (1G) that was used for analog transmissions to the fourth generation (4G) which transmits digital data at speeds up to 15 Mbps. (Speed performance varies by carrier.)

Figure 6.4
Three Types of Cables

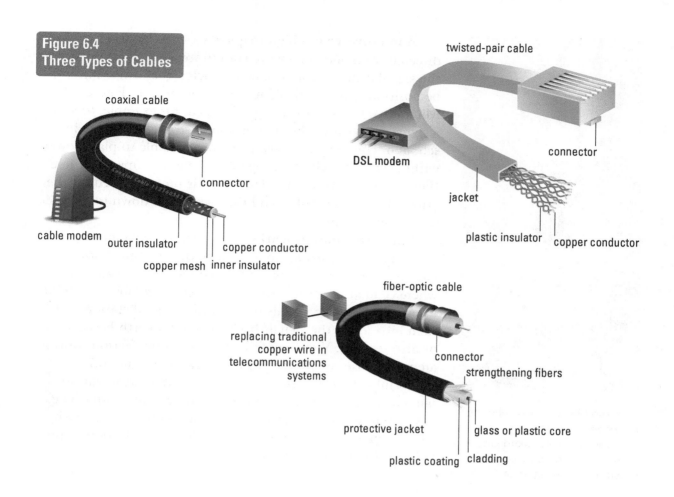

coaxial cable

connector

cable modem

outer insulator

copper mesh   inner insulator

copper conductor

twisted-pair cable

DSL modem

jacket

connector

plastic insulator   copper conductor

fiber-optic cable

replacing traditional
copper wire in
telecommunications
systems

connector

strengthening fibers

protective jacket

glass or plastic core

plastic coating   cladding

Figure 6.5
Cellular Technology

A cell phone sends a signal that travels along a series of cell towers until the data reaches the intended recipient.

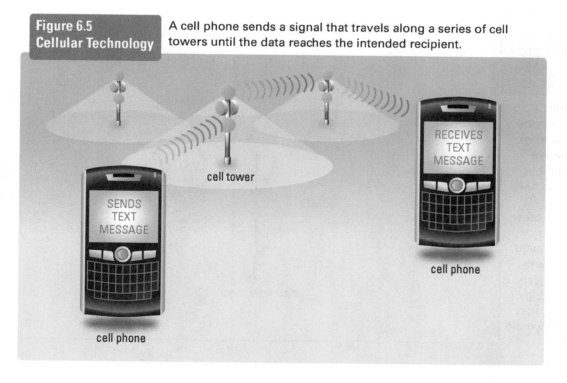

cell tower

RECEIVES
TEXT
MESSAGE

SENDS
TEXT
MESSAGE

cell phone

cell phone

To avoid physical obstructions between them, some microwave towers send signals up to a satellite to be bounced down to the target tower.

A **microwave** is a high-frequency radio signal that is directed from one microwave station tower to another. Because the signal cannot bend around obstacles, the towers have to be positioned in line of sight of each other as in Figure 6.6. Microwave transmission might be used, for example, to send a signal from towers located on top of several buildings in a school or company campus. If it's not possible to place towers within sight of each other, signals can be sent upward where there are no obstructions. The signal is then bounced off the atmosphere or a satellite and then sent back down to another microwave tower.

Satellite communication uses space-based equipment, and is typically used for longer range transmissions, for international communications, and for connectivity in rural areas where cellular or microwave towers aren't available. A satellite receives microwave signals from an earth-based station and then broadcasts the signals back to another earth-based station or dish receiver. Video conferences and air navigation control are typical uses of satellite communication (Figure 6.7).

In July 2011, the Indian Space Research Organization launched a communications satellite from south India. The new satellite will link doctors and teachers from cities with rural India to help with medical diagnoses in addition to providing telecom and television services.

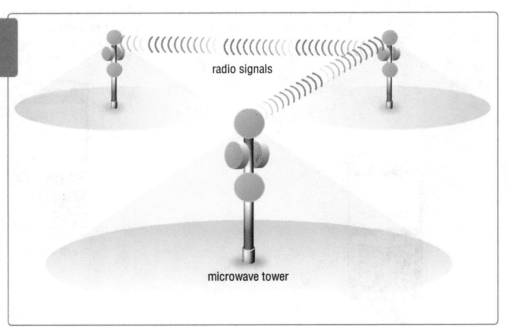

Figure 6.6 Microwave Technology

Radio signals travel through the atmosphere from one microwave tower to another. These towers have to be relatively close to each other because radio signals can't bend around the earth or around objects such as buildings. Alternatively, they can be bounced off a satellite.

radio signals

microwave tower

Our Digital World

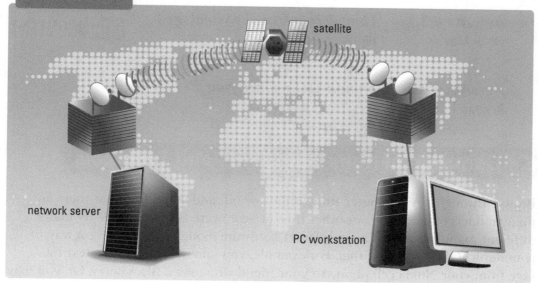

Figure 6.7 Satellite Communications Communications satellites are solar powered. They use transponders to receive signals from the ground, then retransmit them to a specific location on the ground.

satellite

network server

PC workstation

The Changing World of Voice Communications

Digital networks are upending the old ways of human networking, and will continue to change the dynamics of person-to-person communication for years to come, according to technology journalist Dwight Silverman.

Electronic voice communication grew steadily from the time of Alexander Graham Bell until recent years, when people have started to turn away from phone calls in favor of email, texting and other services like Facebook messaging.

"We're seeing a slow death of voice communications," said Silverman.

He even foresees a day when telephone numbers could disappear entirely.

When people do engage in voice communication, increasingly they're doing it in new ways, such as Skype, an Internet-based communications system.

Listen to the Chapter 6 Spotlight on the Future podcast, and then be prepared to answer these questions:

Talk about It

1. According to Silverman, why are people starting to reject electronic voice communication?

2. Why might telephone numbers disappear?

3. Do advances in "Internet telephony" signal a renaissance in voice communications?

4. Will video calling, like that offered by Apple FaceTime, become the norm?

5. What might be the "next big thing" in the way people use technology to network with each other?

Take the Next Step *online*

Activity 6.3.1
Flash Movie
How does infrared technology work?

CORE CONTENT

Activity 6.3.2
Research
Should you replace your POTS?

6.4 Communications Standards and Protocols

Browse through any computer store, online or off, and you'll find that there are many models of computers or other Internet-connected devices made by many different manufacturers. These different hardware models have to have a way to communicate with one another. For example, you may want to send a text message from your Nokia cell phone to your friend who uses a BlackBerry. Or, you may attach a document to an email message and send it from your HP laptop to a customer who uses a Mac. You may even want to send data or a picture from your cell phone to your computer.

To allow all these different devices to talk to each other, the computer industry has developed **standards** that address issues of incompatibility among these devices. Organizations such as the **American National Standards Institute (ANSI)** and the **Institute of Electrical and Electronics Engineers (IEEE)** (pronounced "eye-triple-e") develop and approve these standards, which specify how computers access transmission media, speeds used on networks, the design of networking hardware such as cables, and so on.

A standard that specifies how two devices can communicate is called a **protocol**. A protocol provides rules such as how data should be formatted and coded for transmission.

Hardware manufacturers design their devices to meet network standards that relate to the types of tasks their devices handle. Data sent from one device to another travels across a wired system, a wireless system, or a combination of both wired and wireless using a variety of standards.

Exploring Network Transport Standards

The way that data is transported in a network relates to the standard that is used. There are three primary standards to consider: Ethernet, token ring, and TCP/IP.

Ethernet is a common wired media standard. The Ethernet standard specifies that there is no central device controlling the timing of data transmission. With this standard, each device tries to send data when it senses that the network is available. Ethernet networks are inexpensive and easy to install. If you have a high-speed cable modem or DSL modem at home, chances are you use an Ethernet cable to connect your computer to the networking equipment.

Token ring is another standard that allows computers and other devices accessing a network to share a signal. This signal, called a **token**, is passed from device to device, and only the device that holds the token can transmit data at that time. The token ring standard determines the physical design of the network, including which cables, network cards, and other hardware should be used.

TCP/IP is a protocol that specifies the order in which data is sent through the network. With the TCP/IP standard, instructions are given to divide data into small units called **packets** that are passed along the network. Packets are simply smaller pieces of data combined with information about the sender and intended receiver of the data. The process of breaking data into packets, sending, and then reassembling the original data is called **packet switching**. TCP/IP is the network standard upon which Internet communications are based.

Wireless Networking Standards

Getting rid of wires gives people the freedom to move around and get their connections on the go. This process is important whether you're part of a mobile workforce, or just like to use Twitter or email from your local coffee shop. Improvements in wireless technologies continue to enable mobile users to increase their access to different types of data, as shown in the statistics in Figure 6.8, but just how do they work?

Wireless transmissions can use a variety of networking standards, including Wi-Fi, WiMAX, Bluetooth, and Radio Frequency Identification.

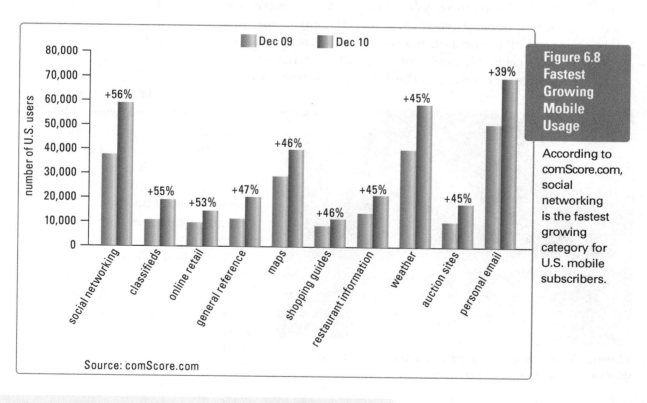

Source: comScore.com

Figure 6.8 Fastest Growing Mobile Usage

According to comScore.com, social networking is the fastest growing category for U.S. mobile subscribers.

Wi-Fi stands for wireless fidelity and refers to a network that is based on the **802.11 standard** in its various versions such as 802.11 a, g, or n. Wi-Fi is a popular choice for setting up a wireless home network. This standard tells wireless devices how to connect with each other using a series of access points and radio frequencies to transmit data.

Computers and portable computing equipment come equipped with built-in Wi-Fi capability. Many public spaces, such as airports, coffee shops, restaurants, and malls, are now being equipped with Wi-Fi access points so you can connect with the Internet from your laptop, tablet, or smartphone. A location, such as a coffee shop, that makes Wi-Fi access available is called a **hotspot**. Operating systems such as Windows and Mac OS X are capable of automatically detecting hotspots and connecting to them.

WiMAX stands for Worldwide Interoperability for Microwave Access (also known as 802.16) and uses the 4G standard that is faster and can work over a longer range than Wi-Fi. WiMAX-capable computers or devices use radio waves and a WiMAX tower to connect with other devices. This method of connecting, which doesn't require the expense of cabling, is expected to attract 50 million users by 2014 according to a 2009 report from Juniper Research. The latest 4G networks used by cell phone providers also use WiMAX. One factor driving the growth of WiMAX is its ability to reach areas that lack cable infrastructure, such as Africa, China, and the Middle East.

Bluetooth is a network protocol that offers short-range connectivity (3 to 300 feet, depending on a device's power class) via radio waves between devices such as your cell phone and car. Bluetooth-enabled devices can communicate directly with each other. Many cars now come with Bluetooth connectivity integrated into their car systems for hands-free cell phone operation. This is partially the result of more and more states and provinces enacting laws against talking on a handheld phone while driving. A variety of devices today contain a Bluetooth chip, such as laptops, smartphones, keyboards, and even digital cameras.

Cell phone users may be able to share the Internet connection of their device via a cable, Bluetooth, or Wi-Fi with another device such as a tablet or laptop. This process is known as **tethering,** and it is useful when access to the Internet via other means is not available for your laptop or tablet. In this case, your mobile phone basically becomes a modem and could possibly service several other computing devices. To be able to tether your mobile device's Internet connection you will need software installed on your mobile phone to support tethering.

Radio Frequency Identification (RFID) is a wireless technology used primarily to track and identify inventory or other items via radio signals. An RFID tag contains a transponder (the part that sends the signal) which is read by a transceiver or

Wireless Bluetooth headsets are popular with cell phone users who want hands-free operation.

RFID reader. As the tag is read, inventory data is automatically updated on the network. The manufacturing and retail worlds track products from production line to the end consumer using RFID tags. This technology is also becoming more widely used as industries embrace the technology to track patients, pets, wildlife, access to parking gates, and toll payments, just to name a few applications.

Wireless Application Protocol (WAP) specifies how mobile devices such as cell phones display online information, including maps and email. Devices using WAP to display web content have to contain a microbrowser, a less robust version of a browser such as Internet Explorer.

Ethics and Technology Blog *online*

Could RFID Tags Be Misused?

RFID tags can be embedded in animals. The same technology could allow these tags to be embedded in humans or planted somewhere on a human to track that person. Anybody with the correct data reader can read any data stored on a tag. Does anybody think that embedding RFID tags in animals or humans could be misused?

Take the Next Step *online*

Activity 6.4.1 Video	What are SMTP, POP, and IMAP?	CORE CONTENT
Activity 6.4.2 Flash Movie	How does Bluetooth work?	CORE CONTENT
Activity 6.4.3 Video	How are businesses using radio frequency technology?	
Activity 6.4.4 Video	What is the Open Systems Interconnection (OSI) model?	
Activity 6.4.5 Team Presentation	What should proper protocol be when a cell phone call is dropped?	

6.5 Network Classifications

Networks have three important characteristics that we'll look at in this section:
- The size of the geographic area in which the network functions.
- The role of computers in the network and how data is shared and stored on the network.
- How devices in a network are physically arranged and connected to each other.

Types of Networks

Networks can be set up to work in your house, your city, or around the world. There are three main types of networks categorized by the area they cover and identified by the catchy acronyms LAN, MAN, and WAN.

Local Area Networks A **local area network (LAN)** is a network where connected devices are located within the same room or building, or in a few nearby buildings (usually not more than a hundred or so feet apart) (Figure 6.9). One computer is designated as the server. In computing terms, a **server** is any combination of hardware and software that provides a service, such as storing data, to your computer. The server in a LAN houses the networking software that coordinates the data exchange among the devices. Shared files are generally kept on that server. A LAN can include a separate print server that manages printing tasks sent from multiple computers to a group printer. Small and home businesses are often networked in a LAN, which can be wired, or wireless. A **wireless LAN** is called (you guessed it) a **WLAN** (a local area network that uses wireless technology).

Metropolitan Area Networks A **metropolitan area network (MAN)** is a type of network that connects networks within a city, university, or other populous area to a larger high-speed network. MANs are typically made up of several LANs that are managed by a network provider. If you connect to a network through your phone or cable company, then you probably connect through a MAN.

Wide Area Networks A **wide area network (WAN)** services even larger geographic areas (Figure 6.10). WANs are used to share data between networks around the world. The Internet is, in essence, a giant WAN. WANs might use leased T1 or T3 lines, satellite connections, radio waves, or a combination of communications media.

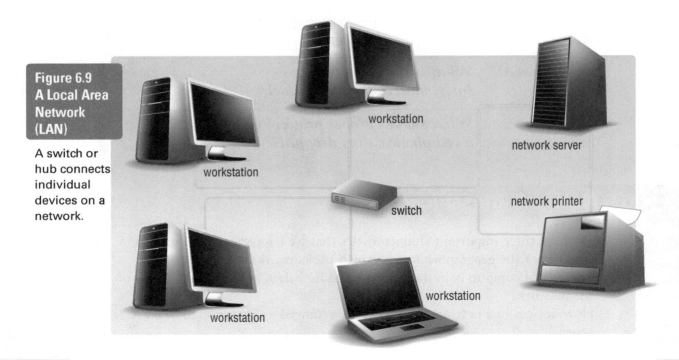

**Figure 6.9
A Local Area
Network
(LAN)**

A switch or hub connects individual devices on a network.

workstation

network server

workstation

network printer

switch

workstation

workstation

workstation

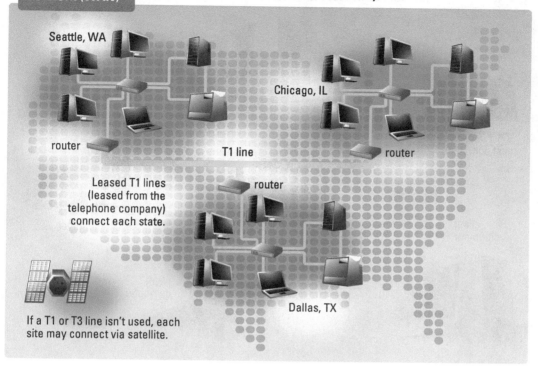

**Figure 6.10
A Wide Area
Network (WAN)**

Here three branches of a company located in different cities share resources through a WAN; a router directs network traffic to each city.

Seattle, WA

Chicago, IL

router

T1 line

router

Leased T1 lines
(leased from the
telephone company)
connect each state.

router

Dallas, TX

If a T1 or T3 line isn't used, each
site may connect via satellite.

Network Architecture

In the noncomputer world architecture relates to the design of a building—where doors go, how walls connect to each other, and so on. **Network architecture** relates to how computers in a network share resources. The two major architectures are client/server and peer-to-peer.

In a **client/server network** (Figure 6.11), a computer called the server stores programs and files that any connected device (called a **client**) can access. Client/server is considered to be a **distributed application architecture** because it distributes tasks between client computers and server computers. For example, on the Internet, a typical client, such as your computer, makes a request of an email server. The sending and receiving of messages to and from your email account is handled on the server, and never makes requests of your computer.

In a **peer-to-peer (P2P) network** (Figure 6.12), each computer in the network can act as both server and client. Each computer can initiate requests of other clients and can act on requests initiated by others. A peer-to-peer network is simple to design and install, but won't function well in a network with heavy user demand. In a busier network, data flow becomes gridlocked like a busy traffic intersection because any computer on the network may request services of any other computer.

A modification of peer-to-peer used on the Internet to share files is **Internet peer-to-peer (P2P) network**. While users are logged onto a P2P connection, they can share and access files from their computers. Each user can both upload files (act as a server) or view uploaded files (act as a client).

**Figure 6.11
Client/Server
Architecture** A client sends information to or requests a service from a server. The
server sends the information on to another client located on that same
network or processes the service request.

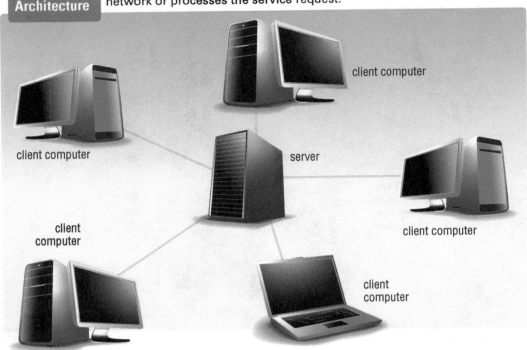

client computer

client computer

server

client
computer

client computer

client
computer

client
computer

**Figure 6.12
Peer-to-Peer
Architecture** In a peer-to-peer network, any computer can be
both a client and a server.

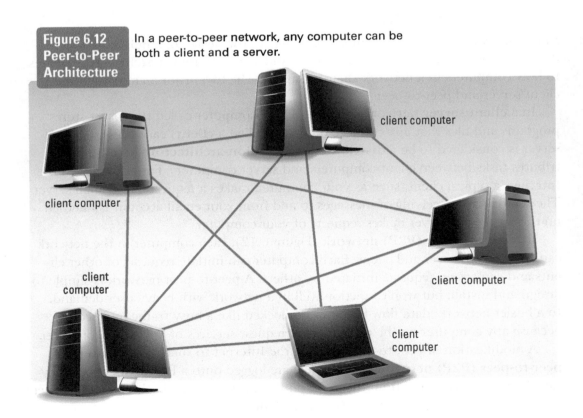

client computer

client computer

client
computer

client computer

client
computer

Our Digital World

Network Topologies

Just as a floor plan describes the arrangement of furniture in a room, the arrangement of computers, servers, and other devices in a network is described as its topology. **Topology** relates to the physical layout but doesn't reflect how the data moves around the network. Three commonly used topologies are bus, ring, and star.

Bus Topology In a **bus topology**, all the computers and other devices, such as printers, are connected by a single cable, like the bulbs that are connected to a single cable in a string of holiday lights. In a network the cable, called the bus, transmits data and instructions for delivering that data to and from computers along the network (Figure 6.13). The address of the device that is intended to receive the data is included in the transmission, so the data arrives at the correct destination. On a bus network, if one device malfunctions, it has no effect on other devices located along the bus cable (unlike your holiday lights!).

Ring Topology A **ring topology** has computers and other devices connected, one after the other, in a closed loop (Figure 6.14). Data transmitted on a ring network travels in one direction from one computer to the other until it reaches its destination. With this setup, if one device on the ring fails, all devices after that device on the loop won't be able to receive data. Though a ring network can work over larger distances, it's not nearly as easy to install as a bus network.

Star Topology In a **star topology** all the devices on the network connect to a central device (Figure 6.15). The central device is usually either a hub or a switch. Data is transmitted from a device to the hub or switch and can then be passed to another device on the network. If one device fails, no other devices are affected. However, if the hub/switch fails, the entire network goes down.

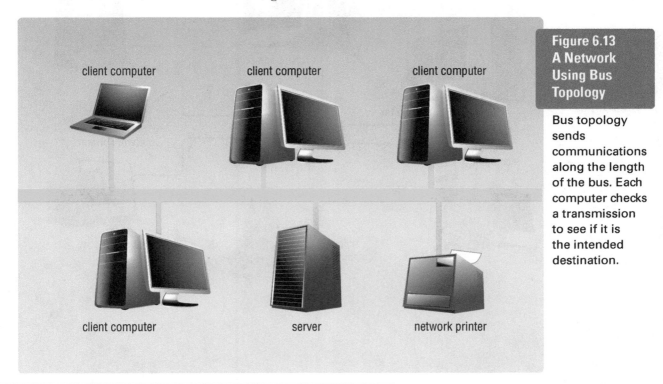

client computer   client computer   client computer

client computer   server   network printer

Figure 6.13 A Network Using Bus Topology

Bus topology sends communications along the length of the bus. Each computer checks a transmission to see if it is the intended destination.

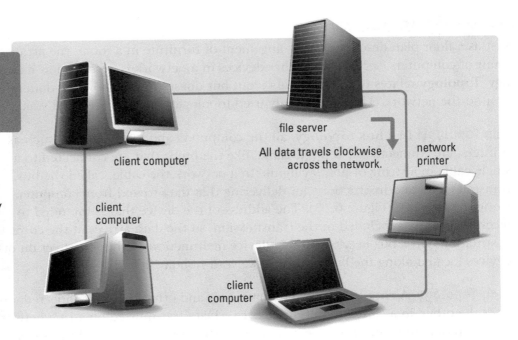

Figure 6.14 A Network Using Ring Topology

A token is passed from one computer to another within a closed loop. Only the device that holds the token has the ability to send data over the network.

file server

All data travels clockwise across the network.

network printer

client computer

client computer

client computer

Figure 6.15 A Network Using Star Topology

Star topology links all computers in the network to a host computer through a **hub or switch**, which is the device through which data transmissions are managed.

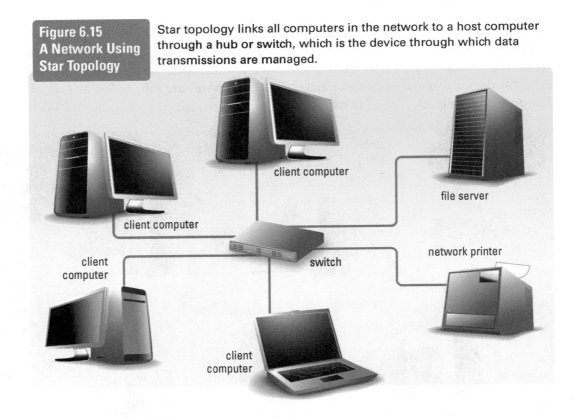

client computer

client computer

file server

client computer

client computer

switch

network printer

client computer

Take the Next Step *online*

Activity 6.5.1 Flash Movie	*What's the role of a hub and switch in a star network?*
Activity 6.5.2 Research	*How does file sharing work on a network?*
Activity 6.5.3 Research	*What is a virtual private network (VPN)?*

CORE CONTENT

6.6 Networking Devices and Software

It's useful to understand the physical elements of a network in case you set up one yourself someday. Setting up a network involves several types of hardware and may involve a network operating system.

Network Devices

Each device connected to the network is called a **node**. Networking devices include hardware that facilitates the exchange of data from your computer to a transmission medium such as a cable connection, and hardware that enables various devices on a network to communicate with each other.

Modems to Send and Receive Signals As you learned earlier, a modem is the piece of hardware that sends and receives data from a transmission source such as your telephone line or cable television connection.

A **dial-up modem** works with phone transmissions. These devices change or manipulate an analog signal so that it can be understood by a computer or fax machine, which only understand digital signals. Dial-up modems typically take the form of adapter cards that are inserted in your computer motherboard.

A **DSL modem** also sends and receives data using lines on the telephone network. This modem modulates and demodulates data transmitted with analog signals, and filters out incoming voice signals. A DSL modem allows you to connect to your existing telephone system and separates voice from data traffic so you don't lose the use of your telephone while your computer is transmitting or receiving data.

A **cable modem** sends and receives digital data using a high-speed cable network based on the cable television infrastructure found in many homes.

A cable modem allows your computer to send and receive digital data via a broadband connection.

A mobile broadband stick is a USB device that acts as a modem to give your computer access to the Internet.

A **wireless modem** typically takes the form of a PC card that you slot into a notebook computer, netbook, or other portable device to provide it with an antenna that can pick up a connection to the Internet. Mobile broadband sticks (also called dongles) have become popular for mobile users who want broadband flexibility while on the go. A **mobile broadband stick** is a USB device that acts as a modem to give your computer access to the Internet. These wireless modems can be moved easily between devices. Powered by the computer itself, a mobile broadband stick does not need to be recharged.

Hardware That Provides Access to a Network

A **network adapter** is a device that provides your computer with the ability to connect to a network. A **network interface card (NIC)** (pronounced "Nick") is one kind of adapter card. The NIC processes the transmission and receipt of data to/from the communications system.

In most recent computers, NICs take the form of a circuit board built into the motherboard. NICs enable a client computer on a LAN to connect to a network by managing the transmission of data and instructions sent by the server. At home, you plug one end of a cable into your desktop or laptop NIC card and the other into a DSL or cable modem.

A **wireless interface card** functions in the same way as a NIC, except that a wireless interface card uses wireless technology to make the connection.

> " The most compelling reason for most people to buy a computer for the home will be to link it to a nationwide communications network. We're just in the beginning stages of what will be a truly remarkable breakthrough for most people—as remarkable as the telephone. "
>
> ▶▶ Steve Jobs, former CEO, Apple Computing

Devices That Connect Devices to Each Other on a Network

There are several devices that help other devices on a network to communicate with each other.

A **wireless access point** is a device that contains a high-quality antenna (Figure 6.16). This antenna allows computers and mobile devices to transmit data to each other or to exchange data with a wired network.

A **router** is a device that allows you to connect two or more networks in either a wired or wireless connection (in which case it is referred to as a **wireless router**). In a home, for example, a router allows you to connect multiple devices on a home network to the Internet using one high-speed connection. Routers used to connect business networks have many ports and are faster and more sophisticated than the routers you use in a home network. A mobile hotspot combines cellular network access with a wireless router, enabling multiple computers or devices to have wire-

Our Digital World

A router (top left), switch (top right), hub (bottom left), and gateway (bottom right) are devices that networks may use to connect and send data.

Figure 6.16 Wireless Access Point in a Network

A wireless access point sends the data to computers or other devices equipped with wireless adapters.

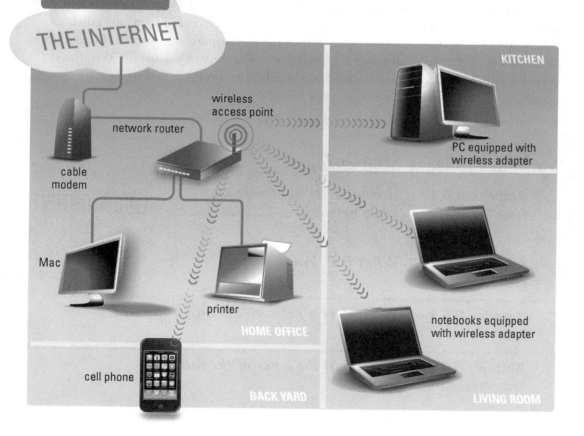

less Internet access. Older models worked on 3G networks, while the newer models support 4G LTE mobile broadband.

A **repeater** is an electronic device that takes a signal and retransmits it at a higher power level to boost the transmission strength. A repeater can also transmit a signal to move past an obstruction, so that the signal can be sent further without degrading, or losing quality.

A **hub** is used on older LAN networks to coordinate the message traffic among nodes connected to a network.

A **switch** has a similar role to a hub. Switches join several nodes together to coordinate message traffic in one LAN network. However, a switch can check the data in the packets it receives, which helps to deliver each packet to the correct destination.

Gateways and bridges are devices that help separate networks to communicate with each other. A **gateway** is used when the two networks use different topologies, and a **bridge** is used to connect two networks using the same topology.

Network Operating Systems

Networks use a few different types of software to function, one of which is a network operating system.

A network uses a network operating system to add features that are essential to managing the network. In a network, a **network operating system (NOS)** is installed on the central server. A network operating system includes programs that control the flow of data among clients, restricts access to resources, and manages individual user accounts.

Some popular network operating systems are Microsoft Windows Server in various editions, Open Enterprise Server (OES), Linux Server in various editions, and Mac OS X Server. Another open source network operating system is ReactOS. Note that an NOS typically isn't required for a peer network. Current Windows versions and Mac OS X have networking capabilities built in, making it easy to set up a basic wireless peer network in your home or office.

Take the Next Step *online*

Activity 6.6.1 Flash Movie	*How do I set up a wireless home network?*	**CORE CONTENT**
Activity 6.6.2 Research	*What is Z-Wave?*	
Activity 6.6.3 Research	*What does a network administrator do?*	
Activity 6.6.4 Team Presentation	*What will the home of the future be like?*	

Our Digital World

6.7 Securing a Network

Whether on a home network or large company network, security is a vital concern today. That's because criminals and malicious hackers can find ways to break into a network to steal data and cause problems. They may locate sensitive financial information, plant viruses that destroy data, or modify settings in ways that cost you time and money.

Network security is managed through a combination of techniques involving hardware and software such as a **firewall**, which stops those outside a network from sending information into it or taking information out of it (Figure 6.17). On your home network, you may be the administrator (operating systems such as Windows allow you to set up administrator privileges) and set up your own firewall. In business, network security is an in-demand career specialty.

Chapter 8 explains computer security in more detail.

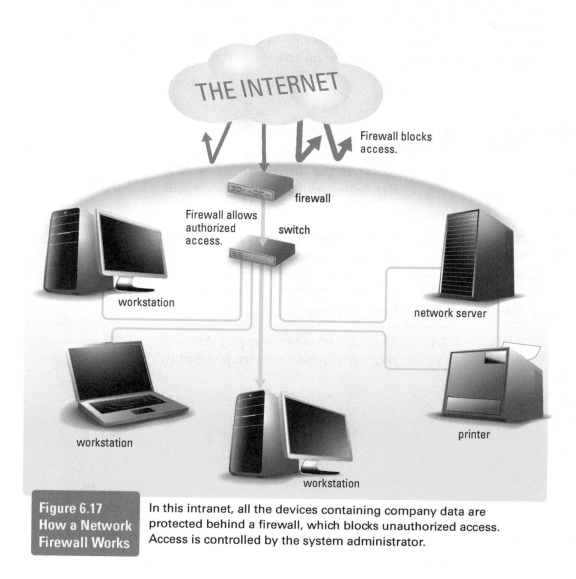

Figure 6.17 How a Network Firewall Works In this intranet, all the devices containing company data are protected behind a firewall, which blocks unauthorized access. Access is controlled by the system administrator.

Ethics and Technology Blog  *online*

Is Stealing Time Online OK?

I hear a lot of companies crack down on employees who use the company network to conduct personal business. What's all the fuss about?

Computers in Your Career

Computer security is a hot field for those seeking a career working with computer technology. More and more companies understand that protecting their information and their customers' records and privacy is essential to their success, and those in the IT department who deal with security are seen as vital partners. According to the Bureau of Labor Statistics' *Occupational Outlook Handbook* for 2010-11, the specialty of computer security is growing rapidly. Security specialists will be employed to assess a system's vulnerability and implement security measures. Additionally, computer analysts and developers will develop new antivirus software, programs, and procedures.

Take the Next Step *online*

Activity 6.7.1 Video	*What is the difference between a hardware and software firewall?*	**CORE CONTENT**
Activity 6.7.2 Research	*How can mobile devices threaten corporate security?*	
Activity 6.7.3 Research	*What network security do you have in place?*	
Activity 6.7.4 In-Class or Blog Discussion	*Do you get what you pay for with free virus and spyware programs?*	

Two key buzzwords in networking circles today are *mobility* and *the cloud*. In fact, the trends are complementary, as both allow computer users more freedom in accessing what they need to get their work done from anywhere and at a lower cost.

Mobility and VoIP

Many companies have built or are building Wi-Fi and Voice over Internet Protocol (VoIP) into their internal computer networks. This means that employees can use their cell phones both inside the company's building and in the wireless networks outside the building without dropping a call as they move from one environment to the other. Also, VoIP is being used by companies to save money.

Cloud Computing

In the past, elements of the network that were kept invisible to users were considered to be in the cloud—that is, software installed on a network server that you simply open and use without having to install it on your computer.

Web 2.0 has ushered in an online cloud where software and services are accessed on the Internet (Figure 6.18). In previous chapters you were introduced to cloud computing as a way to access storage and software applications as services online. This is part of cloud computing, which relies on the concept of Software as a Service, or SaaS. By

> " So therefore, what is your purpose? What are you supposed to do? How are you supposed to educate? How are you supposed to create jobs? I feel that that is what Cloud is, that is what social media is going to do. "
>
> ▶▶ Mark Benioff, CEO, Salesforce.com

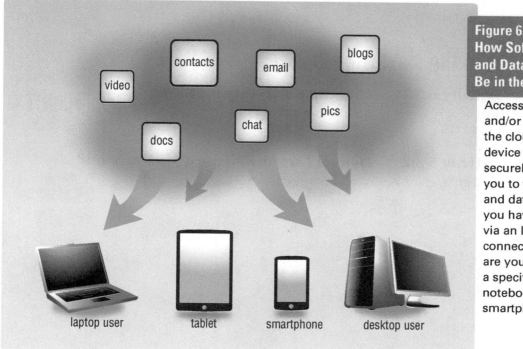

Figure 6.18 How Software and Data Can Be in the Cloud

Accessing software and/or storing data in the cloud means your device is the tool that securely connects you to the services and data for which you have subscribed via an Internet connection. No longer are you tethered to a specific desktop, notebook, tablet, or smartphone.

having applications installed, maintained, and updated outside their walls in the "cloud," companies save money.

Some basic cloud services such as Office Web Apps and Google Docs are free for individual users, but more advanced cloud services cater to larger organizations. Such a cloud service has three features that differentiate it from software located on your computer or network:

- It is sold on demand and generally billed by the minute or by the hour.
- People can use as much or as little of a service as they want at any given time.
- The service is fully managed and maintained by the provider (the end user only uses a computer and his/her Internet access to work with the service).

In the report titled *Reimagining IT: The 2011 CIO Agenda*, Gartner research reports that cloud computing ranks number one on CIO's technology priority list for the year. The report surveyed responses from 2,014 CIOs in 50 countries. Gartner Research predicts that in as little as four years, companies will have 43 percent of their IT efforts running in the cloud.

Long Term Evolution (LTE) Standards

With the explosion of mobile Internet usage, world mobile experts have had to be out in front in developing network standards that will support all the wireless mobility technologies that consumers desire. **Long Term Evolution (LTE) standards** are standards intended to help the mobile phone networks be prepared for new technologies and involves areas such as improving bandwidth efficiency, cost control, providing better service, and integrating standards. Providers will continue to work on future standards that will lead to mobile networks that are faster, more efficient, and able to handle the huge amounts of data and applications used by consumers.

Take the Next Step *online*

Activity 6.8.1 Video	*How can cloud computing save businesses money?*	CORE CONTENT
Activity 6.8.2 Research	*How do I set up and use a VoIP account?*	

Summing Up

How Does the World Use Networking?

A **computer network** consists of two or more computing devices connected by a communications medium, such as a wireless signal or a cable. A network provides a way to connect with others and share files and resources.

Many companies have their own networks, called **intranets**. Intranets are essentially a private Internet within the company's corporate "walls." An **extranet** is an extension of an intranet that allows interaction with those outside the company, such as suppliers and customers.

Exploring Communications Systems

A computer network is one kind of **communications system**. This system includes sending and receiving hardware, transmission and relay systems, common sets of standards so all the equipment can "talk" to each other, and communications software.

Two kinds of signals are used in transmitting data over a computer network: analog and digital. An **analog signal** is formed by continuous waves that fluctuate from high to low. A **digital signal** uses a discrete signal that is either high or low.

If you send data between computers using an analog medium such as a phone line, the signal has to be transformed from digital to analog and back again to digital. Today most new communications technologies simply use a digital signal, saving the trouble of converting transmissions.

The speed of transmission is determined by two factors: 1) **frequency**, which is the speed at which a signal can change from high to low; and 2) **bandwidth**, which refers to the number of bits per second that can be transmitted. Any communications medium that is capable of carrying a large amount of data at a fast speed is known as **broadband**.

Transmission Systems

Wired transmissions send a signal through various media, including:
- **Twisted-pair cable**, which is used for your wired telephone connection at home.
- **Coaxial cable**, the same cable used to transmit cable television signals over an insulated wire at a fast speed.
- **Fiber-optic cable**, a very fast system that uses a protected string of glass to transmit data as beams of light.

Wireless transmissions in use today include cellular, microwave, and satellite. All use radio waves to transmit data.

A **cellular network**, like those used by your cell phone, transmits signals called **cellular transmissions**, by using cell towers. A **microwave** is a high-frequency radio signal that is directed between microwave station towers that are within sight of each other.

Satellite communication uses space-based equipment for longer range transmissions.

Communications Standards and Protocols

To allow different devices to talk to each other, the computer industry has developed **standards** that address issues of incompatibility. A standard that specifies how two devices can communicate is called a **protocol**.

There are three primary wired standards: 1) **Ethernet**, which specifies that there is no central device controlling the timing of data transmission; 2) **token ring**, which allows computers and other devices to share a signal (**token**) that is passed from device to device; and 3) **TCP/IP**, in which **packets** are sent and reassembled by the receiver. TCP/IP is the standard upon which Internet communications are based.

Wireless networking standards include:

- **Wi-Fi** (wireless fidelity), which refers to a network that is based on the **802.11 standard**. A location that makes Wi-Fi access available is called a **hotspot**.
- **WiMAX** (Worldwide Interoperability for Microwave Access, also known as 802.16), which uses the 4G standard.
- **Bluetooth**, a network protocol that offers short-range connectivity (3 to 300 feet, depending on a device's power class) via radio waves between devices such as your cell phone and car. Cell phone users may be able to share the Internet connection of their device via a cable, Bluetooth, or Wi-Fi with another device such as a tablet or laptop. This process is known as **tethering**, and it is useful when accessing the Internet via other means not available for your laptop or tablet.
- **Radio Frequency Identification (RFID)**, a wireless technology primarily used to track and identify inventory or other items using radio signals.
- **Wireless Application Protocol (WAP)**, which specifies how mobile devices such as cell phones display online information including maps and email.

Network Classifications

Networks are classified by three characteristics: 1) the size of the geographic area in which the network functions, 2) how data is shared and stored on the network, and 3) how devices in a network are physically arranged and connected to each other.

Types of networks include:

- A **local area network (LAN)**, a network where connected devices are located within the same room or building, or in a few nearby buildings.
- A **metropolitan area network (MAN)**, a network that connects networks within a city, a university, or other populous area to a larger high-speed network.
- A **wide area network (WAN)**, which services even larger geographic areas.

Network architecture relates to how computers in a network share resources. The two major architectures are client/server and peer-to-peer. In a **client/server network**, a **server** computer stores programs and files that any connected device (**clients**) can access. In a **peer-to-peer (P2P) network**, each computer in the network can act as both server and client.

Three commonly used network **topologies** are bus, ring, and star. In a **bus topology**, all the computers and other devices, such as printers, are connected by a single main cable. A **ring topology** has computers and other devices connected, one after the other, in a closed loop. In a **star topology** all the devices on the network connect to a central device. The central device is either a **hub** or a **switch**.

Networking Devices and Software

Networking devices include hardware that facilitates the exchange of data from your computer to a transmission medium such as a cable connection, or hardware that enables various devices on a network to communicate with each other. Each device connected to a network is called a **node**.

A **modem** is the piece of hardware that sends and receives data from a transmission source such as your telephone line or cable television connection. Types of modems include **dial-up**, **cable**, **DSL**, and **wireless**. A **mobile broadband stick** is a USB device that acts as a modem to give your computer access to the Internet.

A **network adapter** provides your computer with the ability to connect to a network. A **network interface card (NIC)** is one kind of adapter card. NICs support Ethernet.

A **wireless interface card** functions in the same way as a NIC, except that a wireless interface card uses wireless technology to make the connection.

Wireless access points contain a high-quality antenna that permits wireless devices to transmit data to each other or to exchange data with a wired network.

A **router** allows you to connect multiple networks (or multiple devices if used in a home) in either a wired or wireless connection.

A **repeater** is an electronic device that takes a signal and retransmits it at a higher power level to boost the transmission strength.

A **hub** is used on older LAN networks to coordinate the message traffic among nodes connected to a network.

A **switch** has a similar role to a hub, however, a switch can check the data in the packets to ensure delivery to the correct destination.

Gateways and **bridges** help separate networks to communicate with each other.

A **network operating system (NOS)** includes programs that control the flow of data among clients, restrict access to resources, and manage individual user accounts.

Securing a Network

Network security is managed through a combination of hardware and software such as a **firewall**, which stops those outside a network from sending information into it or taking information out of it.

Interesting Trends in Networking

Many companies are building Wi-Fi and Voice over Internet Protocol (VoIP) into their internal networks. In addition, use of cloud computing is expected to continue to grow rapidly in the business world. Cloud computing is where software and IT services are accessed on the Internet and are usually billed as a service rather than by application license. By having applications installed, maintained, and updated outside their walls in the "cloud," companies save money. **Long Term Evolution (LTE) standards** for wireless broadband have evolved to ensure that network capabilities will keep up with consumers' data and service needs.

Terms to Know

How Does the World Use Networking?
computer network, 168

extranet, 168

intranet, 168

Exploring Communications Systems
communications system, 168

network protocol, 168

analog signal, 169

digital signal, 169

modem, 170

frequency, 170

bandwidth, 171

broadband, 171

kilobit per second (Kbps), 171

megabit per second (Mbps), 171

gigabit per second (Gbps), 171

terabit per second (Tbps), 171

petabit per second (Pbps), 171

Transmission Systems
twisted-pair cable, 172

coaxial cable, 172

fiber-optic cable, 172

cellular network, 172

cellular transmissions, 172

microwave, 174

satellite communication, 174

Communications Standards and Protocols
standards, 176

American National Standards Institute (ANSI), 176

Institute of Electrical and Electronics Engineers (IEEE), 176

protocol, 176

Ethernet, 176

token ring, 177

token, 177

TCP/IP, 177

packet, 177

packet switching, 177

Wi-Fi, 178

802.11 standard, 178

hotspot, 178

WiMAX, 178

Bluetooth, 178

tethering, 178

Radio Frequency Identification (RFID), 178

Wireless Application Protocol (WAP), 178

email server, Activity 6.4.1

webmail, Activity 6.4.1

Network Classifications

Networking Devices and Software

Securing a Network

Interesting Trends in Networking

Concepts Check

Concepts Check 6.1 Multiple Choice
Take this quiz to test your understanding of key concepts in this chapter.

Concepts Check 6.2 Word Puzzle
Complete this puzzle to test your knowledge of key terms in this chapter.

Concepts Check 6.3 Matching
Test your understanding of terms and concepts presented in this chapter.

Concepts Check 6.4 Label It
Use the interactive tool to identify components in a local area network.

Concepts Check 6.5 Label It
Use the interactive tool to label the parts of these cables.

Concepts Check 6.6 Matching
Use the interactive tool to identify the topologies.

Projects

Check with your instructor for the preferred method to submit completed work.

Project 6.1 Wireless Coup

Project 6.1.1 Individual

To familiarize yourself with the broadband wireless connection WiMAX, watch the video *What Is WiMAX?* at www.emcp.net/WiMAXvideo. Then read the article "How WiMAX Works" at www.emcp.net/WiMAXarticle. Based on the information you learned from the video and article, prepare a brief summary of bulleted points listing key facts about WiMAX. Now that you have an understanding of this broadband wireless standard, imagine that you work as a marketing manager for a local cable service provider. Your cable company has a large penetration of household subscribers, with the latest estimates showing that your organization has 60% of the broadband market. Consider how your company will respond to the influx of WiMAX technology in your territory. Create a document that outlines the strategies you will adopt to retain your market share.

Project 6.1.2 Team

In a team setting, present your marketing strategies for the retention of the 60% market share that your cable company holds. Discuss the advantages, disadvantages, and cost implications to your company of each team member's suggested strategies. Then vote on the top three strategies, and prepare a slide presentation that can be used to pitch your team's marketing plan at the next company board meeting.

Project 6.2   Public Connectivity

Project 6.2.1   Team

Research the public spaces within your community (outside the school) that offer free wireless connectivity for accessing the Internet. If you have a wireless-enabled laptop, visit these Wi-Fi locations or hotspots and log in to the free network to test the ease of connectivity and the network's speed. Write a summary of the results of your research and testing experience.

Project 6.2.2   Team

Your team works at a local property management company that primarily leases commercial space for offices. The CEO of the company has been considering the idea of providing free wireless access in all of the buildings the company manages. To determine the feasibility of this plan, the CEO has asked your team to investigate the benefits and drawbacks of wireless accessibility, including the cost, security, and other factors for its implementation. Prepare a slide presentation for the executive board that supports or discourages this plan, and provide a rationale for your team's position.

Project 6.3   Solar-Powered Networks

Project 6.3.1   Individual

Watch the video Alcatel-Lucent: Alternative Energy Pilot Site for Wireless Networks at www.emcp.net/SolarPower. Consider the possible applications of solar-powered wireless technology in areas where it is not cost-effective or otherwise feasible to set up a traditional network. Now that you have an understanding of wireless solar-powered technology, assume you are a venture capitalist who is considering a proposal from an entrepreneur to sell this technology in remote areas not currently supported with cost-effective high-speed Internet access. Prepare a document with a series of questions that you would like to ask the entrepreneur during an upcoming meeting to discuss possible funding. Below each question, provide a rationale for why you think the question is important.

Project 6.3.2   Team

Assume your team has been hired by the entrepreneur seeking funding in Project 6.3.1. Review the questions that have been prepared by each team member. Then choose five questions that your team deems most valuable to ask. Using these questions to guide your investigation, conduct research on solar-powered wireless networks to find the answers the entrepreneur should provide. Keep a list of the references that you used when gathering your information. Then prepare a slide presentation that provides a separate slide for each question and its subsequent response. Conclude your presentation with a summary slide that lists the URLs for the reference articles used in your team's research.

Project 6.4   RFID — Cure or Curse?

Project 6.4.1   Individual

Read the article "RFID: Tracking Everything, Everywhere" (available at www.emcp.net/spychips) and record how RFID, or Radio Frequency Identification, is being used by businesses and government. Using this background information, create a survey on RFID technology to conduct among 10 friends or relatives. Try to sample a heterogeneous population in terms of gender, age, and education level. On each survey, provide a brief explanation of RFID technology and its potential uses. Then ask each participant the following questions:

- What concerns do you have about the potential widespread applications of RFID?

- What limits would you propose on how much information could be collected or monitored from embedded RFID tags?

Prepare a document that briefly summarizes the results of your survey. Determine if any trends in your results can be traced to factors such as gender, age, and education level.

Project 6.4.2   Team

Review the surveys compiled by each team member from Project 6.4.1, and discuss the results with your team. Given the positive impact RFID could have for businesses and other organizations that need to track products, come up with strategies or policies that a company could adopt that will address the privacy issues raised by RFID opponents.

Project 6.5   Wiki — Networking Devices and Terms

Project 6.5.1   Team

Your team will be assigned to research and write a brief explanation on one or more of the following devices or terms commonly associated with corporate networks: router, hub, switch, bridge, repeater, gateway, TCP/IP, T1 line, T3 line, or Asynchronous Transfer Mode (ATM). Prepare a posting to the course wiki site for your assigned topic(s). Include an explanation of the device or term along with examples or images, if possible, to aid comprehension. Be sure to compile a list of references for your sources of information.

Project 6.5.2   Team

Your team is assigned to edit and verify the content posted on the wiki site from Project 6.5.1. If you add or edit any content, make sure you include a notation within the page that includes the team members' names and the date you edited the content—for example, "Edited by [team members' names] on [date]." Keep a list of references that you used to verify your content changes. When you are finished with your verification, include a notation at the end of the entry—for example, "Verified by [team members' names] on [date]."

Project 6.6   Wiki — Acceptable Use of Computers and Networks at Work

Project 6.6.1   Individual or Team

Due to ongoing issues regarding the improper use of company-owned computing equipment, the executive board has asked you or your team to draft a new corporate policy on acceptable computer and network practices. You will be assigned to write a section for the new policy on one or more of the following topics:

Gaming

Personal email and IM

Social networking sites (Facebook)

YouTube

Blogging

Access to high-quality color printers

Access to long-distance telecommunications

Company-provided computing equipment (laptop, smartphone)

Internet surfing or shopping

Texting

When you have finished writing your assigned section, post your topic and its accompanying text to the course wiki site.

Project 6.6.2   Individual or Team

You or your team has been asked to comment on the content posted on the wiki site from Project 6.6.1. Post your commentary followed by a notation that includes your name or the team members' names and the date you commented—for example, "Comment by [your name or team members' names] on [date]."

Class Conversations

Topic 6.1 GPS-Enabled Phones—Can You See Me Now?

Location-Based Services (LBS) available for GPS-enabled telephones have opened new doors to managers who want to keep a watchful eye on their mobile workers. Service agreements are available with a company's cellular provider to log employees' movements, including enabling tracking when the employee has entered or exited a predefined region (called GeoFencing) and to send an alert when a specified speed limit has been exceeded. While LBS has obvious safety benefits (such as locating a mobile worker who may be lost or in need of assistance), is there a point at which an individual's right to privacy is at risk with this technology? If yes, where would you suggest this tracking technology has the potential to invade an employee's privacy? Assume you are a manager at a company that subscribes to LBS. How will you address any privacy issues raised by your employees about the data you will receive from the mobile device?

Topic 6.2 Can Broadband Access Be Meaningful?

The Digital Divide (the gap between people with access to digital technology and communications and those with limited or no access) has been a focus of discussion among business, government, and individuals since the 1990s. Closing the gap was originally thought to mean that computers and connectivity needed to be given to those without access due to economics or lack of infrastructure. However, this view is starting to change. Consider the example provided at DigitalDivide.org: *"...when a local youth in a Cambodia village ignores his schoolwork and instead spends his evenings playing violent video games with his peers, he is not really benefiting from digital technology."* DigitalDivide.org is advocating that future innovations to close the gap need to engage the concept of *meaningful broadband (MB)*, which DigitalDivide.org defines this way: *"[MB] refers to high-speed Internet infrastructures and applications that fit three criteria: usable, affordable and empowering. In other words, MB refers to the quality of broadband."* In this context, governments of emerging markets will be allowed to regulate against innovations that are deemed to be meaningless or addictive and reward only those that will benefit their society. Discuss the concept of meaningful broadband. In your own experience with access to high-speed connectivity, how would you differentiate between uses of that network that are meaningful and those that are not? What criteria do you think helps you to make this judgment? Do you agree that governments need to regulate against addictive technologies in emerging markets? Why or why not? Should governments adopt the same strategies in the United States and Canada where access is limited or not available to lower income or rural areas? Why or why not?

Topic 6.3   What Happens When the Network Is Down?

For some, being connected 24/7 can be both a positive and a negative influence in their lives. Have you ever logged in to your computer and become agitated because the network connectivity was slow or—even worse—down altogether? With increasing reliance on digital networks, what happens when the network goes down? If you try to contact someone over a network and receive no response, how do you react? Does work stop, or does work become more productive because employees are not distracted with constant email or other online interruptions? How long would you be content with no connectivity in your day?

The Social Web
Opportunities for Learning, Working, and Communicating

What You'll Accomplish

When you finish this chapter, you'll be able to:

- Describe the evolution of social technologies and online collaboration and how they are changing the way our society functions.

- Explain the terms social Web, open content, blog, social networking, social bookmarking, wiki, and media sharing.

- Discuss the ways in which social technologies are being used by individuals, educators, corporations, and organizations.

- Explain what media sharing is and how it's being used.

- Examine the ethical issues surrounding the new technologies of the social Web.

Why Should I Care?

Social networking sites such as Facebook have seen phenomenal growth in the past several years. In a single year (2008) Facebook grew 153 percent and in 2011 it had more than 750 million active users. If Facebook was a country it would be the world's third largest country and more than twice the size of the United States in population. But connecting with friends on social networking sites is only one aspect of a trend toward a more collaborative online environment. Social technologies are also being used by businesses to help employees connect with each other and communicate with customers, by nonprofit groups to document trends and promote social causes, by schools to involve students in collaborative projects and interactive learning, and in many other settings. You are part of a revolution in the way that people share and collaborate, and by choosing to embrace that revolution you may reap benefits in many areas of your life.

7.1 The Social Web Phenomenon

You may have a page on Facebook or have visited sites such as Twitter, YouTube, ChaCha, or Flickr, or have read about these sites in the news. All of these are social sites, where people go to share their thoughts in text, video, or photos. Taken together these sites form the **social Web**, a revolution in how people connect with each other, how news is delivered, and how our collective knowledge is formed. Social sites and the tools they offer create a vehicle for a two-way dialog between people and groups rather than a one-way communication from media to the public, store to customer, or teacher to student.

> " Facebook will not be the preeminent social network by 2015. It will be smashed by fragmentation. "
>
> ▶▶│ Michael Ossipoff, Director of Capability and Innovation, Telstra

The social Web is still defining itself, and as such is likely to include more types of websites and services than you think. Any site that allows users to interact with each other and share information or content can be considered, at some level, to be social. A website that allows you to share contacts and build a network of "friends" is a **social networking site**. Services that allow you to share media are media sharing sites. Online dating services and special interest sites such as those that cater to genealogy or sports fans, when they allow interaction and communication among members, are social sites. Most of these have content almost entirely driven by the members, though the site owners put the infrastructure, communication tools, and rules for behavior in place.

online ✓ **Take a Survey**

What are you doing on the social Web?

7.2 Social Technology Comes of Age

In Chapter 2 you read about the concept of Web 2.0 as a phase of the development of the Web associated with user involvement and collaboration. This collaboration happens through interactive web services such as Wikipedia (an online encyclopedia) and Facebook (a communication site that connects people to one another). These web services provide users with a way to share information, exchange ideas, and add or edit content. The social Web is one of the most publicized and successful examples of Web 2.0.

How the Social Web Was Born

Since the days before the commercially available Internet, people have been interacting online through tools such as discussion boards and email, but the social Web took that interaction much further. The concept of Web 2.0 appeared in 2001, and understanding the trends it describes is important in understanding how the social Web came to be. In the late 1990s, the open source movement allowed individuals to contribute to the source code of software such as the Linux operating system.

Social sites allow users to share ideas and content online.

This collaboration produced a freely available piece of software. Open source was to software development what **open content** is to the social Web, where anybody can freely share their knowledge about topics in online collections such as Wikipedia or WetPaint (a collection of content focused on a variety of areas of interest to users).

At about the same time that the open source and open content movements were growing, in 1997 one of the first true social networking sites appeared called SixDegrees.com. Though prior to that time users created **profiles** where they published information about themselves and could create lists of friends, SixDegrees was one of the first sites that combined use of profiles and searchable **friends lists** in one service. Social networking was born.

SixDegrees failed, perhaps in part because its concept was ahead of its time. Meanwhile blogging sites surfaced in 1999, adding one more key tool to social interaction in the form of online journals called **blogs** (a term created from web + log). A few more social networking sites appeared, many incorporating a blogging component, until, in 2003, the phenomenon exploded with sites such as MySpace, Flickr, Facebook, and LinkedIn, all launching within months of each other. In 2010, SixDegrees launched as a members-only site. The latest social network, Google+, was launched on June 29, 2011, and in less than two months hit the 10 million user mark. Figure 7.1 presents the timeline of social networking sites.

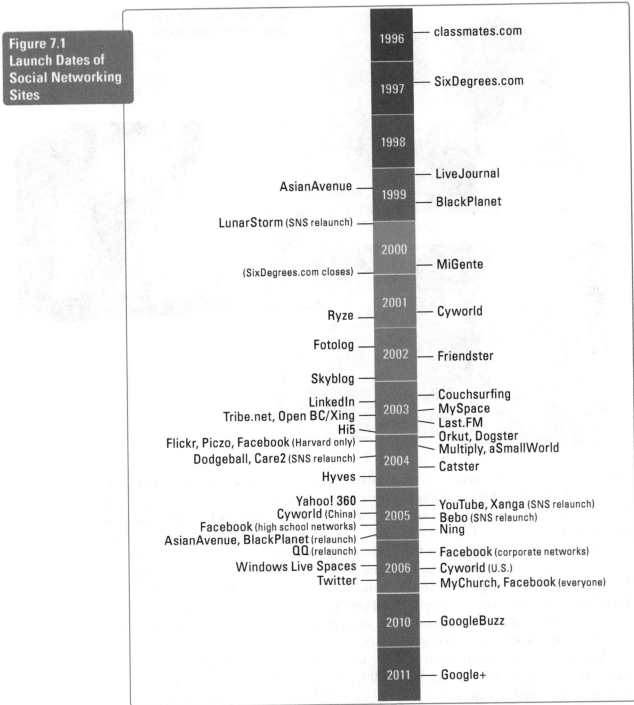

"Social Network Sites: Definition, History, and Scholarship" by Boyd and Ellison, *Journal of Computer Mediated Communication*.

Ethics and Technology Blog *online*

Design by Crowdsourcing

Crowdsourcing involves getting lots of people to contribute to a work online. If a graphic designer gets ideas from others and then sells that work as his or her own, is it wrong? Maybe it's just "social" creativity?

Go2Web20.net offers an index of Web 2.0 applications.

Overview of Social Technology Today

Today, the social Web has expanded to be accessible by a variety of devices such as cell phones and gaming devices. These devices allow people to connect with their social sites to post text, video, and photos and interact with their friends on the go.

If you perform a search for the social Web or visit a site such as Go2Web20.net, you will see the incredible variety of social sites and applications available to you. The function of these sites is as varied as the people and organizations who use them. Social causes use the social Web to muster support in times of crisis, such as raising money to help victims of natural disasters. Businesses use social marketing, driving their branding and sales messages to the public by participating in all kinds of social networking sites. Harvard, MIT, and other schools host classes on virtual worlds like Second Life. Politicians hold online dialogs on political and social issues to gather votes and support. Artists create visual and musical pieces by sharing media and building new pieces of art collaboratively. Political demonstrators all over the globe have used social media to organize their efforts and communicate about incidents and developments.

The social Web is growing and evolving rapidly, with changes happening daily. Functions and features of the different social websites overlap, making it challenging to define the technologies precisely. However, grouping them into the following broad categories provides a way to examine them and understand their value in our digital world:

- blogging
- social networking
- social bookmarking
- wikis
- media sharing

Each of these categories of social media is explored in this chapter in terms of how the technology works, who uses it, and for what purposes.

Khan Academy is a site that provides students with videos, practice exercises, and assessments for free.

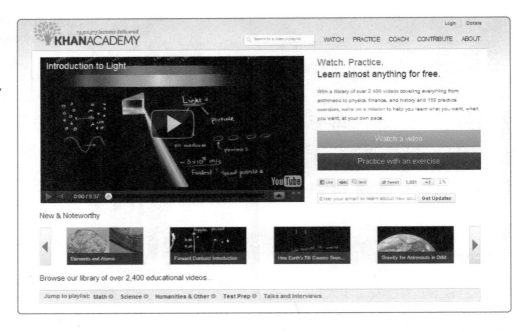

The Future of Social Technology

By the time you read this chapter, social technology will have changed. That's one of the most exciting things about Web content driven by the masses; it morphs very quickly because anybody can suggest an idea that becomes the next great trend rather than having trends dictated by business or the media. Still, it's possible to speculate about some future directions for the social Web that are already emerging.

One predicted trend is the ability to carry your **identity** (the profile you create when you join a service) with you from site to site. There will be a connection among all the social sites you now use separately. You will have one set of friends who have access to your page, and one set of **preferences** (such as privacy settings).

Another trend is the ability to gather together content from a wide variety of services. For example, a service like TweetDeck allows you to create categories of information and collect comments from contacts on services such as Twitter and Facebook in one place.

It's been suggested that in the future all websites will have social networking features, and in fact that movement is already underway. For example, Windows Live, which started as an email and calendar service, now allows you to build a friends network, as do some bookmarking sites. You may also be able to use your social media account to log in to interactive features of other media websites, such as the comments feature for online newspapers. Social media has become a real-time reporting tool. Recent changes in government regimes in the Middle East spread through the use of social media. What could that mean to the way we share knowledge, do business, become aware of global social causes, and report the news?

> " Social networking in the enterprise will break down . . . barriers and provide equal access to information across levels and job functions. "
>
> ▶▶▎Luosheng Peng, CEO Gageln

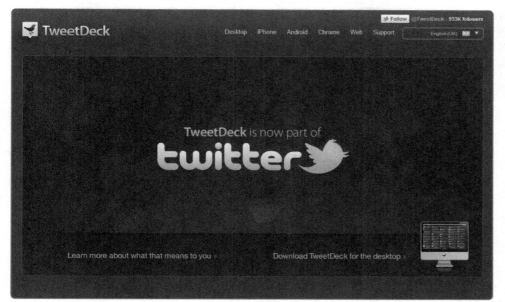

TweetDeck, owned by Twitter, allows you to gather contacts and content from various sites in one place.

Take the Next Step *online*

Activity 7.2.1 Flash Movie	*How can TweetDeck help you organize your communications?*	**CORE** CONTENT

| Activity 7.2.2 Research | *What is changing in social technology?* | |

7.3 Blogging: The Internet Gets Personal

A blog is an online journal that anybody can use to express ideas and opinions online. A blog may be focused around a particular topic, such as animal rights, or simply be a random collection of personal thoughts. Blogs can contain text, images and videos, and links to other online content. Most sites that host blogs allow bloggers to set a level of privacy that determines who can view their content.

People who read blogs can post comments about blog entries. Blogs and responses to them are typically listed in reverse chronological order, with the most recent posting at the top.

How Blogging Has Evolved

Blogging was begun on a small scale in the mid-1990s, but gained popularity in 1999 when blogging tools became more generally available to the public with blog hosting services such as LiveJournal.com and Blogger.com.

Over time blogging has moved into many online settings. Today you may create your blog on a blog hosting site, or you may post to a blog that is part of a social

Blogging on technology trends is a popular use of the blog technology.

networking site such as Facebook or Bebo. Companies often host blogs on their websites where they can share information with their customers and listen to their customers' opinions through product reviews. Experts write columns on sites such as ZDNet and The Huffington Post, finding a new way to reach a readership.

Blogs are incredibly popular, but it's interesting to consider some of the consequences of people posting their opinions and thoughts before millions of others. Blogging has been the subject of lawsuits when postings slander another person or organization. Some governments have cracked down on political blogs that challenge government policy. Job seekers have begun to realize that employers read personal information they have posted online and consider that content in their hiring decisions.

Computers in Your Career

If you have an interest in journalism as a career, you'll find that your chosen world is undergoing major changes. Journalism once provided a "one speaking to many" model, but blogging has brought a new dynamic of two-way communication. Old models of print newspapers are being challenged, but the Internet is also bringing new opportunities. For example, mobile phone journalism (MoJo) offers the ability to report instantly from the field via mobile phones. According to John S. Carroll, former editor of the *Los Angeles Times*, "Journalism…is now a conversation with millions of participants, which gives us access to new facts and new ideas. Thanks to hyperlinks, you can write accordion-like stories that can be expanded to match each reader's degree of interest. The journalism of the future will be flexible, making fluid use of video, audio, and text to tell stories as they can best be told." Though these possible future opportunities may be stimulating to consider, for now journalism is a field fraught with uncertainty.

The Many Uses of Blogs

Many blogs are simply personal journals chronicling a person's day or opinions. But today blogs are also used in many other settings. Blogs have now taken on a role in reporting news stories and providing a soapbox for experts or "pundits" on topics from politics to the environment. Governments of various countries such as Israel host official blogs where citizens can voice their opinions. People who spot technology and social trends find huge audiences for their blogs, as do entertainers such as Oprah and other TV and movie stars. According to BlogPulse, as of 2010 there were 152 million blogs on the Internet.

A fascinating use of blogging is the use of the social Web by Egyptian protestors during the country's change in leadership. As foreign journalists were literally locked up in hotel rooms and websites were blocked, citizens sent messages to others to post on sites such as Facebook and Twitter. It was social networking that exposed the reality of the conditions in Egypt despite government attempts at repression of information.

Sites such as Twitter (referred to as **microblogging** or **social journaling** sites) are a newer form of social site. These sites focus on small details of everyday life by encouraging brief postings (140 characters maximum on Twitter) about a user's daily activities. Twitter established hope140.org to promote social movements to help the nation and the world. The popularity of microblogging is shown in its statistical growth. For example, it took three years, two months and one day for Twitter to reach its billionth tweet. In 2011, there are one billion tweets a week. On average, Twitter users are sending 50 million tweets per day.

> " So forget about blogs and bloggers and blogging and focus on this—the cost and difficulty of publishing absolutely anything, by anyone, into a global medium, just got a whole lot lower. And the effects of that increased pool of potential producers is going to be vast. "
>
> ▶▶| Clay Shirky, New Media Professor, New York University

Playing It Safe

On many sites that host blogs there are good policies regarding behavior, and blog moderators are there to keep contributors from acting abusively towards others. On other sites there is little supervision and therefore more risk for abuse by other bloggers, which usually takes the form of cyberbullying. You should choose sites that offer the support and control that fits your style and comfort level.

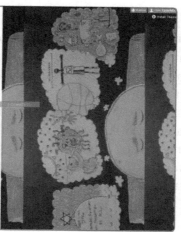

Some blogs combine artwork with text.

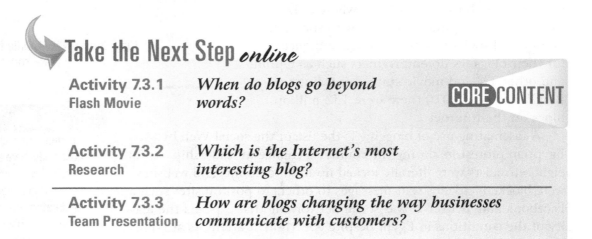

My Country Right or Wrong

Some people in more repressive countries use blogs to get ideas and information out to the world, even though that may be illegal. When is it OK for somebody to decide their country is in the wrong and violate its laws?

Take the Next Step *online*

| Activity 7.3.1 | *When do blogs go beyond* |
| Flash Movie | *words?* |

CORE CONTENT

| Activity 7.3.2 | *Which is the Internet's most* |
| Research | *interesting blog?* |

| Activity 7.3.3 | *How are blogs changing the way businesses* |
| Team Presentation | *communicate with customers?* |

7.4 Social Networking

A social networking site typically includes a blogging feature and the ability to share media, but what has traditionally differentiated social networking sites from other social sites is the ability to share contacts and build a network of friends.

However, when sites such as YouTube (a media sharing site) and Windows Live (traditionally an email service that has recently grown to include some social features) provide a way to build a list of friends, it's hard to identify what a social networking site is anymore. The lines get blurred as the ability to socialize is being built into a huge number and different types of websites.

The Amazing Growth of Social Networking

Online socializing began somewhere in the late 1970s when Usenet, ListServ, and the bulletin board system (BBS) appeared. These went from gathering places for those working on special government research projects to gathering places for those with shared interests.

In the 1980s, early Internet service providers such as CompuServe incorporated next generation bulletin boards called discussion forums. Discussion forums encouraged interaction with postings and responses displayed in discussion series called strings. Classmates.com came along in 1995 with a focus on providing virtual online class reunions. AOL then pushed social boundaries further with its use of searchable member profiles that allowed users to connect with each other. This allowed a sense of an online community, which was fundamental for the social networking phenomenon to come.

Friendster became one of the first social networking sites to catch on with the public in 2002. (The site's popularity in the United States dwindled, but it is still popular in Asia.) This was followed in 2003 by LinkedIn, which has a focus on career networking, and MySpace. In 2004, three Harvard University students launched Facebook as a college-student-only service. The site opened to the general public in 2006.

Launched in 2011, there is a new social network that has created a great deal of interest. The discussion is that Google+ will compete with Facebook, the most popular social networking site. Google+ introduced new features including Circles, Sparks, Hangouts, Huddles, and instant uploads on an Android mobile device. These features are designed to give the user more flexibility in what and how to share.

Today the social networking landscape is rich with a variety of social networking options besides Facebook or Google+. Some of the other popular social networks include LinkedIn, Grouply, Bebo, and ELGG. Many other sites include social features such as profiles, friends' lists, and media sharing capabilities.

> " As more companies and their workers tap into the world of Twitter, blogs and Facebook, employers are reacting with a command and control approach to social media. "
>
> ▶▶ Michael Fertik, Founder, Reputation.com

Interesting Trends for Social Networks

More than 148 million people use social networks and are integrating them into daily life. It is predicted that by 2013, social networking will be saturated and the growth in the percentage of Internet users accessing social networks, at least once a month, will level off. However, as social networking tools are being incorporated into nonsocial networking settings suggests that the social aspect of the Internet is here to stay in some form. The future is anyone's guess, but we can cite some of the current trends in social networking.

The growth of social networking has expanded to location-based mobile devices. Foursquare, a social media site, makes it possible to share your location with your friends. In addition, Foursquare allows users to locate interesting restaurants, activities, and businesses so they can share real world experiences. Foursquare and Google Places allow people to check in on a regular basis. In 2011, there were over 10 million Foursquare users.

One trend that's surfaced recently is higher usage of social networks by older people. Even though social networking is popular with young people, the real growth in social networking has occurred among users 50 and older. The social networking phenomenon continues to change the way generations use the social media technology. According to the Pew Research Center, Internet users between the ages of 18 and 29 showed a slight growth in social media

Playing It Safe

People typically want a lot of friends, but having too many friends on a social networking site can be problematic. Be cautious of allowing friends of friends to have access to your page. Remember that a friend of a friend is often a stranger. Protect your privacy accordingly.

use—13 percent. There has been an 88 percent growth in using social networking by Internet users between the ages of 50 and 64 years, and 100 percent growth for those over the age of 65 years.

Figure 7.2 illustrates how the demographic of social networking is changing in the different generational groups.

Facebook began as a college student social networking site. Today, even federal organizations such as NASA have a Facebook page.

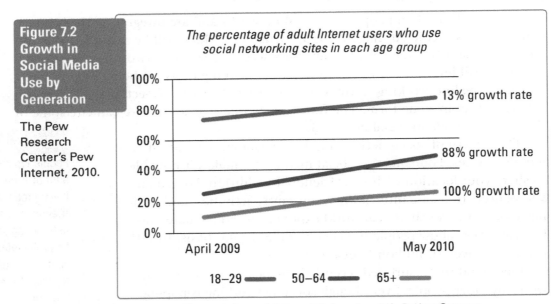

Figure 7.2 Growth in Social Media Use by Generation

The Pew Research Center's Pew Internet, 2010.

The percentage of adult Internet users who use social networking sites in each age group

13% growth rate
88% growth rate
100% growth rate

April 2009   May 2010

18–29   50–64   65+

Source: Pew Research Center's Internet & American Life Project Surveys, September 2005–May 2010. All surveys are of adults 18 and older.

Our Digital World

What Is the Future of Facebook?

With more than 750 million registered users, Facebook is the world's dominant Internet social network. Will Facebook always be the leading social network? Can anyone mount a serious challenge to Facebook?

Knocking Facebook off its perch is possible but not likely anytime in the near future, according to technology journalist Dwight Silverman.

"Facebook is the place most of us go to connect with friends and family online because it does a good job facilitating our impulse to be social in a vast, disorderly medium where we don't see each other in person," says Silverman. "It takes the chaos of the Web and tames it."

It's the social connections we've already made through Facebook that will ensure we keep using the service in the foreseeable future, even as many users find plenty they don't like about Facebook. "It's very much like putting roots down in a small town—you're hesitant to leave because all of your friends are there," says Silverman.

Still, technology and Internet companies have a way of seeming dominant until something unexpected makes them less attractive.

"There may be something we don't see yet about Facebook's model that, when something new comes along, it will not be able to respond to or it will not fit," according to Silverman.

Listen to the Chapter 7 Spotlight on the Future podcast and then be prepared to answer the following questions.

Talk about It

1. How did Facebook become so dominant?
2. Can you name a company that once ruled the Internet but then seemingly lost its way?
3. What's one development in technology that could give Facebook trouble?
4. What is Silverman's opinion about the future of Google+?
5. Does Silverman consider Twitter to be a major player in the social media scene?

Another trend reported is the rapid adoption of mobile use of social networks (so-called **social mobile media**), spurred in large part by iPhone and Android smartphone users. This trend is illustrated in Table 7.1. People are using mobile phones to access their social networking pages, upload pictures and videos they capture with their phones, ask questions through sites such as ChaCha, and send thoughts on the fly to their blogs.

Social networks are reaching beyond online communication to connect with events in our offline lives. Sites such as Socializr, Punchbowl, and Evite have become popular for organizing social events. People post events, send RSVPs, and later post event photos which they can pull onto the event site from Facebook or Flickr.

Table 7.1 A Comparison of Minutes per Day Spent on Social Networking on Mobile Devices and PC Desktops

Social Network	Minutes per Day	
	Mobile Internet	PC Internet
Facebook	45.2	32.4
Bebo (AOL)	39.6	22
MySpace	8.2	7.5
Twitter	19.6	7.2

Source: GSMA/ComScore, January 2010.

A new term has emerged in social networking. **Mocial** refers to using a social networking engine such as Facebook, Twitter, foursquare, or Google Places through any mobile device. The mobile device is used to connect with others and to use apps that are designed to search for people, events, or businesses. Mocial is gaining popularity as a device used by businesses to reach customers on the go. They are using email, Facebook, Twitter and other services to reach their customers.

A new trend involving services such as Groupon, Living Social, and Vouchercloud, provides users with discount coupons/vouchers that may be delivered through a mobile device. These services also provide users the opportunity to share these coupons with friends.

Computers in Your Career

Many people today use social tools to market themselves to employers. They use networking sites such as LinkedIn to connect with other professionals, and spend time posting comments on blogs on sites related to their career interest to create online credentials potential employers make note of. Some produce podcasts or upload videos about their area of expertise on media sharing or job posting sites to get noticed, or to post an online portfolio on their own websites. Next time you're job hunting, consider using the social Web to help you land a job.

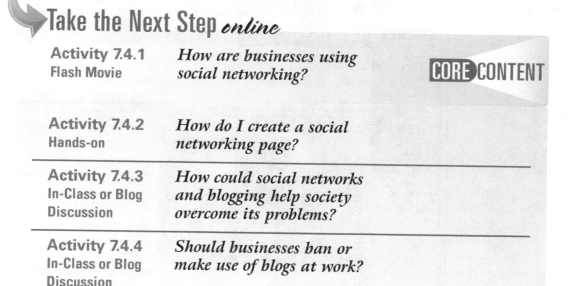

Take the Next Step *online*

Activity 7.4.1 Flash Movie	*How are businesses using social networking?*	CORE CONTENT
Activity 7.4.2 Hands-on	*How do I create a social networking page?*	
Activity 7.4.3 In-Class or Blog Discussion	*How could social networks and blogging help society overcome its problems?*	
Activity 7.4.4 In-Class or Blog Discussion	*Should businesses ban or make use of blogs at work?*	

7.5 Social Bookmarking

Though the social Web is in flux, one thing everybody can agree on is that the Web contains a huge number of websites and a wealth of content. One form of social networking that helps users organize and recommend content to each other is social bookmarking. Using sites such as Symbaloo and StumbleUpon, people can share online content that they feel is useful with individuals and groups, and organize that content in personal libraries.

How Social Bookmarking Works

Social bookmarking allows you to make note of online content in the form of tags, called **bookmarks**, and share those bookmarks with others. The technology uses **metadata**, which is essentially data about data. In other words, metadata describes the location or nature of other data, allowing software such as a browser to organize and retrieve that data easily.

Bookmarking sites save bookmarks as tags rather than saving links in folders as the Favorites features of some browsers do. A **tag** is a keyword assigned to information on the Web that is used by social bookmarking sites to locate and organize content references. Because you can sort through and organize tags, this makes social bookmarks much easier to search and catalogue.

> " Social bookmarking has become a phenomenon in the last couple of years. As more individuals join these social networks, the news and what is deemed important is now driven by consumers—a fundamental shift on how information was prioritized in the past. "
>
> ▶▶ Michael Fleischner, Internet Marketing Expert

The Web is riddled with logo links like these that allow you to connect with bookmarking and other types of social services.

StumbleUpon helps you discover and share online resources.

A Wealth of Social Bookmarking Services

Today you will find tools on many sites that allow you to bookmark them instantly. Look for logos for services such as Digg, Reddit, StumbleUpon, and Amplify on your favorite website, or locate a Share icon that, when clicked, displays a variety of tools that allow you to share your recommendations.

Take the Next Step *online*

| Activity 7.5.1 Video | *How are people using social bookmarks?* | CORE CONTENT |
| Activity 7.5.2 Hands-on | *How can a social bookmarking site such as Diigo help you research a topic?* | |

7.6 Wikis

The social Web isn't only for swapping personal stories or photos. **Wikis** provide a way to share knowledge about every topic under the sun in the form of online visual libraries, encyclopedias, and dictionaries. Wikis enable people to post content and edit content in a way that creates a living network of knowledge to which anybody can contribute.

What's a Wiki?

According to http://wiki.org, a wiki "is a piece of server software that allows users to freely create and edit web page content using any web browser." The wiki technology supports hyperlinks and enables users to create links between internal pages. Wikis allow users to not only edit the content, but change the organization of that content as well. Wiki content can then be searched by users to find the information they need.

The wiki "open editing" model encourages anybody and everybody to contribute his or her experience and knowledge in text, audio, or video format. When you use the edit feature in a wiki, it opens the content as a document that you can modify. You can add and edit text or graphics and insert links to other documents. You then save your changes so that others can view and edit the updated document.

This open editing model can make the accuracy of the content less verifiable. Some sites, such as Wikipedia, have systems in place to monitor postings and edits and note where additional clarification or authentication is needed.

A wiki can be a valuable learning tool that can be integrated into courses for students of all ages.

Who's Using Wikis?

You can use wikis to coordinate projects, trips, parties, or build online stores of shared information in the form of encyclopedias or dictionaries. Authors, artists, collectors, journalists, educators, scientists, researchers, technologists, and business people are making use of wikis to collaborate on creative works or build business policies and procedures. People who share interests are using wikis to build content communities. In business, where companies often have to get client approval of designs or campaigns, wikis help streamline the process and keep everybody in the loop.

Here are some interesting uses of wikis you might want to check out:

- Memory-Alpha.org is a wiki where anybody can contribute and edit an encyclopedia about all things Star Trek.
- WikiTravel.org is an open content travel guide with advice and information from thousands of travellers.
- Wiktionary is an open, web-based dictionary that provides definitions, pronunciations, and the history (etymology) of words contributed by users.
- Anatowiki.wetpaint.com is a wiki about human anatomy that grew out of a class project.

What interesting wikis can you find online?

Take the Next Step *online*

7.7 Media Sharing

Just as people want to share stories in blogs and knowledge in wikis, people are also sharing files. When you view, download, or exchange media files such as music, videos, or photos, it's referred to as **media sharing**. Sites such as YouTube, Flickr, Picasa, and Slideshare are examples of media sharing sites.

The media sharing trend began with MP3 music file sharing in the late 1990s using services such as Napster and Gnutella. MP3 sites have gone through some legal challenges because they have distributed the work of musicians and artists freely, sometimes violating copyright protections.

Sites such as YouTube tap into the grassroots version of media sharing where individuals freely post their content in a bid for a moment of online fame. Many media sharing sites use **live media streaming**, a technology that allows them to send the content over the Internet in **live broadcasts**.

Playing It Safe

When sharing media or any content over the Internet, be aware of copyright laws and requirements. Some sites, such as Wikipedia, allow you to freely copy and share their content. Others, such as YouTube, allow you to direct people to shared content by using links to their site, but do not allow you to distribute user content yourself.

A conversation focused on shared images on Voicethread.

How Media Sharing Works

You can easily create your own media and share it with others online. Some sites allow you to record your media right from the site; others require that you record it offline using a camera, voice, or video recorder. Media that you create in the form of a digital file can be shared as an email attachment, sent through instant messages, or posted on sites where people can then download the file.

Media is shared on many social networking sites and blogs, in web-based communities, social bookmarking sites, as well as on more specialized media sharing sites such as Flickr and YouTube.

Voicethread is an interesting example of a site that combines media sharing with the ability to hold a conversation about the media. You can even record voice comments from your computer or any phone, including cell phones, and navigate the site through voice commands.

> "At CUNY's Graduate School of Journalism . . . we just told the students that they no longer need to commit to a media track—print, broadcast, or interactive. We believe this is the next step in convergence. All media become one."
>
> ▶▶ Jeff Jarvis, *Columbia Journalism Review*

How People Are Using Media Sharing

People are using media sharing in a variety of ways. Some artists are promoting their work by sharing it in online portfolios. People collaborating on projects such as website design may share media in environments that allow each person to comment or annotate the media file. Some media sharing sites and software allow you to build personal playlists of the media you find online.

A popular trend is to post product reviews or tutorials, for example, showing features of new cell phone models. Businesses and nonprofit organizations can use services such as Radian6.com to troll the Internet and find content related to a theme. For example, they can find posted videos that relate to their products or brand so they can learn what their customers think of them. In response to this feedback, they can make changes or improvements.

Sites such as FriendFeed allow you to import playlists from several services and even let you share your content through Twitter and Facebook. You can also post your customized list of media content on your own website or blog.

FriendFeed lets you share media with colleagues or friends.

Ethics and Technology Blog *online*

Posting Photos of Others to a Media Sharing Site

Do you think it's OK to take a picture or video of another person and post it online without permission?

Take the Next Step *online*

Activity 7.7.1 Flash Movie	*How do you share video online?*	**CORE CONTENT**
Activity 7.7.2 Research	*How do you find what you want on media sharing sites?*	
Activity 7.7.3 In-Class or Blog Discussion	*How did your parents or grandparents share images?*	

Review and Assessment *online*

Social Technology Comes of Age

Any site that allows users to interact with each other and share information is a social site, and together, these social sites make up the **social Web**. A site that allows you to share contacts and build a network of "friends" is a **social networking site**. Using social media technology, people can blog, network, post wikis, and share media such as photos, videos, and music.

Blogging: The Internet Gets Personal

A **blog** (short for web log) is an online journal that may be focused around a particular topic or simply be a random collection of personal thoughts. Blogs can contain text, images and videos, and links to other online content. Many blogs focus on the written word, but there are also blogs that use other kinds of content, such as **artblogs**, **sketchblogs**, and **photoblogs**.

People who read blogs can post comments. Blogs and comments are listed in reverse chronological order, with the most recent posting at the top.

You may create your blog on a blog hosting site, or you may post to a blog that is part of a social networking site. Companies often host blogs on their websites, and blogs have taken on an important role in reporting news stories. Sites such as Twitter that use brief comments are called **microblogging** sites.

Social Networking

Social networking sites typically include a blogging feature and the ability to share media, but what differentiates them from other social sites is the ability to share contacts and build a network of friends. Many websites today include social networking types of features such as profiles, friends' lists, and media sharing capabilities.

Social networking trends include higher use by older people and the rapid adoption of **social mobile media**. The social Web is also creating some great opportunities for businesses and organizations which have their own pages on sites such as Facebook where they can interact with their customers. The term **mocial** means using a social networking engine such as Facebook, Twitter, foursquare, or Google Places through any mobile device.

Social Bookmarking

Social bookmarking helps users organize and recommend content to each other. This technology uses **metadata**, which is data about data. Bookmarking sites save users' **bookmarks** as **tags**. Because you can sort through and organize bookmark tags, it's easy for you to search and catalogue information.

Wikis

Wikis are a way to share knowledge about any topic in the form of online visual libraries, encyclopedias, and dictionaries. Wikis enable people to post content and edit content in a way that creates a living network of knowledge to which anybody can contribute.

Media Sharing

Viewing, downloading, or exchanging media files such as music, videos, or photos is referred to as **media sharing**. Many media sharing sites use **live media streaming**, a technology that allows them to send the content over the Internet in real-time broadcasts.

Media is shared on many social networking sites and blogs, in web-based communities, social bookmarking sites, and in more specialized media sharing sites such as Flickr and YouTube.

Terms to Know

CORE CONTENT

Media Sharing

media sharing, 224
live media streaming, 224
live broadcast, 224

Concepts Check

Concepts Check 7.1   Multiple Choice
Take this quiz to test your understanding of key concepts in this chapter.

Concepts Check 7.2   Word Puzzle
Complete this puzzle to test your knowledge of key terms in this chapter.

Concepts Check 7.3   Matching
Test your understanding of terms and concepts presented in this chapter.

Concepts Check 7.4   Arrange It
Use the interactive tool to identify the steps for creating a blog.

Projects

Check with your instructor for the preferred method to submit completed project work.

Project 7.1   Using Social Technologies in Business

Project 7.1.1   Individual
Identify a company that is using some form of social technology, such as blogging, microblogging, wikis, social bookmarking, social networking, or media sharing. Determine the types of social websites that the company uses, its strategies in maintaining these sites, the use of these sites to reinforce the messages on the company's website, and the ability of these sites to attract interest from diverse age-groups.

Project 7.1.2   Team
As a team, brainstorm a start-up business that you would like to launch. Write down the name of your business and the types of products or services that your company will offer. Establish your target audience and recognize your market competition. Discuss the ways in which social technology could be an effective communications and marketing tool to attract potential customers. Then document the various steps that a business would take to operate a business page on Facebook. Prepare a web-based presentation that introduces your business venture and outlines your Facebook business plan.

Project 7.2   Gaining Experience with Blogging

Project 7.2.1   Individual

To understand the purposes, types, benefits/drawbacks, and popularity of blogging, research a variety of blogs on the Web. Join a blog that interests you, and actively engage in a dialog with other users by posting information and commentary. Prepare a memo that identifies your blog and describes your blogging experience. Include a transcript of your dialog exchange in the memo.

Project 7.2.2   Team

Go to the Chapter 7 class blog. As a group, find a news story of interest, and summarize the story on the class blog. Then have each team member respond to the summary by posting a blog entry once a day for a week. At the end of the week, prepare a transcript of the blog. Be prepared to discuss your exchange of ideas and opinions in class. Submit the transcript as well as your reference source for the news article to your instructor.

Project 7.3   How Are Social Networking Sites Being Used Today?

Project 7.3.1   Individual

Many colleges and universities today have their own social networking sites for their students. Go to your college home page, and locate the school's social networking site. If your college does not have a social networking site, find a school that does have one. Where did you find the site? Is it current? Are there many participants? Does the site contain text, audio, photos, and/or videos? Prepare a summary of your findings.

Project 7.3.2   Team

As a team, investigate the impact of social networking on the 2011 change in leadership in the Middle East. Determine the types of sites that were used, the topics that were discussed, the number of participants, and so on. Then, based on your research, predict the role that social networking might play in the future global political arena. Prepare a presentation of your team's findings and predictions.

Project 7.4   Sharing Through Media

Project 7.4.1   Individual

Create a slideshow résumé. Post your presentation on www.slideshare.net. Adjust your privacy settings so that your presentation can only be shared with your instructor and your class.

Project 7.4.2   Team

Using a video recording device, create a team video about one of the topics presented in this chapter. Upload your video to YouTube and share the link with your instructor.

Project 7.5   Wiki—Building an Online Policy

Project 7.5.1   Team

You are employed at a large publishing company that produces newspapers and magazines. Recently, several of your publications have been posted online, and your company has created blogs on these sites. You are in charge of writing the blogging policies. Write a policy on the class wiki that addresses the following user issues:

- standards for appropriate behavior or content
- reporting of inappropriate behavior or content
- privacy safeguards

Before you begin writing, review the policies of mainstream blogging sites for ideas. When you have finished your blogging guidelines, submit the document to your instructor. Be sure to include any references that you used in creating your document.

Project 7.5.2   Team

As a team, use the tools in PollDaddy or SurveyMonkey to create a survey on the use of social technology. For example, you may want to ask your survey participants how they are using personalized start pages or how blogging has benefited their business. Have each team member distribute the survey to 10 friends or family members. Share your survey results on the class wiki. When you post or edit content, make sure you include a notation within the page that includes your name or the team members' names and the date you posted or edited the content—for example, "Posted/edited by [your name or team members' names] on [date]."

Class Conversations

Topic 7.1   What Privacy Issues Does the Social Web Create?
The social Web is used by millions of people from many cultures and backgrounds. With so many people using these technologies, one issue that users face is privacy. What privacy protections do social networking sites offer? What is meant by your social footprint? How could what you post on the Web today have an impact on your future?

Topic 7.2   How Could You Use Social Technologies to Make a Better World?
You work for a nonprofit organization working for a cleaner environment. How could you use social technologies to raise awareness and get new members and support? Discuss ways to use a wiki, blogs, media sharing, microblogging, and social bookmarking in a campaign to encourage people to take public transportation or walk rather than drive a car.

Topic 7.3   Business Use of the Social Web
People have jumped on the social Web to connect with each other, but businesses are beginning to use these tools to sell products and services to people. Should businesses be allowed to insert advertising into what was meant to be a way to hold a social dialog?

Digital Defense
Securing Your Data and Privacy

What You'll Accomplish

When you finish this chapter, you'll be able to:

- Recognize and protect against risks associated with operating a computer connected to a network and the Internet.
- Explain various types of malware and tools used to protect against them.
- Understand how to identify a trusted online site.
- Understand security risks associated with mobile devices.
- Identify risks to hardware and software and develop strategies to reduce the risk of physical or economic loss.

Why Should I Care?

Would you leave your bank card and PIN number sitting on an empty table in a food court at the mall? Would you leave your home for a vacation and not bother to lock the doors or windows? Most people who are used to protecting their wallets or houses may not take steps to guard their digital information against common threats. Even if you protect your computer with antivirus software, you might overlook routine tasks that can leave you vulnerable to losing important data. Everybody should learn the basic skills of computer security because replacing a computer is easy—replacing valuable data is not.

Chapter 8 Digital Defense: Securing Your Data and Privacy

Protecting the data on your computer and your personal information online are important concerns in our digital age. From firewalls and antivirus software to corporate security planning and protecting your mobile devices, learn about the tools available to stay secure.

ANTISPYWARE

Do a search on a news website any day of the week and you'll come up with stories like these:

- Spring 2011 saw technology giant Sony Corporation the target of a lawsuit after the company was forced to shut down its PlayStation 3 network because hackers accessed the network and stole data from more than 100 million users.
- In June 2011, Citibank reported that hackers had viewed account information for approximately one percent of its North American credit card customers, or an estimated 200,000 accounts.
- Google Inc. identified that hackers in China had broken into several hundred personal Gmail accounts, including those of account holders such as senior U.S. government officials, military personnel, and political activists.
- Two security professionals showed off an unmanned airplane they built for less than $10,000 at the August 2011 Black Hat cybersecurity conference in Las Vegas. According to its creators, the plane "can fly over a Starbucks and steal the personal information of everyone connected to the coffee shop's free Wi-Fi network. It can intercept your cell phone conversations and even reroute your calls to another number. It can trace the location of specific people and follow them home."

Computer security and safety are very much in the news and on the minds of both company executives and individual computer users. Just what's involved in computer security?

Computer Security: Where's the Threat?

Computer security, also referred to as information security, involves protecting the boundaries of your home or business network and individual computing devices from intruders. An important part of computer security is **data loss prevention (DLP)**, which involves minimizing the risk of loss or theft of data from within a network.

Security threats can come from malware (such as computer viruses). In some cases, companies find that employees' own negligence can cause a company to simply lose data, in which case you face the hard fact that your people have been your own worst enemy. Cyber attackers may damage or steal data and can come individually or in groups. Attacks may come from malicious **hackers** or organized crime, corporate spies, unethical employees, disgruntled colleagues, or, in the case of your home computer, from an ex-friend out to cyberbully you.

Finally it's important to recognize that proper security practices are not just a matter of individual protection but are also critical for the overall security of the Internet. If you allow your own PC to be co-opted by criminals to scam or spam others, you have become part of a bigger problem.

Figure 8.1 shows some of the measures you should put in place to keep your own digital world more secure.

What can happen if your information security is compromised? Companies can face enormous costs resulting from the theft of their intellectual property. Consider these

online ✓ **Take a Survey**
How secure is your computer?

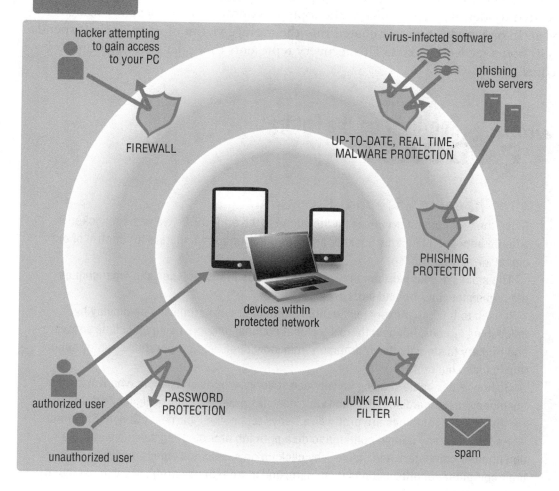

**Figure 8.1
The Secure PC**

Computer security is all about keeping data, from your company's recipe for soup to your own bank account information, safe from threats and loss.

findings from a report released in March 2011 by Ponemon Institute LLC (a research center for privacy, data protection, and information security policy):

- Among U.S. companies, about 85 percent have experienced one or more data breaches.
- The $35.3 million breech that was most expensive represented a 15 percent increase over the prior year's costliest breach.
- The average cost per incident to businesses for exposing data such as Social Security and credit card numbers increased 7 percent to $7.2 million.

In January 2010, Google admitted that it had been the target of an **advanced persistent threat (APT)** in what has been dubbed Operation Aurora by security company McAfee. An APT is a highly targeted, sophisticated attack tailored to a specific organization usually to gain access to sensitive information. Operation Aurora capitalized on a vulnerability in Microsoft's Internet Explorer to infiltrate Google and 30 other companies to obtain intellectual property. Security provider FireEye, Inc., in its white paper titled *Advanced Malware Exposed*, warns that targeted APTs are evading today's network defenses as criminals with profit motives or political agendas are behind the explosion of advanced malware.

For individuals, the primary security risk is identity theft (ID), and the associated costs are tallied not only in dollars but in time as well. According to the Federal Trade Commission (FTC), 19 percent of complaints received in 2010 were related to identity theft, which is the topmost concern for the eleventh straight year. In one study, it was estimated that the average victim of identity theft spends 330 hours recovering data. This recovery represents time spent on a full-time job equal to 8.25 weeks!

online Spotlight on the Future PODCAST

The Changing Face of Online Crime

Since the first computer viruses hit the scene in the early 1970s we've been locked in a battle between malicious hackers and guardians of our computers for control of our digital infrastructure.

The stakes are higher than they've ever been, as profit replaces showmanship as the prime motivator behind most attacks.

It used to be that hackers just wanted to put their nerd credibility on display by unleashing viruses, but now there's a global criminal network using malicious software and trickery to steal digital information from individuals and corporations—information that leads to big profits.

So how is this battle shaping up between security experts and people who would steal our money, credit card numbers, and very identities using the tools of digital warfare?

"At the moment things are pretty dire," says technology journalist Dwight Silverman.

As long as many people continue to do a poor job of protecting sensitive information on their computers and online—by clicking on suspicious emails, not keeping their computer security settings up to date, and more—things aren't likely to get much better, according to Silverman.

"People need to wise up when it comes to computer security."

Listen to the Chapter 8 Spotlight on the Future podcast and then be prepared to answer the following questions.

Talk about It

1. What are some recent digital attacks that Silverman references?
2. What is Silverman's opinion about the future of computer and network security?
3. What steps does Silverman advocate for improving computer security?
4. Does Silverman think there's a "magic bullet" that will greatly reduce computer crime? If so, what is it?
5. What is "spearfishing" in the context of computer crime?

Basic Tools of Computer Security

The tools you can use to protect your personal computer and information are similar to tools corporations use to protect their intellectual property. Both individuals and companies can implement authentication processes, security technologies, and user procedures to keep data safe.

Authentication involves the use of passwords and in some cases other identifiers such as fingerprints to make sure that the people accessing information are who they claim to be. For example, on your personal computer you can create a user name and password to ensure that others do not have access to your user account.

Technologies that help keep intruders out or defend against dangerous computer code include firewalls, encryption, and antivirus software, to name some key examples.

User procedures may be as simple as teaching your kids not to click on a link online that might download a virus, or as robust as a company-wide policy identifying who can access data and establishing procedures for backing up files to avoid data loss. Recent high-profile hacks into companies such as Sony and Google have companies reviewing, updating, and improving their security procedures. Operation Aurora initially started with employees clicking a link that took them to a malicious website where the Internet Explorer vulnerability was exploited to download malware onto the employees' computers. All computer users need to be suspicious of unsolicited links and follow their company's defined security practices daily.

McAfee antivirus software is one of the products people use to protect their personal computers from damaging viruses.

8.2 When Security Gets Personal

The increasing number of households connected to the Internet has also resulted in an increased need for vigilance by individuals to defend against cyber attacks, identity theft, and other types of fraud. In addition, loss or damage to data resulting from damaging programs inadvertently downloaded to a computer can be frustrating and costly. To date, most security problems have dogged Windows users, but as Mac and perhaps Linux grow their market shares, those systems are also becoming the target of criminals.

The increased use of mobile devices has turned hackers' attention to mobile apps. Android users were 2.5 times more likely to encounter malware on their device in

August 2011 than they were six months earlier. Mobile security firm Lookout reported that Android apps infected with malware rose from 80 in January to more than 400 in June.

Mobile security involves more than just worrying about downloading infected apps. Bluetooth users must also beware. Although Bluetooth connections are short-range, data can be intercepted and people can send files or viruses via these connections.

Protecting Your Home Network

If you have set up a home network that enables your computers to connect to the Internet and you haven't thought about security, it's as if you just installed a back-door to your house that's left wide open 24/7. An unprotected network means that anybody who is near your home can "piggyback" on your Internet connection, track your online activities, and possibly even hack into your computer.

There are several simple steps you can take to secure a home network. Wi-Fi home networks use an access point or router, a piece of equipment that comes with a preset password. The bad news is that these default passwords are pitifully predictable and simple. The good news is that you can go to your device manufacturer's website and find instructions for changing the password to something that is harder to guess.

Another important step in securing a home network is to use **encryption**, a part of cryptography, which is the study of

Routers have some built-in protections for your network, if you know how to use them.

creating algorithms and codes to protect data. Encryption scrambles a message so that it's unreadable to anybody who doesn't have the right key. Say you want your friend to send you a message that will contain data you want to protect. You use your computer to generate a **public key**, which you send to your friend. Your friend applies the key, which encrypts the message, and sends the message to you. Your computer then applies a **private key**, known only to you, to decrypt the message. Because the message is encrypted, nobody but the intended recipient can read it. Figure 8.2 shows this example of the **public key encryption** process. Two popular forms of encryption are **Wi-Fi Protected Access (WPA)** and **Wired Equivalent Privacy (WEP)**.

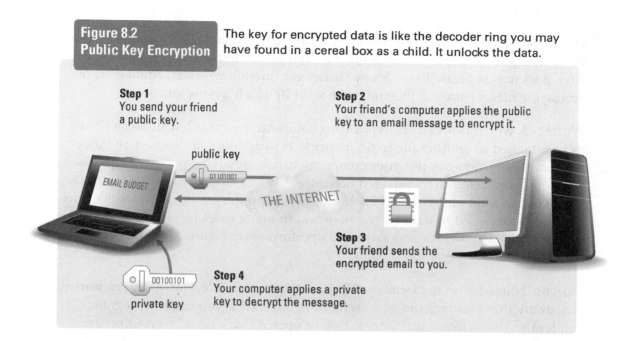

Figure 8.2 Public Key Encryption

The key for encrypted data is like the decoder ring you may have found in a cereal box as a child. It unlocks the data.

Step 1
You send your friend a public key.

Step 2
Your friend's computer applies the public key to an email message to encrypt it.

Step 3
Your friend sends the encrypted email to you.

Step 4
Your computer applies a private key to decrypt the message.

EMAIL BUDGET

public key

THE INTERNET

private key

The Menace of Malware

Collectively, nasty computer programs such as viruses and spyware are called **malware** (*mal* meaning bad or evil in Latin and *ware* referring to software). Malware installs itself on your computer without your knowledge and consent. Malware can do anything from pelting you with pop-up window advertisements to destroying your data or tracking your online activities with an eye toward stealing your identity or money.

In the early days of computers, individual hackers often planted viruses just to aggravate people or exploit a technological weakness. Today, most malware is created by less-than-ethical businesses, organized gangs, or criminals who aim to download dangerous code to your computer, co-opt your email contact list to send out **spam** (mass emails), or perform other illegal activities for profit-based motives. Here are descriptions of some common forms of malware.

Viruses A computer **virus** is a type of computer program that can reproduce itself, which is the way it spreads from computer to computer, by attaching itself to another, seemingly innocent, file. Viruses duplicate when the user runs an infected program. A typical scenario is that a virus is part of an attachment to an email.

Ethics and Technology Blog *online*

Taking Advantage of an Unsecured Network

My apartment is next door to a café that offers Internet access. I hardly ever go to the café, but because I can pick up its Internet connection from my apartment, I do. It saves me lots of money. Does anybody think that's a problem?

When the user opens the attachment, the program runs and the virus is duplicated. If the user does not open the attachment—and therefore run the program—the virus does not duplicate itself. Many viruses eat through your data, damaging or destroying files. Figure 8.3 illustrates the ways in which a virus attacks.

Worms A **worm** is also a self-replicating computer program but it doesn't have to be attached to another file to do its work. A worm does not require the user to do anything. You can put your computer at risk merely by powering up your computer connected to an infected network. A worm has the nasty ability to use a network to send out copies of itself to every computer on the network. Worms are usually designed to damage the network, in many cases by simply clogging up the network's bandwidth and slowing its performance. Figure 8.4 shows how a worm attacks.

Trojans Named after the infamous Trojan horse of Greek legend, a **Trojan horse** is malware that masquerades as a useful program. When you run the program, you let the Trojan into your system. Trojans open a "back door" to your system for malicious hackers, just as the Trojan horse allowed invaders to enter a city and then attack from within. Figure 8.5 shows how a Trojan horse attacks. Trojans are becoming more sophisticated, often disguising themselves as authentic operating system or antivirus warning messages that, when clicked, download the Trojan malware to your computer or mobile device.

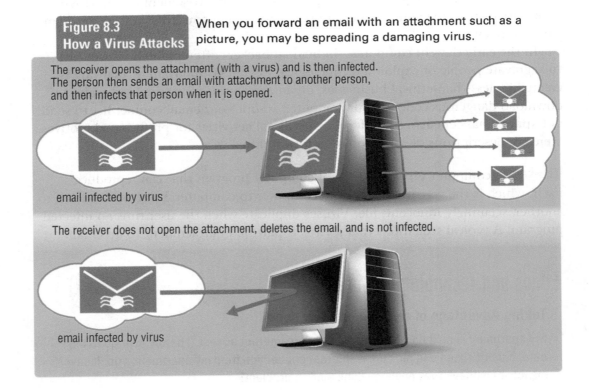

Figure 8.3 How a Virus Attacks When you forward an email with an attachment such as a picture, you may be spreading a damaging virus.

The receiver opens the attachment (with a virus) and is then infected. The person then sends an email with attachment to another person, and then infects that person when it is opened.

email infected by virus

The receiver does not open the attachment, deletes the email, and is not infected.

email infected by virus

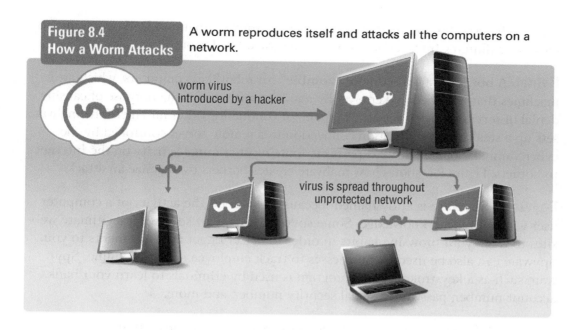

Figure 8.4 How a Worm Attacks

A worm reproduces itself and attacks all the computers on a network.

worm virus introduced by a hacker

virus is spread throughout unprotected network

Figure 8.5 How a Trojan Horse Attacks

A Trojan horse pretends to be a useful program but ends up opening your system to hackers.

hacker

Step 1
A hacker introduces a Trojan horse virus.

Step 2
The Trojan horse virus opens a "back door."

Step 3
The hacker gains access to computer through "back door."

Macro Viruses and Logic Bombs Other malicious programs such as macro viruses and logic bombs are small pieces of code embedded in a program. A **macro virus** is usually found in documents such as word processing and spreadsheets and can corrupt the computer when the user opens the document and executes the macro (a recorded series of keystrokes that can be played back to perform a task). A **logic bomb virus** might be placed in a software system to set off a series of damaging events if certain conditions are met (for example, if you try to delete a set of files).

Rootkit A **rootkit** is a set of programs or utilities designed to gain access to the "root" of a computer system or the system software that controls the hardware and software. With this access, a hacker can then monitor the user's actions. This can take place on an individual system or on a network system. An important aspect of a rootkit is that it cannot be detected, at least not easily, by the user (or the administrator, in the case of a network). While rootkits can serve harmful purposes, they can also be used for legitimate purposes. For example, programs used by parents to monitor children's Internet activities can be considered rootkits.

Botnet A **botnet** is a collection of "**zombie**" (or robotlike) computers, which are machines that have been taken over by malware software for the purpose of causing denial-of-service attacks, generating spam, or conducting other mischief. The malware sets up a stealth communication connection to a remote server controlled by the cybercriminal. Some security experts attribute most criminal activity on the Internet to botnets. Figure 8.6 shows how malware creates botnets to organize an attack.

Spyware **Spyware** is aptly named, because it spies on the activity of a computer user without his/her knowledge. Some spyware is used by somewhat legitimate websites to track your browsing habits in order to better target advertisements to you. Spyware can also be used by businesses to track employee activities online. Spyware such as a keystroke logging program is used by criminals to learn your bank account number, passwords, social security number, and more.

Adware **Adware** is a piece of software designed to deliver ads, often in pop-up form and usually unwelcome, to users' desktops. A related software is called ad-supported software, which shareware writers allow to be included in their programs to help pay for development effort and time.

Scareware **Scareware** is a scam where an online warning or pop-up convinces a user that his or her computer is infected with malware or has another problem that can be fixed by purchasing and downloading software. In reality, the downloaded software may not be functional or may itself be malware. These scams primarily are used to steal the user's money and credit card information. One scareware attack in May 2011 targeted Mac computers long thought to be safer, but attacks on Macs are on the rise.

Figure 8.6 How Malware Uses Botnets Your computer can be taken over by bots and used to send spam or malware to others.

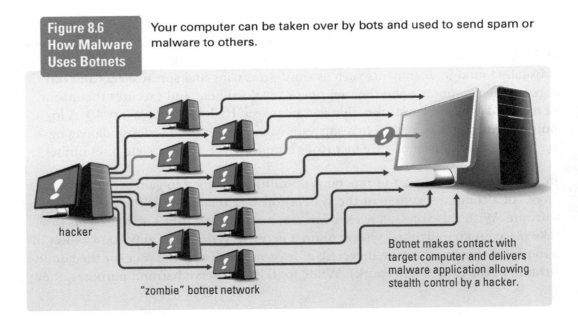

hacker

"zombie" botnet network

Botnet makes contact with target computer and delivers malware application allowing stealth control by a hacker.

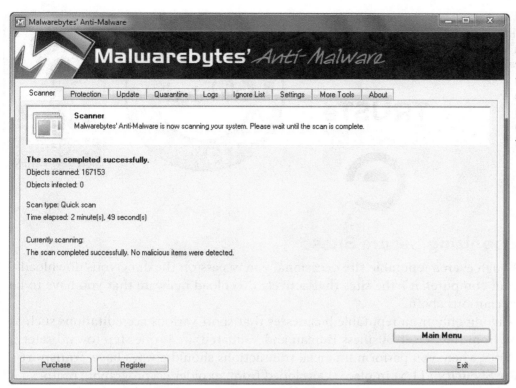

Products such as Malwarebytes' Anti-Malware scan your computer for any malware; some help prevent it from downloading in the first place.

How Is Malware Spread?

There are several ways in which malware, depending on its nature, can be spread:

- You can infect your computer by clicking on an email attachment that contains an executable file.
- Pictures you download can carry viruses stored in a single pixel of the image.
- Visiting an infected website can spread malware.
- Viruses can spread from a computer storage device such as a DVD or flash drive that you use on an infected computer and then insert into another computer drive.
- Worms can spread by simply connecting your computer to an infected network.
- Mobile devices can be infected by downloading an app, ringtone, game, or theme that carries malware.
- A mobile device with Bluetooth enabled in "discoverable mode" could be infected simply by coming within 30 feet of another Bluetooth device that has been infected and is running the same operating system.

Security threats are a reality in our digital world. What's also true is that several programs and technical tools are available to protect your computer against these potential hazards, as you'll read about later in the chapter. In addition, knowing how to recognize trustworthy websites and how to manage cookies are two proactive strategies everyone can use.

Playing It Safe

Be especially cautious when you receive a chain letter via email. These are often simply devices for delivering malware or collecting email addresses for the purpose of building spam lists.

Look for these symbols from various organizations that verify the secure practices of sites.

Recognizing Secure Sites

Although even a reputable site occasionally may pass on the dangerous download to your computer, it's the sites that actively download malware that you have to be most cautious about.

Buying only from reputable businesses that sport various accreditations such as those from the Better Business Bureau and ValidatedSite is one step toward safety.

Sites where you perform financial transactions should always have **Transport Layer Security (TLS)** in place. Developed from an older cryptographic protocol called **Secure Socket Layer (SSL)**, TLS is a protocol that protects data such as credit card numbers as they are being transmitted between a customer and online vendor or payment company. In more recent web browser versions, you can tell when you are using TLS, in two different ways: "http" in the address line is replaced with "https," and a small closed padlock appears next to the address bar or in the status bar of the window.

Another useful tool is a product such as McAfee Site Advisor, or similar tools built into browsers and security programs. These display an icon next to sites in your search results indicating websites that are known to have doubtful business practices or to routinely pass on malware to visitors.

It may be safer to do business with retailers you know from the "brick-and-mortar" world, and always type a URL into your browser to go to a site rather than clicking on a link in an email or advertisement.

Managing Cookies (Hold the Milk)

A **cookie** is a file stored on your computer by a web server to track information about you and your activities. Cookies can be completely harmless and perhaps helpful. For example, if you shop at an online store often, when you next visit that site you might find that the store knows your name and has suggestions of items that might interest you. Sites can provide this personalized service by reading the information stored in the cookie.

Playing It Safe

When browsing online, your best defense is common sense. Free offers aren't really free and often mask dangerous downloads. Clicking on links in advertisements may buy you malware. Clicking on an attachment in an email you weren't expecting can get you a world of computer trouble. Don't leave your common sense behind when you go online.

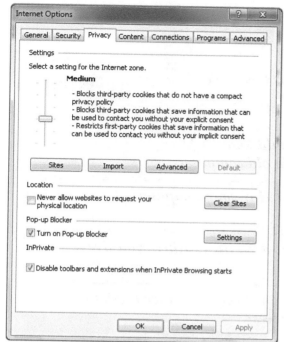

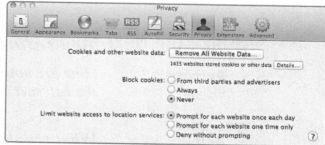

Both PC- and Mac-based browsers allow you to set privacy levels that in part control how cookies should be handled.

However, some companies or individuals plant cookies on your computer for other reasons. They may be trying to track your activities to gather enough information to steal your identity, for example.

Every major browser has tools and settings for dealing with cookies. For example, in Internet Explorer, you can use the Internet Options to set Privacy to accept all cookies, block cookies from certain sources, or block all cookies.

Foiling Phishers (No Catch Today)

Phishing (pronounced *fishing*) refers to the practice of sending email that appears to be from a legitimate organization in an attempt to scam the user into revealing information. Typically, the revealed information is used for identity theft. The email directs the user to click a link, which goes to a bogus website that appears valid, containing logos and color schemes that simulate the real organization's branding. The bogus site prompts the user to update personal information such as the user's user name, password, credit card number, or bank account number. Once you click these links and enter your information, you've basically handed over your sensitive information to criminals.

Delete any messages you receive that ask you to update information in a financial or retail account. Never click links in email messages to bank or other financial websites—always enter the URL into your browser address field yourself.

Phishing is also a problem in social media sites such as Facebook and Twitter. Popular social media sites have a high volume of users, making them frequent targets for new scams. A survey in December 2010 found that 40 percent of social media users had encountered malicious attacks. Antivirus programs do not protect users in social network sites because the malware is operating as part of the social media application. Aryeh Goretsky, a researcher at ESET antivirus aptly says, "*Think before you click.*"

Take the Next Step *online*

8.3 Mobile Security

Computing no longer is just a sit-at-your-desk type of activity—it's mobile! Mobile is convenient, but it also brings its own security risks. Various settings and tools can help you keep your portable device and the information stored on it safer.

Protecting Your Laptop or Tablet and Precious Data

When you bring your computer with you, you're carrying a big investment in both dollars and data, so it's important that you protect it from theft and damage. Corporations are also struggling with protecting IT assets as their workforces begin to carry smaller devices, which can be more prone to being left behind by mistake or stolen. There are several devices, and procedures you can use to physically secure your laptop or tablet computer.

Locks When you ride your bike downtown, you probably secure it with a bike lock. Laptops have a comparable device that you can use to tie them to an airport chair or desk in a field office to deter potential thieves from snatching them. As with bike locks, the determined thief with enough time can cut this cable and get away with the goods, so it's only a slight deterrent.

Remote Tracking/Wiping For stronger protection, consider services such as LoJack for Laptops, which allow you to remotely delete data if your computer is stolen and use GPS to track your wayward laptop or tablet. For example, Norton Mobile Security enables you to track and lock your Android tablet remotely, and the iPad 2's Find My iPad feature enables you to map, lock, or wipe your iPad clean of data. Expect remote security options to increase as tablet technology evolves.

Traditional cable locks allow you to physically tie down a laptop. Fingerprint readers restrict access by matching authorized fingerprints.

Fingerprint Readers Many newer laptops include fingerprint readers. Because fingerprints are unique to each individual, being able to authenticate yourself with your own set of prints to gain access to your computer is a popular security feature. If somebody without a fingerprint match tries to get into the computer data, the system locks up.

Password Protection If you travel with a mobile computer, it's a very good idea to activate password protection and create a secure password. If somebody steals your laptop or netbook and can't get past the password feature, he or she can't immediately get at your valuable data. Activate the passcode/lock feature on your tablet and configure the device to lock automatically if it is inactive for a set period of time. This action could help protect your data since there is a time lag from when you initially become aware of the loss of your device and when you take action. It is during this delayed response time that your data is particularly vulnerable. If your device doesn't include a password or locking feature, you can generally find and download an app that adds that capability.

Mobile Computing Policies for Employees Stopping thieves is one concern when you're on the road, but stopping employees from making costly mistakes regarding company data is another area where companies must take precautions. Making sure that employees who take company laptops or tablets outside of the office are responsible for safe and secure storage offsite is vital to company security. Policies might require them to keep backups of data on physical storage media such as a flash drive, or to back up data to a company network.

Using Wi-Fi Safely

If you travel and access the Internet using a public hotspot (a location that offers Wi-Fi access), you have to be very careful not to expose private information. Anything you send over a public network can be accessed by malicious hackers and cybercriminals. Limit your use of online accounts to times when it's essential. Be especially on guard when accessing your bank accounts, investment accounts, and retail accounts that store your credit card for purchases, and avoid entering your social security number.

Mobile Phone Safety

There are three major security issues when it comes to using mobile phones, which are the most common mobile computing devices in use today. First, you have to protect the phone from theft. Second, you should be cautious if your phone features Bluetooth. Third, you need to avoid mobile viruses.

Public Internet access is incredibly convenient, but in order for businesses such as Internet cafés to provide access to the public, they have to remove vital security settings.

- What can you do if your phone is stolen? You may have stored contact information as well as some passwords to access online sites on your phone, and these are at risk if your phone is stolen. Some services have started up to provide protection for mobile phones. For example, when a phone is stolen, you call the service, and they clear data from the SIM card (the card that holds all phone data such as your contacts), causing the phone to emit a shrill sound, and lock the phone's keypad. Another company is developing software that can track your speech patterns and walking gait—if somebody else is using your cell phone, it can lock up and require a password to proceed.

- How can you protect your phone if you use Bluetooth? Bluetooth technology allows devices in close proximity to communicate with each other. This is useful for some wireless printers to connect with computers, or cell phones to connect with a car Bluetooth system to make handsfree calls. However, once you turn on Bluetooth, anybody in your location with Bluetooth can connect with your device. It's important to turn off Bluetooth when you aren't using it to avoid connection by nefarious people lurking nearby.

- Mobile malware that can attack smartphone operating systems is increasing. Malware writers prefer Android because it is an open platform; however, other mobile devices are also at risk of malware. Install and keep updated mobile security software on your mobile device. Apply the latest updates for your mobile operating system. Finally, be cautious when downloading new apps to your device because you could be inadvertently downloading malware. Avoid third party app stores and be mindful of where you are clicking or tapping while browsing the Web on your device.

When you're on the go, you may be exposed to dangers and too rushed to take precautions, which could be a costly mistake.

Keeping a close watch on your phone and writing down any hardware or SIM card codes you might need to track or identify it are good cell phone safety practices.

Data Privacy in the Cloud

If you store your data in the cloud using a service such as Windows Live SkyDrive or Dropbox, learn about the provider's privacy and security policies with regard to your data. These sites typically allow you to share information only with specific users and to set other policies and permissions. However, there may be unanticipated issues, such as employees at the host site being able to view the contents of your files. Protect yourself by considering the sensitivity of the data before you post it. For example, don't post files such as your tax return, which includes your address and Social Security number, because the exposure of that data would make you vulnerable to identity theft.

Take the Next Step *online*

Activity 8.3.1 Video	*What risks are involved in using Bluetooth?*	**CORE CONTENT**
Activity 8.3.2 Research	*How can you stay safer while traveling?*	
Activity 8.3.3 Team Presentation	*What can you do to keep your tablet or phone safe from thieves and hackers?*	

8.4 Security at Work

Loss of a report to a club or organization you belong to might be annoying, but loss of a company's customer list or secret recipe could be devastating. For that reason, many corporations have sophisticated security strategies and tools in place to protect them against attacks from outside and data loss due to negligence by employees.

Corporate Security Tech Tools

Organizations take advantage of some security tools that most individuals don't need. For example, though encryption is available to the average person when sending a sensitive email, few encrypt the majority of their data and messages. However, a recent U.S. government survey indicated that 71 percent of companies surveyed did use some form of encryption on a regular basis.

Symmetric encryption is often used by companies to ensure that data sent across a network is kept secure from outsiders. Companies can protect stored data and data in transit on the Internet or across a corporate network by designating which computers should be able to share encrypted data and then providing them with the matching keys. The computers use the key to encrypt and decrypt data sent among them. Figure 8.7 shows the process of symmetric encryption in action.

An **Intrusion Prevention System (IPS)** is a robust form of anti-malware program that offers network administrators a set of tools for controlling the system. An IPS detects malware and can block it from entering the corporate network. One type of IPS can also detect suspicious content or unexpected traffic; this is called an **anomaly-based intrusion detection system**.

Many corporations also use tools to audit events on their networks. These audits help to spot random problems or attacks. One technique is to create a so-called **honeypot**, which is a computer set up to be easily hacked into. When an attacker targets the honeypot because it's the easiest prey, companies can find weak spots in their security.

Figure 8.7 Symmetric Encryption Only devices that have the same key that matches the one used to encrypt the message can decrypt the message. The encrypted message can be shared within a network or be sent between two networks.

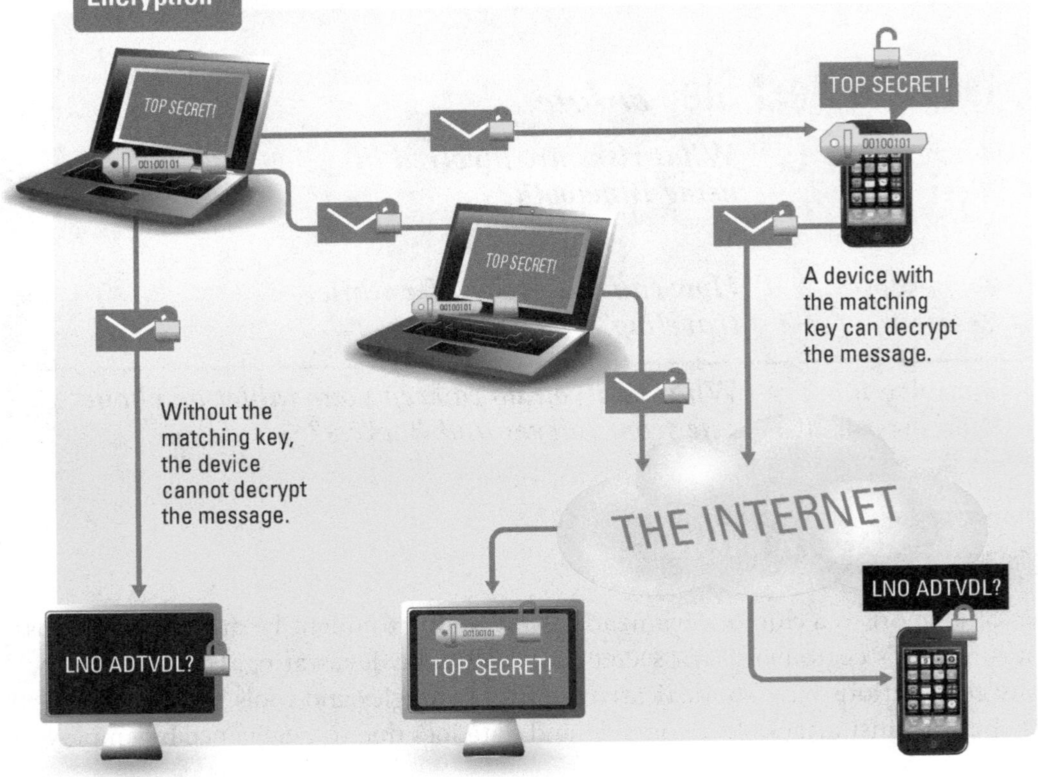

TOP SECRET!

TOP SECRET!

A device with the matching key can decrypt the message.

TOP SECRET!

Without the matching key, the device cannot decrypt the message.

THE INTERNET

LNO ADTVDL?

LNO ADTVDL?

TOP SECRET!

Preventing Unauthorized Access

Those targeting a company range from criminals trying to steal corporate secrets or customer credit card numbers, to disgruntled employees. Stopping unauthorized access to the most sensitive data may involve both physical security (for example, locking the door to the network server room) and an authentication system that requires users to identify themselves. Employee training to prevent con artists known as **social engineers** from talking an employee into giving up corporate secrets or passwords is also important.

Physical security is an obvious starting point in protecting data. Companies should ensure that they have locked server rooms, secured offices, and controlled access to buildings. Physical access may be controlled by using security cards that have to be swiped through a card reader or passed in front of a reader panel to gain access. Closed-circuit TV monitors managed by security officers also help control physical access. When employees lose their jobs for whatever reason, corporations typically follow a specific procedure to keep company information and property secure. This policy might involve checklists to ensure that all employee access cards and keys are returned, and that passwords are changed.

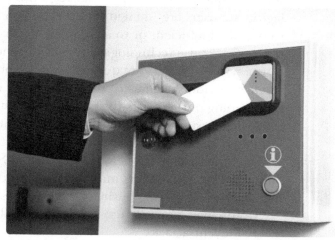

Anyone who has ever lost their security card knows that getting back into the office can be a challenge—which is exactly the point!

Authentication of users is one of the most essential elements in any corporate security plan. There are several levels of authentication, ranging from the input of a simple user name and password to using **biometrics**, which involves devices such as a fingerprint reader or face or voice authenticator to identify individuals by a unique physical characteristic.

Criminals constantly try to find ways around authentication systems that require simple user names and passwords. For example, **spoofing** is a technique used by malicious hackers to make it appear that they are someone else and convince a user to give up valuable information. Corporations have become more and

Our eyes are as unique as our fingerprints, so retinal scans are good proof of an individual's identity.

more aware of such social engineering attacks. For example, a criminal might call into the company office at midnight, tell a security officer that he is an employee working on the road, providing enough personal information gained by various means to convince the officer. The story usually goes that while on a business trip he lost his access information to get into the network where vital files reside for his meeting the next morning. The officer goes to the requested office, locates secure information, and provides access to the network. The crook is in and can have a field day with company data.

Denial-of-Service Attacks

A **denial-of-service (DoS) attack** targets a corporate system with continuous service requests, so constant that response time on the system slows down and legitimate users are "denied service." A DoS attack typically causes an Internet site to become inefficient or to completely crash (fail). Essentially, the perpetrators of these attacks use technological means to send a constant stream of requests to the target system. Targets are quite often high-profile sites such as banks or Internet service providers such as AOL. Attacks may involve a set of distributed computers all pumping out requests to the target system, until the system slows or fails. A DoS attack can result in slow performance of a site, unavailability of a site, or a huge number of spam emails being received.

What are the motives for DoS attacks? Some are launched by spiteful individuals or groups. Others may be terrorist attacks, or an assault by a competitor to damage the competing business. Figure 8.8 shows how a DoS might occur.

Companies typically use a three-pronged approach to combat DoS attacks:
- Prevent attacks.
- Detect intrusions.
- Block malicious actions.

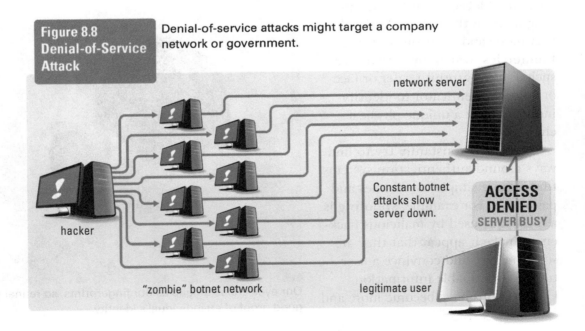

Figure 8.8 Denial-of-Service Attack

Denial-of-service attacks might target a company network or government.

network server

Constant botnet attacks slow server down.

ACCESS DENIED
SERVER BUSY

hacker

"zombie" botnet network

legitimate user

Many software tools are available to address the three parts of this strategy, and the security industry is continually developing new programs to counteract the latest DoS threats. Network administrators often use a combination of firewalls, antivirus products, and the like to prevent attacks. Detection software looks for behavior patterns and characteristics of known attack types. Ideally, products recognize the content of network traffic quickly enough to block attacks.

Data Protection in Disastrous Times

Just as individuals have a first aid kit and some extra water and a flashlight around in case of disaster, companies typically have a data **disaster recovery plan (DRP)** in place. Damage of records, from paper to electronic files, can happen on a large scale when an earthquake or hurricane hits or when an unauthorized user gains access to the company network.

Companies typically set up their networks to back up regularly, which may be daily or more often so all information stored on their computers is kept safe. Individuals may also use automated backup features to run at regular intervals, or back up manually to a storage medium such as a DVD or flash drive.

To back up company servers that might contain a great deal of vital company data, there are three options:

- A **cold server** is simply a spare server you can use to take over server functions.
- A **warm server** is activated periodically to get backup files from the main server.
- A **hot server** receives frequent updates and is available to take over if the server it mirrors fails. (The process of redirecting users to this spare server is called **failover.**)

Many large corporations use an off-site backup. For example, a television or movie company might create copies of their programming and store them at another facility in case an original is lost or damaged or there is a natural disaster.

To avoid loss of data from a sudden surge in power such as might occur during a thunderstorm, individual computers can be plugged into a **surge protector.** In addition, an **uninterruptible power supply (UPS)** can provide a battery backup that takes over in the case of a power failure. UPS systems typically provide backup for about 15 minutes and require an auxiliary power supply to kick in during that time.

Disasters that can destroy important company data come in all shapes and sizes, and are best prepared for by backing up data.

Employee Training

The final piece of corporate security is to train employees in the procedures that will keep corporate intellectual property and other data safe.

Employees are more likely to comply with security policies if they understand why they are needed. Security measures include using strong passwords changed frequently; using a swipe card to access the company premises; and keeping certain company information, such as network access codes, confidential. Many IT departments offer employees regular security training to educate them about the latest cyber attack methods and best practices for keeping data secure.

Ethics and Technology Blog *online*

Protecting Company Assets

My employer recently instituted new data security rules, stating that employees would be responsible for any sensitive data such as company secrets exposed to the public or any lost company property. I often take information home with me on a flash drive so I can work after hours or on weekends. If I make an honest mistake and lose data or property while I'm trying to do my work at a more convenient time, should I be held liable?

Computers in Your Career

Cyberforensics, also known as computer forensics or digital forensic science, is an up-and-coming field. If you worked in this field, you would spend your day extracting information from computer storage that can be used to provide evidence in criminal investigations or identify terrorists. This might involve decrypting data, or finding residual data on a hard drive that somebody has tried to wipe clean. **Mobile forensics** relates to finding data saved or sent via a mobile device. Several colleges offer majors in the field, so if you like to solve mysteries, consider cyberforensics as a career.

 Take the Next Step *online*

Activity 8.4.1 Flash Movie	*How does encryption work?*	
Activity 8.4.2 Team Presentation	*What are the major causes of data loss?*	
Activity 8.4.3 In-Class or Blog Discussion	*What is the role of employees in keeping data secure?*	

Whether protecting a large business or your personal laptop, there are certain security defenses available that help to prevent attacks and avoid data loss, including firewalls, software that detects and removes malware, and strong password protection.

Building Firewalls

As you learned in Chapter 6, a firewall is a part of your computer system that blocks unauthorized access to your computer or network even as it allows authorized access. Firewalls can be created by using software, hardware, or a combination of software and hardware. You can use a firewall feature in Windows, for example, that you turn on and off from within the Windows control panel.

Firewalls are like guards at the gate of the Internet. Messages that come into or leave a computer or network go through the firewall, where they are inspected. Any message that doesn't meet preset criteria for security is blocked. You can set up trust levels that allow some types of communications through and block others, or designate specific sources of communications that should be allowed access.

Keeping Viruses and Spyware under Control

All computer users should consider using **antivirus software** and **antispyware software** to protect their computers, data, and privacy. In fact, there are several free products that do a very good job.

Antivirus products require that you update the **virus definitions** on a regular basis to ensure that you have protection from new viruses as they are introduced. Once you have updated definitions, you run a scan and have several options: to quarantine viruses to keep your system safe from them, to delete a virus completely, and to report viruses to the antivirus manufacturer to help keep their definitions current. Antispyware performs a similar function regarding spyware.

Most people are using software that deals with both viruses and spyware in one package. Some can be set to protect your computer in real time, meaning that they detect an incoming threat, alert you, and stop it before it is downloaded to your computer. Microsoft provides free downloads of Microsoft Security Essentials which includes real-time protection for a home or small business computer to protect against viruses, spyware, and other malware.

In addition to using antivirus and antispyware software, consider allowing regular updates to your operating system. Companies such as

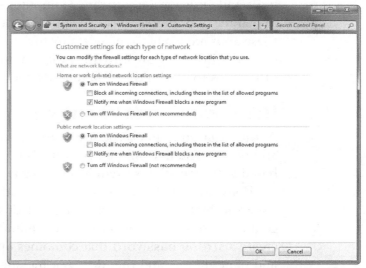

Windows Firewall blocks unwanted intruders from reaching your computer or network. This is an example of a software firewall.

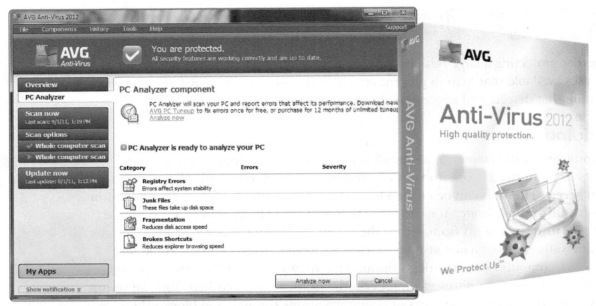

In addition to for-sale antivirus software, AVG offers a free version of its antivirus program.

Microsoft release periodic updates that address flaws in their shipped software or new threats that have come on the scene since their operating system shipped. Windows Update is a feature of the Windows operating system that you can set up to automatically download these updates or alert you when they become available and let you choose which updates to download. Although Macs are not as popular a target for malware, Apple provides updates and security enhancements in a similar method as Windows. When new software has been released to address a potential security threat, you are prompted in the Software Update window that new software is available to be installed.

Protect your mobile device such as your smartphone or tablet with mobile antivirus and antispyware software. Computer security companies such as McAfee and Symantec offer mobile security apps. In addition to protecting you from malware, these apps are likely to include a feature to lock and wipe your device remotely. Consider installing an antivirus program on your mobile device before you add any other apps to ensure that you're protected from the get-go.

Using Passwords Effectively

Authentication is an excellent way to ensure that user access, often the weakest link and biggest risk in computer security, is managed effectively. However, a password-based authentication system is only as good as its users' passwords.

Passwords can be surprisingly weak and easily determined with automated password-breaking tools. For example, a dictionary attack can scan through every common word in the language in just minutes. The best system requires a user to create a **strong password** that combines uppercase and lowercase letters, numbers, and punctuation, and that does not include three or more repeating numbers or letters (333, for example) because these patterns are easy to discern.

In addition, a good password system requires that users change passwords frequently, and provides password validation questions that are not easily discovered. For example, asking you to verify your place of birth or mother's maiden name is a weak system, because both facts are in the public record. Asking you your favorite vacation spot or piece of music is stronger because, although some close friends might know this information, the average criminal might have trouble figuring it out from publicly available records.

People should also create a system for themselves to keep track of passwords. Good passwords don't have to be hard to remember, just hard to guess. If you have a favorite phrase from a movie or song, type it in backwards and add a few numbers, rather than entering a random jumble of letters and numbers or your birthdate. The first is hard to remember, and the latter easy to guess. Also, it's okay to write down passwords, but don't keep them near your computer or mobile device where an intruder might find them.

Take the Next Step *online*

| Activity 8.5.1
 Flash Movie | *How do you use digital certificates and digital signatures to protect data in transit?* | **CORE** CONTENT |

| Activity 8.5.2
 Video | *What makes a strong password?* |

The Role of Security and Privacy in Your Digital World

Computer security, also referred to as information security, involves protecting the boundaries of your home or business network and individual computing devices from intruders. An important strategy is **data loss prevention (DLP)**, which involves minimizing the risk of loss or theft of data from within a network. Next generation malware incorporates **advanced persistent threats (APTs)** where highly targeted, sophisticated attacks tailored to a specific organization or group of organizations are used to gain access to sensitive information.

The tools for protecting your personal computer and information are similar to tools corporations use to protect their intellectual property: **authentication**, special software and hardware, and user procedures.

When Security Gets Personal

The increasing number of households connected to the Internet has resulted in a growing number of cyber attacks, identity theft, and other types of fraud. In addition, loss or damage to data resulting from damaging programs inadvertently downloaded to a computer can be frustrating and costly.

If you have set up a home network that connects to the Internet, it is important to protect the network with a password.

Another important step in securing a home network is to use encryption. **Encryption** technologies protect stored data and data in transit. When you send an email, for example, you apply an **encryption key**. **Public key encryption** involves the use of a **public key** to encrypt data and a **private key** to decrypt it.

It is also important to protect your computer against **malware**. Some common forms of malware are **viruses**, **worms**, **Trojan horses**, **macro viruses**, **logic bomb viruses**, **rootkits**, **botnets**, **spyware**, **adware**, and **scareware**. Malware is most often spread via the Internet, so an important way to protect your computer is by knowing how to spot a trusted site and avoiding those that are known to spread malware.

Sites where you will perform financial transactions should always have **Transport Layer Security (TLS)** protection in place. TLS is a protocol—evolved from **Secure Socket Layer (SSL)**, an earlier protocol—that protects data such as credit card numbers as they are being transmitted between a customer and an online vendor or payment company.

Other important skills include understanding how to manage **cookies** and not being caught by **phishing** scams.

Mobile Security

Mobile computing carries its own security risks. There are several devices and procedures you can use to physically secure your laptop or tablet computer including locks, fingerprint readers, and password protection. Companies may provide mobile computing policies for employees.

If you travel and access the Internet using public hotspots (locations that offer Wi-Fi access), be very careful not to expose private information. Anything you send over a public network can be accessed by hackers and criminals.

There are three major security issues when it comes to using mobile phones: first, protect the phone from theft; second, use caution if your phone features Bluetooth because nearby users can use this technology to track your communications or infect you with a virus; and third, avoid downloading malware which can result in the loss or theft of personal data.

Security at Work

Many corporations have sophisticated security strategies and tools in place to protect them against outside attacks and internal negligence by employees.

Using **symmetric encryption,** companies can protect stored data and data in transit on the Internet or across a corporate network by designating which computers should be able to share encrypted data and then providing them with matching decryption keys.

An **Intrusion Prevention System (IPS)** is a robust anti-malware program that offers network administrators a set of tools for controlling access to the system. Many corporations also use audit tools to help spot random problems or attacks. One type of IPS called an **anomaly-based intrusion detection system** can also detect suspicious content or unexpected traffic.

Stopping unauthorized access to the most sensitive company data may involve both physical security (for example, locking the door to the network server room) and a user authentication system. Employee training to prevent con artists, known as **social engineers**, from talking an employee into giving up corporate secrets or passwords is also important.

Criminals constantly try to find ways around authentication systems that require user names and passwords. For example, **spoofing** is a technique used by malicious hackers to make it appear that they are someone else and convince a user to give up valuable information.

A **denial-of-service (DoS) attack** involves assaulting a corporate network with a constant stream of requests that causes the system or website to slow down or even crash.

Major damage of paper and electronic records can happen when an earthquake or hurricane hits. Backup systems using **cold servers**, **warm servers**, or **hot servers** may prevent the loss of data. Off-site storage is another good option for companies.

Corporate IT departments may provide regular training for employees to keep them up to date on types of cyber attacks and the strategies to combat them.

Security Defenses Everybody Can Use

A firewall serves as a gatekeeper, blocking suspect access and allowing authorized access to your computer or network. Firewalls use software, hardware, or a combination of software and hardware to inspect incoming and outgoing communications. Any communication that doesn't meet preset criteria for security is blocked.

All computer users should use **antivirus software** and **antispyware software** to protect their computers, data, and privacy. Manufacturers of antivirus products provide regular virus definition updates to ensure that you have current information and therefore the best protection. In addition to using antivirus and antispyware software, consider allowing regular updates to your operating system.

Some passwords can be easily determined with automated password-breaking tools. The best system requires a **strong password**, which combines uppercase and lowercase letters, numbers, and punctuation, and does not allow three or more repeating numbers or letters because these patterns are easy to discern. A good password system requires users to change passwords frequently and provides password validation questions that are not easily discovered.

Terms to Know

CORE CONTENT

The Role of Security and Privacy in Your Digital World

computer security, 236
data loss prevention (DLP), 236
hacker, 236

advanced persistent threat (APT), 237
authentication, 239

When Security Gets Personal

encryption, 240
public key, 240
private key, 240
public key encryption, 240
Wi-Fi Protected Access (WPA), 240
Wired Equivalent Privacy (WEP), 240
malware, 241
spam, 241
virus, 241
worm, 242
Trojan horse, 242
macro virus, 243

logic bomb virus, 243
rootkit, 243
botnet, 244
zombie, 244
spyware, 244
adware, 244
scareware, 244
Transport Layer Security (TLS), 246
Secure Socket Layer (SSL), 246
cookie, 246
phishing, 247

Security at Work

symmetric encryption, 252
Intrusion Prevention System
    (IPS), 252
anomaly-based intrusion detection
    system, 252
honeypot, 252
social engineer, 253
biometrics, 253
spoofing, 253
denial-of-service (DoS) attack, 254
disaster recovery plan (DRP), 255
cold server, 255

warm server, 255
hot server, 255
failover, 255
surge protector, 255
uninterruptible power supply (UPS), 254
cyberforensics, 256
mobile forensics, 256
decryption, Activity 8.4.1
digital rights management (DRM),
    Activity 8.4.1

Security Defenses Everybody Can Use

antivirus software, 257
antispyware software, 257
virus definitions, 257

strong password, 258
digital certificate, Activity 8.5.1
digital signature, Activity 8.5.1

Concepts Check

CORE CONTENT

Concepts Check Activity 8.1   Multiple Choice
Take this quiz to test your understanding of key concepts in this chapter.

Concepts Check Activity 8.2   Word Puzzle
Complete this puzzle to test your knowledge of key terms in this chapter.

Concepts Check Activity 8.3   Matching
Test your understanding of terms and concepts presented in this chapter.

Concepts Check Activity 8.4   Label It
Use the interactive tool to identify a trusted online site.

Concepts Check Activity 8.5   Label It
Use the interactive tool to identify what threat each security measure is designed to protect against.

Projects

Check with your instructor for the preferred method to submit completed work.

Project 8.1 Wireless Networks at Home

Project 8.1.1 Individual

Watch the video titled *Why You Should Protect Your Wireless Network with WPA* at www.emcp.net/ProtectWirelessNetworks. After watching the video, research Wi-Fi Protected Access (WPA) and Wired Equivalent Privacy (WEP) wireless security standards. Prepare a brief summary comparing WPA to WEP security. Include the URLs of the source material you used.

Project 8.1.2 Team

As employees of a new IT security company, your team has found that the typical homeowner is unaware of the risks of using a wireless network at home. To educate homeowners about these security issues, your company has decided to create a short video that presents a convincing demonstration of the need for wireless security. As a team, create a video storyboard that shows a wireless network being breached by an outsider. Following this sequence of scenes, devote the remaining scenes of your storyboard to an explanation of security measures that a homeowner can take to avoid being victimized by a cybercriminal. When you are finished with the storyboard, film and edit the video; then share the video with your class.

Project 8.2 Mobile Device Security

Project 8.2.1 Individual

Read the article titled "10 Best Practices for Mobile Device Security" at www.emcp.net/MobileSecurity. Prepare a one-page document in a checklist format that lists each of the 10 practices. Next to each practice, provide a brief description of the practice in your own words. Then, using the checklist, interview a parent, friend, or relative who uses a smartphone for work and determine which best practices the interviewee follows. After you have completed the checklist, ask the interviewee if his or her place of employment has a mobile security policy. If so, modify the checklist to include any practices that are not on the original form. Prepare a summary of the interview that details which practices were and were not followed. Submit the completed checklist and summary to your instructor.

Project 8.2.2 Team

A local company has hired your team to develop a mobile device security policy to protect its IT assets. The company employs five consultants who travel around the country conducting training presentations on public accounting government reporting requirements. Each consultant travels with a company smartphone, laptop, and in some cases a tablet and is typically away from the office for three days. To prepare you for writing the company's mobile security policy, read the article titled "Hefty Price Tag for Lost Laptop: Nearly $50,000" at www.emcp.net/LostLaptop. Using this article as a starting point, discuss with your team how to safeguard the company from the disruption in service and large costs associated with lost mobile devices. Refer to the best practices checklist in Project 8.2.1 for guidance in creating effective security procedures for mobile employees. Prepare a presentation for the company's executive board that outlines your team's recommended mobile device security policy for smartphones, laptops, and tablets.

Project 8.3 Thwarting Social Engineers

Project 8.3.1 Individual

You have been asked by your company's human resources department to prepare a training proposal for employees on the security threats posed by social engineers. Read the article titled "Social Engineering Fundamentals, Part I: Hacker Tactics" at www.emcp.net/HackerTactics. When you have finished, locate and read two additional articles that address the manipulative practices of social engineers. Now that you have some background knowledge on social engineers, consider the content that needs to be covered in your employee training program in order to safeguard your company's confidential information. What topics should be included in the training? What would be the best training method? How will you ensure that employees comply after the training? Prepare a training proposal that includes a rationale for the training, an outline of the content, a description of the methodology you would use, and suggestions for ensuring employee compliance after training. At the end of the proposal, include references to the two additional articles you read for this project.

Project 8.3.2 Team

Your IT manager has decided she wants to perform a test to evaluate the company's social engineering training that was recently completed. The manager has targeted two positions that she believes are the most vulnerable targets of social engineers: the help desk staff and the front desk receptionists. Develop a script for a telephone conversation in which a social engineer calls the help desk and attempts to get a staff member to reveal the user name and password of an employee. Develop another script for a face-to-face conversation in which a social engineer walks into the main reception area of the company and tries to obtain the name of the IT manager from a front desk receptionist.

Project 8.4 The Best Defense Is a Good Offense

Project 8.4.1 Individual

Read the article titled "Assessing Internet Security Risk, Part One: What Is Risk Assessment?" at www.emcp.net/RiskAssessment. Then review the five questions that the author recommends that company computer users ask themselves in order to develop their Internet security risk profile. Using those same five questions for guidance, establish a security risk profile for your home computer and network. Aside from examining Internet-based risks, consider factors such as theft or damage to your equipment as well as other risk variables whose solutions will cost more than the estimated losses. Create a table with the risk identified in the first column, the plan or strategy to address the risk in the second column, and the estimated cost of the strategy in the third column. Submit the completed table to your instructor.

Project 8.4.2 Team

Your team has volunteered to help senior citizens at a local community center. Recognizing that this age-group is easily victimized by social engineers, your team would like to inform these elderly individuals about the manipulative practices of social engineers and the ways in which they can protect themselves. Develop a presentation that demonstrates the tactics that a social engineer uses to obtain private information and that provides tips on managing personal security.

Project 8.5 Wiki — Computer Security

Project 8.5.1 Individual or Team

You or your team will be assigned to research and write a response to one or more of the following FAQs associated with Internet security and safety:

- How can I protect my mobile device from malware?
- How can I tell if an email message is a phishing attempt?
- How can I tell if a checkout page is secure?
- How do I turn on the lock/passcode feature on my tablet?
- How do I hide my mobile device when Bluetooth is on?
- How can I control a website's placement of a cookie on my computer?
- How can I tell if my computer has a virus?
- How do I secure my wireless network at home?
- How can I make sure that all of my personal information is wiped off of the hard drive of a computer that I am donating to charity?
- What can I safely do online at a cyber café?

Prepare a posting to the course wiki site for your assigned question(s). In the posting, include your response and any examples that would aid comprehension. Be sure to include references to the sources of your information.

Project 8.5.2 Individual or Team

Your team is assigned to edit and verify the content posted on the wiki site from Project 8.5.1. If you add or edit any content, make sure you include a notation within the page that includes your name or the team members' names and the date you edited the content—for example, "Edited by [your name or team members' names] on [date]." Keep a list of references that you used to verify your content changes. When you are finished with your verification, include a notation at the end of the entry—for example, "Verified by [your name or team members' names] on [date]."

Class Conversations

Topic 8.1   What Are the Biggest Threats to Workplace Networks?

Watch the video interview titled "Kevin Mitnick on Security for Enterprise and Small Business" at www.emcp.net/Mitnick. In the interview, Mitnick speaks about what he believes are the biggest threats to the future of network security. Discuss ways in which businesses should gear up to respond to more sophisticated worms and viruses as described by Mitnick.

Topic 8.2   Do You Want Advertisers to Get Into Your Head?

Read the article titled "Ads Follow Web Users, and Get More Personal" at www.emcp.net/CookieData. Discuss the pros and cons of businesses tracking consumers and providing customized web content. Do you like this practice or feel that because of this practice you may not see everything you want to see on the Internet? Is this practice a violation of your privacy? Why or why not?

Topic 8.3   How Common Is Data Theft by Employees?

Read the article titled "Data Theft Common by Departing Employees" at www.emcp.net/DataTheft. Do you agree today's increasingly mobile workforce has less loyalty to employers? Why or why not? Do you believe employees who leave a company are entitled to take some data away with them? If yes, what data would be acceptable to take and what data would not be acceptable to take? Do employers rely too heavily on non-disclosure agreements? If yes, how should an employer harden his/her termination procedure to protect company data?

Glossary

802.11 standard A communications standard used in Wi-Fi networks that tells wireless devices how to connect with each other using a series of access points and radio frequencies to transmit data. Ch 6

A

access speed The speed with which data in RAM can be accessed and processed by a computer. Ch 3

advanced persistent threat (APT) A highly targeted, sophisticated attack tailored to a specific organization usually done to gain access to sensitive information. Ch 8

adware Software that is supported by advertising and is capable of downloading and installing spyware. Ch 8

alpha version The first stage of testing a software product. Ch 5

American National Standards Institute (ANSI) One of the organizations that establishes network communications standards. Ch 6

analog computer A computer that uses mechanical operations to perform calculations, as with an older style car speedometer or handheld calculator. Ch 1

analog signal An electronic signal formed by continuous sound waves that fluctuate from high to low. Your voice is transmitted as an analog signal over traditional telephone lines at a certain frequency. Ch 6

Android A Linux-based operating system from Google that is used on mobile devices such as tablets and smartphones. Ch 4

animation software Software used to create a series of moving images. Ch 5

anomaly-based intrusion detection system A type of intrusion prevention system that detects suspicious content or unexpected traffic. Ch 8

antispyware software Software used to prevent the downloading of spyware to a computer or network, or to detect and delete spyware on the system. Ch 8

antivirus software Software used to prevent the downloading of viruses to a computer or network, or to detect and delete viruses on the system. Ch 8

application software Includes the software products you use to get tasks done, from producing reports for work to creating art or playing games. Ch 5

artblog A blog where people post creative works such as music, photos, or paintings. Ch 7

assistive technology device A variety of devices and methods that enable physically challenged computer users to control their computer and provide input. Ch 3

audio software Software that allows you to record and edit audio files. Ch 5

authentication The use of passwords or other identifiers such as fingerprints to make sure that the people accessing information are who they claim to be and that they have permission to get such access. Ch 8

B

bandwidth The number of bits (pieces of data) per second that can be transmitted over a communications medium. Ch 6

bar code reader An input device that optically scans a series of lines, or a bar code, using a light beam. Ch 3

beta version The second stage of testing a software product. Ch 5

binary system A system consisting of two possible values, 0 and 1, called binary digits, or bits. Ch 1

biometrics Technology that uses devices such as fingerprint readers or retinal scanners to identify a person by a unique physical characteristic. Ch 8

BIOS Code that checks and starts up computer devices such as memory, monitor, keyboard, and disc drives and directs the hard drive to boot up and load the operating system (OS) to memory. Ch 3

bit The smallest unit a computer can understand and act on. An abbreviation for binary digit. Ch 1

blog An online journal; short for Web + log. Ch 7

Blue-ray disc A type of disc-shaped storage device, mostly used for high-definition movies and games. Ch 3

Bluetooth A network protocol that offers short-range connectivity (3 to 300 feet, depending on a device's power class) via radio waves between devices such as your cell phone and car. Bluetooth-enabled devices can communicate directly with each other. Ch 6

Bluetooth headset A wireless headset that can receive data (including sound) from Bluetooth-enabled devices. Ch 3

bookmark A way to save a reference to a website or web page so that it can be easily visited again. Ch 7

booting The process of starting your computer. Ch 4

bot See zombie. Ch 8

botnet A group of computers that have been compromised (zombies or bots) so they can forward communications to a controlling computer. Ch 8

bridge A device that helps separate but similar networks to communicate with each other. Ch 6

broadband Any communications medium that is capable of carrying a large amount of data at a fast speed. Ch 6

browser An application used to view pages and content on the Web and to navigate among pages. Ch 2

bug A computer industry term for a flaw or failure in software that causes it not to work as intended. Ch 5

bus topology An arrangement where all the computers and other devices on a network, such as printers, are connected by a single cable. Ch 6

business-to-business (B2B) e-commerce A product, service, or payment between two online businesses. Ch 2

business-to-consumer (B2C) e-commerce A product, service, or payment between an online business and individual consumers. Ch 2

byte A collection of 8 bits. Ch 1

C

cable modem A piece of hardware that enables you to send and receive digital data using a high-speed cable network based on the cable television infrastructure found in many homes. Ch 6

cache memory A memory area located on or near the microprocessor chip for the most frequently used data. Ch 1

calendar software Software designed to schedule appointments or events and to set up reminders. Ch 5

CD A disc-shaped storage device from which you can read data, write data, or both. Ch 3

cellular network A transmission system that sends signals through a cell tower. Each cell tower has its own range or cell of coverage. Used to transmit both voice and data in every direction. Ch 6

cellular transmissions Signals sent using a cell tower. Ch 6

central processing unit (CPU) The part of your computer system that interprets instructions and processes data. Also sometimes referred to as the processor or core. Ch 1

Chrome OS A Linux-based operating system from Google that works primarily in web-based applications. Ch 4

client A computer or other device capable of sending data to and receiving data from a server on a network. Ch 6

client/server network A network architecture in which a computer (called the server) stores programs and files that any connected device (called a client) can access. Ch 6

clock speed The speed at which a processor can execute computer instructions, measured in gigahertz. Ch 3

cloud computing A model of software delivery in which software is hosted on an online provider's website and you access it over the Internet using your browser; you don't have to have the source application software actually installed on your computer in order to use the software. Also called utility computing. Ch 5

cloud storage Services that allow users to store documents online. Ch 5

coaxial cable The cable that is used to transmit cable television signals over an insulated wire at a fast speed (millions of bits per second). Ch 6

cold boot Starting a computer from a no-power state. Ch 4

cold server A spare server used to take over server functions. Ch 8

command-line interface Refers to operating systems where you typed in text commands, such as DOS. Ch 4

comma-separated-values (CSV) format A format that separates each piece of data in a file by with a comma. Ch 5

communications system In the context of a computer network, a system that includes sending and receiving hardware, transmission and relay systems, common sets of standards so all the equipment can "talk" to each other, and communications software. Ch 6

computer An electronic, programmable device that can assemble, process, and store data. Ch 1

computer cluster A group of computers joined together to provide higher computing power. Ch 1

computer engineering (CE) The study of computer hardware and software systems, and programming how devices interface with each other. Ch 1

computer memory Temporary storage areas on your computer, including random access memory (RAM) and cache memory. Ch 1

computer network Two or more computing devices connected by a communications medium, such as a wireless signal or a cable. Ch 6

computer science (CS) The study of how to design software, solve problems such as computer security threats, or come up with better ways of handling data storage. Ch 1

computer security Activities that involve protecting the boundaries of your home or business network and individual computing devices from intruders. Also called information security. Ch 8

consumer-to-consumer (C2C) e-commerce A product, service, or payment between two online consumers. Ch 2

contact management software A type of software used to store, organize, and retrieve contact information. Ch 5

convergence device A type of device that combines several technologies, such as the ability to calculate, store data, and connect to the Internet. Examples of this type of device include your cell phone, a GPS navigation system, a digital camera, or an appliance you can program remotely to perform tasks at a certain time. Ch 1

cookie A small file stored on your computer by a web server to track information about you and your activities. Ch 8

copyright Legal ownership of a work or symbol. Ch 2

crawler An intelligent agent that follows a trail of hyperlinks to locate online data. Ch 2

customer relationship management (CRM) software A suite of software or online services used to store and organize client and sales prospect information, and automating and synchronizing other customer-facing business functions such as marketing, customer service, and technical support. Ch 5

cyberforensics A field of study or a career that involves extracting information from computer storage that can be used to provide evidence in criminal investigations. This might involve decrypting encrypted data, or finding residual data on a hard drive that somebody has tried to erase. Ch 8

D

data Raw facts; what you put into a computer. Ch 1

data integration Combining data from several online sources into one search result. In the context of online search, cross referencing various sources of data and including those references in the results. Ch 2

data loss prevention (DLP) Activities that involve minimizing the risk of loss or theft of data from within a network. Ch 8

database software A type of software used to query, organize, sort, and create reports on sets of data such as customer lists. Ch 5

decryption The process of decoding an apparently random sequence of characters into meaningful text. It reverses the process of encryption and takes place as the final step in sending and receiving a secure communication. Ch 8

deep Web Databases and other content on the Web that aren't catalogued by most search engines. A typical search engine won't return links to these databases or documents when you enter a search keyword. Also called the invisible Web. Ch 2

denial-of-service (DoS) attack An attack against a corporate system that slows performance or brings a website down. Ch 8

desktop The background image shown on the screen upon which graphical elements such as icons, buttons, windows, links, and dialog boxes are displayed. Ch 4

desktop computer A non-portable computer whose central processing unit (CPU) might be housed in a tower configuration or in some cases within the monitor, as with the Apple iMac. Ch 1

desktop publishing (DTP) software Software used to lay out pages for books, magazines, and other print materials such as product packaging or brochures. Ch 5

dial-up modem A piece of hardware that works with telephone transmissions and changes or manipulates an analog signal so that it can be understood by a computer or fax machine (which only understand digital signals). Ch 6

digital certificate An electronic document used to encrypt data sent over a network or the Internet. Ch 8

digital computer A computer that represents data using binary code. Ch 1

digital rights management (DRM) A set of technologies used by owners of digital content to control access to, and reproduction of, their material. It is used primarily to enforce copyright protection for digital content. Ch 8

digital signal A discrete electronic signal that is either high or low. In computer terms, high represents the digital bit 1; low represents the digital bit 0. Ch 6

digital signature A mathematical way to demonstrate the authenticity of a digital certificate. Ch 8

disaster recovery plan (DRP) A formal set of policies and procedures that guides the preparation for a possible disaster and subsequent recovery of computer resources and information thereafter. Ch 8

Disk Cleanup A utility included with Windows that gets rid of unused files on your hard disk. Ch 4

distributed application architecture A network architecture that distributes tasks between client computers and server computers. Ch 6

document camera An output device that is often used in educational settings to display text from a book, slides, a 3D object, or any other printed material. Ch 3

domain name An identifier for a group of servers (the domain) hosting a particular website. Ch 2

DOS An early operating system for personal computers which used a command-line interface. An acronym for disk operating system. Ch 4

download To transmit data, such as a digitized text file, sound, or picture from a remote site to one's own computer via a network, such as the Internet. If you are receiving content from the Internet, you are downloading. Ch 2

DRAM Short for dynamic random access memory. The type of memory most commonly found in computers, and works quickly, is compact, and affordable. Requires electricity and is fragile, meaning that the data held in RAM must constantly be refreshed. Ch 1

drive A device that stores data on media. Can be integrated into the computer or be external or removable. Ch 3

driver Software that allows an operating system to interface with specific hardware such as a printer or keyboard. Ch 4

DSL modem A piece of hardware that allows you to connect to your existing telephone system but separates voice from data traffic so you don't lose the use of your telephone while your computer is transmitting or receiving data. DSL stands for digital subscriber line. Ch 6

DVD A disc-shaped storage device from which you can read data, write data, or both. This type of media can store larger quantities of data than a CD. Ch 3

E

e-commerce The transaction of business over the Internet. Ch 2

edutainment Software and/or media that contain both entertainment and educational value. Ch 5

electronic pen A special input device used to write or draw on a Tablet PC screen. Also called a stylus. Ch 3

email A message that is shared over the Internet. Short for electronic mail. Ch 2

email address A unique identifier for an email sender or recipient comprised of user name, domain name of the email service, and domain suffix. Ch 2

email client A program stored on your local computer that is used to manage multiple email accounts and contacts when you connect to your email service. Ch 2

email server A computer dedicated to managing the sending, receiving, and storing of email messages. Ch 6

embedded object An object that has been inserted into software documents using object linking and embedding (OLE) technology. Ch 5

embedded technology Placing computing power in your environment as with, for example, a system in your house that senses and adjusts lighting or temperature. Also called ubiquitous computing. Ch 1

encryption The process of using a key to convert readable information into unreadable information to prevent unauthorized access or usage. Ch 8

entertainment software A category of software that includes computer games you play on your computer or game console. Ch 5

Ethernet A standard that specifies that there is no central device controlling the timing of data transmission. With this standard, each device tries to send data when it senses that the network is available. Ch 6

expansion card A device inserted on the computer motherboard that adds capabilities such as sound, graphics handling, or network communications. Ch 3

export To send data to another document. Ch 5

external hard drive A disk drive that connects to your computer via a cable connected to a port where you can store data and retrieve it from another computer. Ch 3

extranet An extension of an intranet that allows interaction with those outside the company, such as suppliers and customers. Ch 6

F

failover The process of redirecting users to a hot server. Ch 8

fax machine A device used to transmit a facsimile (copy) of a document to another location using a phone line. Ch 3

fiber-optic cable A transmission medium that uses a protected string of glass which transmits beams of light. Fiber-optic transmission is very fast, sending billions of bits per second. Ch 6

file A computer's basic storage unit, which might contain a report, spreadsheet, or picture, for example. Ch 1

file allocation table (FAT) A table maintained by the OS to keep track of the physical location of the hard disk's contents. Ch 4

file extension The part of a file name that identifies the program that is to launch when the file is double-clicked. It is commonly a set of 3 or 4 characters following a period at the end of the file name. For example, for the file index.htm, "index" identifies the file and "htm" is the extension, indicating in this case that a browser such as Internet Explorer would launch to view the HTML (web page) file. Ch 5

firewall Software and hardware systems that stop those outside a network from sending information into the network or taking information out of it. Ch 6

FireWire port Based on the same serial bus architecture as a USB port, this type of port provides a high-speed serial interface, for example for digital cameras, camcorders, set-top boxes, and high-end audio and video. Ch 3

firmware Code built into electronic devices that controls those devices and may include instructions to start the system. Ch 4

flash drive Small, convenient device that lets you store data and take it with you. Also known as a USB stick or thumb drive. Ch 3

flash memory A type of computer memory used to record and erase stored data and transfer data to and from your computer; used in mobile phones and digital cameras because it is much less expensive than other types of memory. Ch 3

freeware Software that is made available to use free of charge. Ch 5

frequency The speed at which a signal can change from high to low; a signal sent at a faster frequency provides faster transmission. Ch 6

friends list The people you have allowed to access your profile on a social network. Ch 7

G

gaming device A piece of equipment such as an Xbox that allows a user to play a computer game using software or an online connection. Ch 3

gateway A device that helps separate but dissimilar networks to communicate with each other. Ch 6

generic top-level domain (gTLD) A top level TLD with three or more characters. Ch 2

geographic information system (GIS) expert A computer profession that helps users capture, manage, analyze, and display geographic data. Ch 1

gigabit per second (Gbps) A transmission at a rate of 1 billion bits per second. Ch 6

gigabytes (GB) The average computer's hard drive capacity for data storage is measured in gigabytes; one gigabyte is approximately one billion bytes. Ch 3

gigahertz (GHz) A measurement of processor speed; one gigahertz is approximately one billion cycles per second. Ch 3

GNU General Public License A policy that specifies polices about creating open-source software, including that source code has to be made available to all users and developers. Ch 5

graphical user interface (GUI) The visual appearance of an operating system that uses graphical icons, buttons, and windows to display system settings or open documents. Ch 4

graphics software Software that allows you to create, edit, or manipulate images. Ch 5

H

hacker A person who has knowledge of computer technology and security settings, which can be used for benign or malicious purposes. Ch 8

handwriting recognition software A type of software that enables a computer to recognize handwritten notes and convert them into text. Ch 5

hard disk The disk that is built into your computer and is the primary method of data storage. The disk rotates under a read/write head that reads and writes data. Ch 3

home page The main page of a website or the page a browser first lands on when you specify a universal resource locator (URL). Ch 2

honeypot As part of a corporate security strategy, a computer set up to be easily hacked into to help identify weaknesses in the system. Ch 8

hot server A spare server that receives frequent updates and is available to take over if the server it mirrors fails. Ch 8

hotspot A location where Wi-Fi access is available. Ch 6

hub Used on older LAN networks to coordinate the message traffic among nodes connected to a network. Ch 6

hyperlink Describes a destination within a web document and can be added to text or a graphical object such as a company logo. Used for navigation. Generally, clicking on a hyperlink sends the user to the specified web document. Ch 2

hypertext Text that represents a hyperlink. Used for navigation. Generally, clicking on hypertext sends the user to the specified web document. Ch 2

I

identity The profile you create when you join a social networking service. Ch 7

iOS A mobile operating system from Apple, Inc. designed for devices such as the Apple iPad and iPod Touch. Ch 4

import To bring content into a document. Ch 5

information Raw facts that are processed, organized, structured, or presented in a meaningful way; what you get out of a computer. Ch 1

information processing cycle A cycle of handling raw data and information that has four parts: input of data; processing of data; output of information; and storage of data and information. Ch 1

information security Activities that involve protecting the boundaries of your home or business network and individual computing devices from intruders. Also called computer security. Ch 8

information systems (IS) A computer profession that bridges the needs of an organization and the way their information is handled to solve business problems. An IS professional considers who needs what data to get work done and how it can be delivered most efficiently. Ch 1

information technology (IT) The study, design, development, or management of computer systems, software applications, and computer hardware. Ch 1

Infrared Data Association (IrDA) port Ports that allow you to transfer data from one device to another using infrared light waves. Ch 3

infrared technology A technology that enables transfer of data over short distances using light waves in the infrared spectrum. Ch 3

input Data that is entered into a computer or other device or the act of reading in such data. Ch 1

input device A device that allows a user to put data into a computing device. Translates into electronic (digital) form. Ch 3

Institute of Electrical and Electronics Engineers (IEEE) One of the organizations that establishes network communications standards. Ch 6

instruction register A holding area on your computer where instructions are placed after the fetch portion of the machine cycle is completed. Ch 1

intellectual property Creations of the mind; inventions, literary and artistic works; and symbols, names, images, and designs used in commerce. Ch 2

interactive whiteboard (IWB) A display device that receives input from the computer keyboard, a pen, a finger, a tablet, or other device. Ch 3

Internet The physical infrastructure that provides us with the ability to communicate with others across a network of computers. The Internet is made up of hardware such as servers, routers, switches, transmission lines, and towers that store and transmit vast amounts of data. Ch 2

Internet law A legal specialty that includes writing the legal terms and policies for websites. Ch 1

Internet Message Access Protocol (IMAP) A communications protocol that receives email from a mail server and delivers it to the proper mailbox. Has replaced POP on some email servers. Messages will not be deleted from the server until requested by the recipient. Ch 2

Internet peer-to-peer (P2P) network A modification of peer-to-peer used on the Internet to share files. Ch 6

Internet Protocol (IP) address A series of numbers that uniquely identifies a location on the Internet. An IP address consists of four groups of numbers separated by a period, for example: 225.73.110.102. Ch 2

Internet service provider (ISP) A company that lets you use its technology to connect to the Internet for a fee, typically charged monthly. Ch 2

intranet A private network within a company's corporate "walls." Ch 6

Intrusion Prevention System (IPS) A robust form of anti-malware program that offers network administrators a set of tools for controlling access to the system and stopping attacks in progress. Ch 8

invisible Web Databases and other content on the Web that aren't catalogued by most search engines. A typical search engine won't return links to these databases or documents when you enter a search keyword. Also called the deep Web. Ch 2

K

keyboard An input device that consists of keys a user types on to input data. Ch 3

keystroke logging software A kind of malware that is used to track the keystrokes typed by a computer user. Ch 3

keywords Words or phrases that you include in search text to look for content using a search engine. Ch 2

kilobit per second (Kbps) A transmission at a rate of 1 thousand bits per second. Ch 6

L

laptop A portable computer with a built-in monitor, keyboard, and mouse along with the central processing unit (CPU) and a battery. Also known as a notebook computer. Ch 1

LCD projector Liquid crystal display projectors are devices that project light through panels made of silicone colored red, green, and blue. The light passing through these panels displays an image on a surface such as a screen or wall. Ch 3

least possible privileges A principle applied by network operating systems that means that each user is only given access to what he or she needs in order to get his or her work done. Ch 4

LED display A display process using light-emitting diodes to both conserve power and provide a truer picture than LCD models. Ch 3

Linux First developed by Linus Torvalds in 1991, Linux is an open source operating system, meaning that the source code for it is freely available and many people can use it and modify it. Ch 4

live broadcast Live, or real-time, delivery of media over the Internet. Also called live media streaming. Ch 7

live media streaming Live, or real-time, delivery of media over the Internet. Also called live broadcast. Ch 7

local area network (LAN) A type of network where connected devices are located within the same room or building, or in a few nearby buildings. Ch 6

logic bomb virus A piece of code that is placed in a software system to set off a series of potentially damaging events if certain conditions are met. Ch 8

Long Term Evolution (LTE) standards A standard for wireless communication of high-speed data for mobile phones and data terminals and involves areas such as bandwidth efficiency, cost control, providing better service and integrating standards. Ch 6

M

machine cycle A cycle a computer uses during which four basic operations are performed: (1) fetching an instruction, (2) decoding the instruction, (3) executing the instruction, and (4) storing the results. Ch 1

Macintosh OS X The operating system produced by Apple Computers. Ch 4

macro virus A form of virus that infects the data files of commonly used applications such as word processors and spreadsheets. Ch 8

malware Collectively, damaging computer programs such as viruses and spyware, which can do anything from displaying pop-up window advertisements to destroying your data or tracking your online activities. Ch 8

media sharing Sharing video, photos, music, or presentations with individuals or groups using the Internet. Ch 7

megabit per second (Mbps) A transmission at a rate of 1 million bits per second. Ch 6

megahertz (MHz) A measurement of RAM access speed; one megahertz is approximately one million cycles per second. Ch 3

memory capacity The amount of memory (RAM) on your computer, which it uses to run programs and store data. Ch 3

metadata Data about other data, which describes that data and how to process it. Ch 7

metasearch engine A type of search engine that can search for keywords across several websites at the same time. Ch 2

metropolitan area network (MAN) A type of network that connects networks within a city or other populous area to a larger high-speed network; typically made up of several LANs that are managed by a network provider. Ch 6

microblogging A form of blogging where brief comments rather than personal blogs are the main form of interaction, as on Twitter. Also called social journaling. Ch 7

microphone An input device for sound. Ch 3

microprocessor A computer chip that can accept programming instructions that tell a computer what to do with the data it receives. Ch 1

Microsoft Windows The operating system produced by Microsoft Corporation. Ch 4

microwave A high-frequency radio signal that is sent from one microwave tower to another. Because the signal cannot bend around obstacles, the towers have to be positioned in line of sight of each other. Ch 6

MIDI A protocol that allows computers and devices, such as musical synthesizers and sound cards, to control each other. Ch 3

mobile broadband stick A USB device that acts as a modem to give users computer access to the Internet. Ch 6

mobile forensics Field of study or career that involves finding data saved or sent via a mobile device to use as evidence in criminal prosecutions. Ch 8

mobile Internet device (MID) A category of devices that fall between netbooks and phones, putting the Internet in a pocket-sized form. Ch 4

mobile operating system Operating system used on mobile phones. Often called mobile OS or mobile platform. Ch 4

mocial A term that refers to using a social networking engine such a Facebook, Twitter, foursquare, or Google Places through any mobile device. Ch 7

modem A piece of hardware that sends and receives data from a transmission source such as your telephone line or cable television connection. The word modem comes from a combination of the words modulate and demodulate. Ch 6

monitor A visual output device that displays data and information as well as provides the ability to view the computer's interface. Ch 3

Moore's Law A theory proposed by Gordon Moore, one of the founders of Intel, which states that over time the number of transistors that can be placed on a chip will increase exponentially, with a corresponding increase in processing speed and memory capacity. Ch 3

motherboard The primary circuit board on your computer that holds the central processing unit (CPU), BIOS, memory, and expansion cards. Ch 3

mouse An input device referred to as a pointing device, that is able to detect motion in relation to the surface you rest it on and provides an onscreen pointer representing that motion. Ch 3

MP3 blog A blog where people post audio or music files. Ch 7

multicore processor A CPU chip that contains more than one processing unit (core), for example dual core (two cores) or quad core (four cores). Ch 3

multimedia software Software that enables you to work with media, such as animation, audio, or video. Ch 5

Multipurpose Internet Mail Extensions (MIME) format A format for messages that are sent over the Internet. MIME permits text, graphics, audio, and video. Ch 2

multitasking The ability to have two or more tasks running at the same time. Also refers to the CPU's ability to execute several processes simultaneously. Ch 4

N

netbook Designed as devices for those who mainly want to browse the Internet or use email. A style of computer that is small in size, usually with screen sizes ranging from eight inches to ten inches or so, and weighing only two to three pounds. Ch 1

network adapter A device that provides the ability for a computer to connect to a network. Ch 6

network architecture The design and layout of the communications system; how computers in a network share resources. Ch 6

network attached storage (NAS) A file-level computer data storage device that connect to a computer network via a wired or wireless connection for the purpose of data storage. Also called a networked external hard drive. Ch 3

network interface card (NIC) One kind of network adapter card. In most current computers, NICs take the form of a circuit board built into the motherboard of a computer that enables a client computer on a LAN to connect to a network by managing the transmission of data and instructions received from the server. Ch 6

network operating system (NOS) Programs that control the flow of data among clients, restrict access to resources, and manage individual user accounts. Ch 6

network protocol A rule for how data is handled as it travels along a communications channel. Ch 6

node A device connected to a network. Ch 6

notebook A portable computer with a built-in monitor, keyboard, and mouse along with the central processing unit (CPU) and a battery. Also known as a laptop. Ch 1

O

object linking and embedding (OLE) A technology that allows content to be treated as objects that can be inserted into different software documents even if they were not created using that software. Ch 5

open content A creative work or other content that anybody can copy or edit online. Ch 7

open source operating system Operating system software built with contributions by users whose source code is free to anybody to modify and use. Ch 4

open source software A type of software whose source code can be used, edited, and distributed by anybody. Ch 5

operating system (OS) A type of software that provides an interface for the user to interact with computer devices and software applications. Ch 4

operating system package Packaged software, such as Windows or Linux, which includes an operating system and utilities (collectively known as system software). Ch 4

optical drive A drive that allows your computer to read and write data using optical technology, such as a DVD or CD drive. Ch 3

optoelectronic sensor Technology used in devices, such as optical drives, which detects changes in light caused by irregularities on a surface. Ch 3

organic light emitting diode (OLED) A display technology that projects light through an electroluminescent (a blue/red/green–emitting) thin film layer made of up of organic materials. Ch 3

organizer software Software that includes multiple features for organizing in one package, for example, schedule, contact, and email management. Ch 5

output The information that results from computer processing or the act of writing or displaying such data. Ch 1

output device A device that allows a computer user to obtain data from a computer. Translates from electronic (digital) form to some other format. Ch 3

P

packaged software Software saved to a physical medium such as a DVD and sold in a box or other package. Ch 5

packet A small unit of data that is passed along packet-switched a network, such as the Internet. Ch 6

packet switching The process of breaking data into packets, sending, and then reassembling the original data. Ch 6

parallelized Software design that allows tasks to run pieces of a task on two or more processors. Ch 3

path The hierarchy of folders that leads to a stored file. Ch 4

PC Card An add-on card that slots into a built-in card reader to provide other kinds of functionality such as adding memory or networking capabilities. Ch 3

peer-to-peer (P2P) file sharing program A program that allows people to share music, video, and other types of files by downloading them from each other's hard drives, rather than from a central location on the Internet. Ch 2

peer-to-peer (P2P) network A network architecture in which each computer in the network can act as both server and client. Ch 6

performance The speed with which your computer functions. Ch 4

peripheral device A device that physically or wirelessly connects to and is controlled by a computer but is external to the computer. Ch 3

petabit per second (Pbps) A transmission at a rate of 1 quadrillion bits per second. Ch 6

petaflop A measure of supercomputing power representing a thousand trillion operations per second. Ch 1

phishing The practice of sending an email that appears to be from a legitimate organization in an attempt to scam the user into revealing information. Ch 8

photo editing software Software designed to enhance photo quality or apply special effects such as blurring elements or feathering the edges of a photo. Ch 5

photo printer An output device that allows you to print high-quality photos directly from a camera's flash memory to the printer without having to upload the photos to a computer first. Ch 3

photoblog A blog used to share amateur or professional photography. Ch 7

physical port A type of port that uses a physical cable to connect a computer to another device. Ch 3

pixel A single point in an image; short for picture element. Ch 1

plasma displays Flat panel displays mainly used for televisions. They use a great deal of power but have a very true level of color reproduction compared with LCDs. Ch 3

platform The hardware architecture of a computer and the operating system that runs on it. Ch 4

platform dependency Applications and hardware that are only designed to work with a particular operating system. Ch 4

player A freely downloadable program that enables you to view or hear various types of online multimedia content. Ch 2

plotter An output device used to print large blueprints and other design or engineering documents. Ch 3

Plug and Play A feature that recognizes and makes available for use devices you plug into your computer, for example into a USB port. The OS installs the correct driver in order for the device to operate if the driver is available. Ch 4

plug-in A freely downloadable program that adds functionality to your browser. Ch 2

podcast A short audio presentation that can be posted online. Ch 5

port A slot in your computer used to connect it to other devices or a network. Ch 3

Post Office Protocol, Version 3 (POP3) A communications protocol that receives email from a mail server and delivers it to the proper mailbox. By default, messages are deleted from the server when the recipient retrieves his/her mail unless the user changes the settings. Ch 2

power supply Switches alternating current (AC) provided from a wall outlet to lower voltages in the form of direct current (DC). Ch 3

preferences Settings on your social networking page, including privacy settings. Ch 7

presentation software Software that enables you to create slideshows that include text, graphics, and multimedia. Ch 5

printer A peripheral device used to produce printed output, sometimes called hardcopy. Ch 3

private key A code key used in encryption that is known to only one or both parties when exchanging secure communications. Ch 8

processing The manipulation of data by the computer to create information. Ch 1

processor speed The speed at which the CPU interprets and carries out instructions that operate the computer and its devices. Ch 3

productivity software Software applications that people typically use to get work done such as a word processor, spreadsheet, database, or presentation software. This type of software is often compiled into suites of applications. Ch 5

profile A blogger or social networking user's information such as name, location, and interests. Ch 7

protocol A standard that specifies how two devices will communicate by providing rules such as how data should be formatted and coded for transmission. The Internet transmission protocol is indicated in the first part of a website's universal resource locator (URL). Ch 6

public key A code key used in encryption. Creates an encrypted message that is decrypted by a private key. Ch 8

public key encryption A system of encrypting and decrypting data using a public key and private key combination. Ch 8

Q

quick response (QR) code A shortcut that users can access to go to a website using a smartphone. Ch 2

R

Radio Frequency Identification (RFID) A wireless technology primarily used to track and identify items using radio signals. An RFID tag placed in an item contains a transponder which is read by a transceiver or RFID reader. Ch 6

random access memory (RAM) A holding area for data while your computer processes information. When you turn your computer off, the data temporarily stored in this holding area disappears; RAM is therefore also referred to as volatile memory. Ch 1

read-only memory (ROM) Memory that holds information such as the BIOS and instructions the computer uses to start up the operating system. Ch 3

release to manufacturing (RTM) version A final version of the software with all identified bugs reconciled so that the software can be duplicated and sold to the public or deployed to internal users. Ch 5

render farm A custom-designed connection between groups of computers joined in a computer cluster. Ch 1

repeater An electronic device that takes a signal and retransmits it at a higher power level to boost the transmission strength. A repeater can also transmit a signal to move past an obstruction, so that the signal can be sent further without degradation. Ch 6

resolution A measurement of the number of pixels on a screen. Ch 1

RFID reader An input device often used in retail or manufacturing settings to scan an embedded tag using radio frequency. Ch 3

rich text format (RTF) A text format that includes only basic formatting information that most software products are likely to be able to open or import. Ch 5

ring topology An arrangement that has computers and other devices connected, one after the other, in a closed loop. Data transmitted on a ring network travels from one computer to the other until it reaches its destination. Ch 6

rootkit A set of programs or utilities designed to allow a hacker to control a victim computer's hardware and software and permit a hacker to monitor the user's actions. Ch 8

router A hardware device that connects two or more networks. Ch 6

S

satellite communication Space-based equipment that receives microwave signals from an earth-based station and then broadcasts the signals back to another earth-based station. Ch 6

scanner A peripheral input device used to create an electronic file from a hard copy document. Ch 3

scareware A scam where an online warning or pop-up convinces a user that his or her computer is infected with malware or has another problem that can be fixed by purchasing and downloading software. Ch 8

screen capture software Software that enables you to capture an entire computer screen or only a portion of it. Ch 5

SDRAM Short for synchronous dynamic random access memory. An updated version of DRAM, which provides significant improvements in access speed. Most modern computer memory is some variation of SDRAM, including DDR-SDRAM, DDR2-SDRAM, and DDR3-SDRAM. Ch 1

search directory A site that allows you to locate web content within categories. Ch 2

search engine A website that catalogs web pages into topics. Ch 2

Secure Socket Layer (SSL) An older cryptographic protocol used to perform communication security of financial transactions over the internet. It is the predecessor of Transport Layer Security. Ch 8

Semantic Web The next (third) phase in online usage, also called the Web 3.0, which will make it possible for websites to "understand" the relationships between elements of web content. Ch 2

serial port A port, built into the computer, used to connect a peripheral device to the serial bus, typically, by means of a plug with 9 pins. Network routers use serial ports for administration, although they are being replaced by web-based administration interfaces. Ch 3

server Any combination of hardware and software that provides a service, such as storing data, to a client, such as your computer. Ch 6

shared feature A small application that cannot run on its own but that allow suites of software products to share functionality such as diagramming or drawing. Ch 5

shareware Software for which you pay a small fee. Ch 5

Short Message Service (SMS) A text messaging service component of a phone, web, or mobile communication systems, using standardized communication protocols that allow the exchange of short text messages between fixed line or mobile phone devices. Ch 2

Simple Mail Transfer Protocol (SMTP) A communications protocol installed on the ISP's or online service's mail server that determines how each message is to be routed through the Internet and then sends the message. Ch 2

sketchblog A blog consisting of drawings and sketches. Ch 7

smartphone Mobile phone devices with a mobile OS and rich feature set that essentially makes them into very small computers. Ch 4

social bookmarking A method of sharing bookmarks with others using tags. Ch 7

social engineer Con artist who employs tactics to trick computer users into giving up valuable information. Ch 8

social journaling A form of blogging where brief comments rather than personal blogs are the main form of interaction, as on Twitter. Also called microblogging. Ch 7

social mobile media Social services accessed from mobile phones. Ch 7

social networking site A site that offers the ability to share contacts and build a network of "friends" along with tools that allow individuals and groups to connect and communicate. Ch 7

social Web The collective description of websites that offer the ability to communicate, interact, and network with others. Ch 7

software as a service (SaaS) A software delivery model where a provider licenses an application to customers to use as a service on demand. Ch 5

software development life cycle (SDLC) The general flow of creating a new software product; includes performing market research and business analysis, creating a plan and budget for implementing the software, programming the software, testing the software, releasing the software to the public, and debugging the software. Ch 5

software engineering (SE) A field involving writing software programs, which might be developed for a software manufacturer to sell to the public, or involve a custom program written for a large organization to use in-house. Ch 1

software on demand A software delivery model where a provider licenses an application to customers to use as a service on demand. Also called software as service (SaaS). Ch 5

software suite A collection of productivity software applications sold as one package that use tools common to all the products in the suite. Ch 5

solid state drive (SSD) A lighter and more durable flashed-based data storage device that replaces an internal hard disk. Ch 3

source code The programming code used to build a software product. Ch 5

spam Mass emails sent to those who haven't requested them, usually for the purpose of advertising or fraud. Ch 8

speaker A device that provides audio output. Ch 3

speech recognition software A type of software that enables a computer to recognize human speech and convert it into text. Ch 5

spoofing Attempting to gain valuable information via electronic communications by misleading a user as to your identity. Ch 8

spreadsheet software An application with which you can perform calculations on numbers and display other data. In addition, most spreadsheet products offer sophisticated charting and graphing capabilities. Ch 5

spyware Software that tracks activities of a computer user without the user's knowledge. Ch 8

SRAM Short for static random access memory. A type of memory that is about five times faster than DRAM. Though dependent upon electricity, this type of memory does not require constant refreshing and is more expensive than DRAM. It is therefore often used only in cache memory applications. Ch 1

standards Allow different devices to talk to one another. Ensure compatibility among devices, specifying how computers access transmission media, the speeds used on networks, the design of networking hardware such as cables, and so on. Ch 6

star topology An arrangement where all the devices on the network, called nodes, connect to a central device. Ch 6

storage A permanent recording of information, data, and programs on a computer's storage medium, such as a magnetic disk or optical disc, so that they can be retrieved as needed. Ch 1

streaming video Video that is delivered to your computer as a constant stream of content, usually requiring a media player. Ch 2

strong password A password that is difficult to break. Strong passwords should contain uppercase and lowercase letters, numbers, and punctuation symbols. Ch 8

stylus A special input device used to write or draw on a Tablet PC screen. Also called an electronic pen. Ch 3

supercomputer A computer with the ability to perform trillions of calculations per second, usually custom-made for a particular use or used as a large server. Ch 1

surface-conduction electron-emitter display (SED) A display technology that uses nanoscopic electron emitters (extremely tiny wires smaller than human hairs) to send electrons that illuminate a thin screen. Ch 3

surge protector Protects an individual device from loss of data caused by a spike in a power, such as might occur during a thunderstorm. Ch 8

swap file A file created when data is stored or "swapped" into virtual memory. Ch 4

switch A hardware device that joins several computers together to coordinate message traffic in one LAN network. Although a switch performs a role similar to a hub, a switch checks the data in a packet it receives and sends the packet to the correct destination using the fastest route. Ch 6

symmetric encryption A system of encrypting and decrypting data where in the sending and receiving computers each have a matching private key. Ch 8

sync An updating of data from one device to another based on changes made to the data of one device. Ch 5

system configuration The entire computing system including the identity of the computer, the devices connected to it, and some essential processes that the computer runs. Ch 4

system files Files that provide instructions needed to run the operating system on your computer. Ch 4

system software Software that includes the operating system and utilities for maintaining a computer and its performance. Ch 4

T

tablet A portable computer that includes a special electronic stylus used to write on the screen. Ink technology allows you to use programs to convert your writing to text or graphic objects. Ch 1

tag A keyword assigned to information on the Web used by social bookmarking sites to locate and organize content references. Ch 7

TCP/IP Short for Transmission Control Protocol/Internet Protocol. A protocol that breaks transmissions into small packets of data that are sent on the network. Each packet specifies the order in which the data is to be reassembled. This is the protocol for the Internet. Ch 6

technological convergence When a device begins to use technologies traditionally thought to belong to another device, as when a cell phone performs tasks traditionally performed by a computer. Ch 1

terabit per second (Tbps) A transmission at a rate of 1 trillion bits per second. Ch 6

tethering Cell phone users who can share Internet connection of their device via cable, Bluetooth, or Wi-Fi with another device such as a tablet or laptop. Ch 6

text message A message between mobile phones and other portable devices written in 160 characters or less. Ch 2

texting The process of sending a text message. Ch 2

TFT active matrix liquid crystal display (LCD) The most prevalent type of monitor technology used today. It uses a thin film transistor (TFT) to display your computer's contents. Ch 3

thermal printer A type of printer that heats coated paper to produce output. Ch 3

thumb drive Small, convenient device that lets you store data and take it with you. Also known as a USB stick or flash drive. Ch 3

token A signal passed from device to device in a token ring network. Ch 6

token ring A standard that allows computers and other devices accessing a network to share a signal. This signal, called a token, is passed from device to device, and only the device that holds the token can transmit data at that time. Ch 6

top-level domain (TLD) The suffix (the period and the letters that follow) of a domain name. Ch 2

topology How devices in a network are physically arranged and connected to each other. Ch 6

touchpad A type of flat mouse or pointing device often used in laptop computers, which senses finger movement. Ch 3

Transport Layer Security (TLS) A protocol that protects data such as credit card numbers as they are being transmitted between a customer and online vendor or payment company. Ch 8

Trojan horse Malware that masquerades as a useful program. When you run the seemingly useful program, you can let this type of malware into your system. It opens a "back door" through which hackers can access your computer. Ch 8

twisted-pair cable A type of cable consisting of two independently insulated wires twisted around one another. This type of cable is used to transmit signals over short distances. Twisted-pair cables are used to connect a home's hardware telephone system or an Ethernet network, for example. Ch 6

U

ubiquitous computing Placing computing power in your environment as with, for example, a system in your house that senses and adjusts lighting or temperature. Also called embedded technology. Ch 1

uniform resource locator (URL) A naming system used to designate unique website addresses that you enter into a browser to navigate to a particular site. Also called web address. Ch 2

uninterruptible power supply (UPS) A battery backup that provides a temporary power supply in case of a power failure. Ch 8

universal serial bus (USB) port A port in the form of a small rectangular slot that can be used to attach everything from wireless mouse and keyboard toggles (the small device that transmits a wireless signal to a wireless device) to USB flash drives for storing data. Ch 3

UNIX A server operating system written with the C programming language. Ch 4

upload To transmit data, such as a digitized text file, sound, or picture from one's own computer to a remote site via a network, such as the Internet. If you are sending content to the Internet, you are uploading. Ch 2

USB stick Small, convenient device that lets you store data and take it with you. Also known as a flash drive or thumb drive. Ch 3

user interface The visual appearance that software presents to a user. Ch 4

utility computing A model of software delivery in which software is hosted on an online provider's website and you access it over the Internet using your browser; you don't have to have the source application software actually installed on your computer in order to use the software. Also called cloud computing. Ch 5

utility software A category of system software that you use to optimize and maintain your system performance and provides information about system resources. Ch 4

V

video blog A blog where people post video content. Also called vlog. Ch 7

video software Software used to create and edit video files. Ch 5

virtual memory A capability of the computer's operating system that handles data that cannot fit into RAM when running several programs at once. When RAM is used up, data is stored or "swapped" into virtual memory. Ch 4

virtual reality system A system that connects you to a simulated world. It creates a connection between user and computer that allows both input and output in various forms and can be used to create sophisticated training programs such as those used by pilots, doctors, and astronauts. Ch 3

virus A type of computer program that is placed on your computer without your knowledge. The key characteristic of a virus is that it can reproduce itself and spread from computer to computer by attaching itself to another, seemingly innocent, file. Ch 8

virus definitions Information about viruses used to update antivirus software to recognize the latest threats. Ch 8

vlog Short for video blog. A blog where people post video content. Ch 7

Voice over Internet Protocol (VoIP) A transmission technology that allows you to make voice calls over the Internet using a service such as Skype. Ch 2

volatile memory A holding area for data while your computer processes information. When you turn your computer off, the data temporarily stored in this holding area disappears. Also referred to as random access memory (RAM). Ch 1

W

warm boot Restarting a computer without turning the power off. Ch 4

warm server A server activated periodically to get backup files from the main server. Ch 8

Web (World Wide Web or WWW) A system that contains the body of content available as web pages that are stored on Internet servers. Ch 2

Web 2.0 An evolution of the Web, considered its second phase, associated with users not only reading content but interacting by writing content. Provides users with a means to collaborate—share, exchange ideas, and add or edit content. Ch 2

Web 3.0 The next (third) phase in online usage, also called the Semantic Web, which will make it possible for websites to "understand" the relationships between elements of web content. Ch 2

web address A naming system used to designate unique website addresses that you enter into a browser to navigate to a particular site. Also called uniform resource locator (URL). Ch 2

web authoring software A type of software that provides tools for creating and editing web pages. Ch 5

web-based mail A process to create and send messages, add attachments, receive and reply to messages, store contact information, and manage services. Ch 2

web conferencing A combination of technologies that allow you to hold meetings online with voice, video, images, and various collaborative tools such as virtual whiteboards. Ch 2

web designer Someone whose job it is to design the layout of websites. Ch 1

web development A career technology path from the World Wide Web that includes programming websites, developing text and visual content, explaining how clients can use tools such as a search engine optimization (SEO) to maximize site traffic, and using social media to promote goods and services. Ch 1

web page A single document on the Web, which may contain text, images, interactive animations, games, music, and more. Several related web pages make up a website. Ch 2

web-based software Software that is hosted on an online provider's website; you access it over the Internet using your browser. This type of software is not installed on your computer. Ch 5

web-based training Learning that typically contains a self-directed element and takes place via the Web using some combination of text, multimedia, and interactive tools. Ch 5

webcam Video cameras that are either built into your computer monitor or that you purchase separately and mount on your computer. Ch 3

webmail A web-based email service such as Hotmail or Gmail that can be accessed from any computer connected to the Internet using a web browser. Ch 6

webmaster Someone whose job it is to make sure website content is delivered to users efficiently. Ch 1

website A collection of related web pages. Ch 2

wide area network (WAN) A type of network that serves larger geographic areas. WANs, such as the Internet, are used to share data between networks around the world. WANs might use leased T1/T3 lines, satellite connections, radio waves, or a combination of communications media. Ch 6

Wi-Fi Short for wireless fidelity. A wireless technology, based on the 802.11 standard in its various versions such as 802.11 a, g, or n, that is used to connect to the Internet via hotspots and radio waves. Ch 6

Wi-Fi Protected Access (WPA) An encryption standard used to protect data sent across a wireless network. Designed by the Wi-Fi Alliance to overcome the security limitations of Wired Equivalent Privacy (WEP). Ch 8

wiki A technology which allows people to contribute and edit content in an online document, such as an encyclopedia or dictionary. Ch 7

WiMAX Short for Worldwide Interoperability for Microwave Access. Also known as 802.16, this standard uses radio waves to connect with other devices using a WiMAX tower; it is faster and can work over a longer range than Wi-Fi. Ch 6

wired data gloves Equipment worn on the hands that allows users to communicate with a virtual reality system. Ch 3

Wired Equivalent Privacy (WEP) An encryption standard used to protect data sent across a wireless network. An older and less secure technology than Wi-Fi Protected Access (WPA). Ch 8

wireless access point A hardware device that contains a high-quality antenna that allows computers and mobile devices to transmit data to each other or to and from a wired network infrastructure. Ch 6

wireless adapter A piece of equipment used to connect a computer to wireless networks. Ch 3

Wireless Application Protocol (WAP) Specifies how mobile devices such as cell phones display online information such as maps and email. Ch 6

wireless interface card A network interface card that uses wireless technology. Ch 6

wireless LAN (WLAN) A local area network that uses wireless technology. Ch 6

wireless modem A piece of hardware that typically takes the form of a PC card that you slot into a device to provide it with an antenna that can pick up a connection to the Internet. Ch 6

wireless router A hardware device that allows you to connect multiple networks using wireless communication signals. Ch 6

word processor software A type of software used to create documents that include sophisticated text formatting, tables, photos, drawings, and links to online content. Ch 5

worm A self-replicating computer program with the ability to send out copies of itself to every computer on a network. Worms are usually designed to damage the network, in many cases by simply clogging up the network's bandwidth and slowing its performance. Ch 8

WYSIWYG (what you see is what you get) An acronym used to describe a system in which content (text and graphics) displayed onscreen during editing appears in a form closely corresponding to its appearance when printed or displayed as a finished product. Pronounced Wiz-e-wig. Ch 5

Z

zombie A computer compromised by malware that becomes part of a botnet and used to damage or compromise other computers. Also called a bot. Ch 8

Index

building into computer to enable
communications, Activity 3.2.3
carrying around, Activity 1.2.3
ethical choices in manufacturing
of, 107
gaming, 4, 13, 78
routing data between applications
and, 115–116
that project computer content,
81–82
dial-up modem, 185
Digg, 222
digital cameras, 7
digital certificates, use of, Activity
8.5.1
digital computer, 4
digital devices, 70, 85
Digital Divide, 202
Digital Millennium Copyright Act, 51
digital signals, 169–170
digital signatures, use of, Activity
8.5.1
digital subscriber line (DSL), 39, 40
Diigo, research on, Activity 7.5.2
direct current, 72
disaster recovery plans (DRPs), 255
discussion forums, 216
disk cleanup, 100
distributed application architecture,
181
document camera, 81
document management software, 145
Dogpile.com, 47
domain name, 43
DOS, 103
Dot-com collapse of 2001, 35
Dragon Naturally Speaking, 78
DRAM, 84
drivers, 102
drives, 74
Dropbox, 15, 75, 251
DSL modem, 185
DVD, 15

E

Earthlink, 40
eBay, 53
eBeam, 82
e-commerce, 52–54
business-to-business, 52–53
business-to-consumer, 52
comparison of kinds of, Activity
2.6.1
consumer safety and, 54
consumer-to-consumer, 53
802.11 standard, 178
electronic pens, 79
ELGG (open source social networking engine), 217
email, 4, 40, 41, 55–56
chain letters on, 245
privacy of, in workplace, Activity
2.7.3

sending and receiving, Activity
2.7.1
email address, 55
email client, 55
embedded object, 155
embedded technology, 10
employees
mobile computing policies for, 249
role of in keeping data secure,
Activity 8.4.3
training of, 256
encryption, 239, 240
process of, Activity 8.4.1
public key, 240–241
symmetric, 252
entertainment software, 143
Ethernet, 172, 176
Evite, 219
expansion cards, 71, Activity 3.2.2
Expedia, 47
export, 154
external hard drives, 74–75
extranet, 168

F

Facebook, 53, 205, 208, 209, 214,
215, 217, 218, 220, 225
future of, 219
phishing as problem in, 247
failover, 255
fax machines, 81
Federal Trade Commission, on identity theft complaints, 238
Fertik, Michael, 217
fiber-optic cable, 172, 173
file allocation table (FAT), 116
file names, 130
files, 16
format saved in, Activity 5.4.2
managing, 116–117
saving, 15
sharing, Activity 5.4.2
on networks, Activity 6.5.2
financial applications, 144
financial scams, 55
fingerprint readers, 249
FireEye, Inc., 237
Firefox, 41
firewalls, 40, 41, 189, 239
building, 257
differences between hardware and
software, Activity 6.7.1
FireWire port, 73
firmware, 100
first generation (1G), 172
flash drives, 7, 15, 16, 73, 75
flash memory, 75
flatbed scanners, 78
Fleischner, Michael, 221
Flickr, 208, 209, 220, 224, 225
flops, 5
Food Force, 143
forensics, computer, 146

4G LTE mobile broadband, 188
4G (fourth generation) technology,
40–41, 172, Activity 4.4.1
foursquare, 217, 220
freeware, 152
frequency, 170
FriendFeed, 225
friends lists, 209
Friendster, 217

G

gaming devices, 4, 13, 78
gaming models, 87
gateways, 5, 87, 188
generic top-level domains (gTLDs), 43
GeoFencing, 202
geographic information system
expert, 11
gigabytes, 16, 85
gigahertz, 84
Gmail, 55
Gnutella, 224
Google, Inc., 51, 121, 147, 150, 236
Calendar, 140
Chrome, 5, 7, 41
Google +, 209, 217
Google.com, 45
Google Docs, 31, 135, 153, 192
Google Places, 217, 220
Google Squared, 36, 37, 45
Google Video, 47
as target of Operation Aurora,
237, 239
Goretsky, Aryeh, 247
Go2Web20.net, 211
GPS navigation systems, 4, 7, 9
Graham, Philip, 51
graphical user interface (GUI), 103
graphics software, 141
green computing, 95–96
Grouply, 217
Groupon, 220
Guest Tracker, 145
Gupta, Gopal, 10

H

hackers, 238, 243
defined, 236
keeping tablets and mobile
phones safe from, Activity
8.3.3
handwriting recognition software, 155
advances in, Activity 5.4.3
hard disks, 74
external, 74–75
hardware
for accessing Internet, 39–41
for accessing networks, 186
configuring, 110–111
help system, 118
Hertz (Hz), 14
Hewlett-Packard, 4, 121
TouchPad, 6

Our Digital World

capacity of, 84
flash, 75
needed amount of, 84–85
random access, 14, 71, 84, 113,
    115, Activity 1.4.1, Activity
    3.2.5
read-only, 71, 113
virtual, 113
volatile, 14
Memory-Alpha.org, 223
metadata, 221
metahertz, 85
metasearch engine, 47
metropolitan area networks (MAN),
    180
microblogs, 31, 215
    comparison with blogs, wikis and,
        Activity 7.6.1
microphone, 13, 79, 112
microprocessors, 14, 71, 103
Microsoft, 97, 100, 102, 103, 104,
    106, 150, 154, 178, 189
    Access, 138
    Bing, 45
    comparison of Mac OS X and,
        Activity 4.2.2
    evolution of, Activity 4.1.1
    Excel, 136, 147
    Expression Web, 142
    features offered by, Activity 4.3.1
    Internet Explorer, 41
    Office, 86, 135, 154
    Office 365, 150
    Office Web Apps, 135, 192
    Outlook, 55, 141
    PowerPoint, 138–139, 154
        importing files into Word from,
            Activity 5.4.1
    PowerPoint Mobile, 147
    Project, 144
    Publisher, 142
    Security Essentials, 143, 257
    Word, 147
        importing files into PowerPoint
            from, Activity 5.4.1
Microsoft Windows, 102, 105
    file management for, 117
    Windows 7, 7
    Windows 8, 105, 108
    Windows 2000, 105
    Windows Live, 141, 212, 216
    Windows Live SkyDrive, 251
    Windows Media Player, 48
    Windows Movie Maker, 142
    Windows Update, 258
    Windows XP, 105
microwave, 174
MIDI, 74
Mimio, 82
minus symbol, 46
mobile applications, 147
mobile broadband sticks, 40, 186

mobile computing policies for
    employees, 249
mobile devices, computer security on,
    248–251, Activity 6.7.2
mobile forensics, 256
mobile hotspots, 186
mobile Internet devices, 78–79
mobile malware, 250
MobileMe, 55, 56
mobile operating systems, 120–121
mobile phones, 4
    keeping safe from thieves and
        hackers, Activity 8.3.3
mobile safety, safe use of, 250–251
mocialo, 220
modems, 169–170
    cable, 185
    dial-up, 185
    DSL, 185
    wireless, 186
Mo Jo (mobile phone journalism), 214
monitors, 14–15, 79–81
    new technologies in, Activity 3.3.3
Moore, Gordon, 84
Moore's Law, 84
motherboard, 70–71, 100, 101, 185
Motorola XOOM, 6
mouse, 13, 76–77, 112
    elimination of, Activity 4.3.4
Movie Maker, 142
MP3 players, 7
MP3 sites, 224
MS-DOS, 103
multicore processor system, Activity
    3.2.1
multimedia models, 87
multimedia software, 142
MySpace, 209, 217

N

nanotechnology-enabled robots, 32
Napster, 224
NASA Quest, 30
navigation bar, 34
NEMO, 9
netbooks, 6–7, 74
    costs of, 87
net neutrality, 62
network adapter, 186
network administrator, 255
    job of, Activity 6.6.3
network attached storage (NAS), 75
network interface card (NIC), 186
network routers, 73
networks, 179
    architecture of, 181–182
    connection of devices to com-
        puter, Activity 3.2.4
    devices in, 185–186, 188
    file sharing on, Activity 6.5.2
    hardware that provides access to,
        186

operating systems for, 188
protocols for, 168
securing, 189
security on, Activity 6.7.3
sending messages over, Activity
    6.2.1
speed of connection, Activity 6.2.2
tasks handled by operating soft-
    ware, Activity 4.2.1
transport standards, 176–177
trends in, 191–192
types of, 180
typology of, 183
    bus, 183, 184
    ring, 183, 184
    star, 183, 184
Nielsen Online, 38
Nintendo's Wii Fit, 143
nodes, 185
Norton, 143
    Mobile Security, 248
notebook computers, 6
number pad on smartphone, 13
Numbers for the Mac, 136

O

object linking and embedding (OLE),
    155
obsolescence, 130
online auctions, 54, 87, Activity 2.6.2
    eBay and, 53
    PayPal and, 54
online crime, changes in, 238
online scheduler, scheduling team
    meeting using, Activity 5.3.5
online trainer, 35
open content, 209
Open Enterprise Server (OES), 107,
    188
OpenOffice, 136
Open Office Writer, 105
OpenProj, 144
open source, 104, 209
    evolution of, Activity 5.3.2
    operating system, 108
    software for, 152
Open Systems Interconnection (OSI)
    model, Activity 6.4.4
Opera, 41
Opera Mobile, 42
operating systems, 86, 100, 116,
    Activity 3.4.5. *See also specific by
    name*
    cloud, 122
    customizing, Activity 4.3.3
    future of, 109
    history of, 102–103
    mobile, 120–121
    packages for, 102
        maintenance features in, 119
        perusing popular, 104–109
        tasks of, 110–119